NOW *with* ENTHUSIASM
Charism, God's Mission and Catholic Schools Today

enthusiasm (n.)
> c. 1600, from Middle French *enthousiasme*, and directly from Late Latin *enthusiasmus*, from Greek *enthousiasmos* 'divine inspiration, enthusiasm (produced by certain kinds of music, etc.),' from *enthousiazein* 'be inspired or possessed by a god, be rapt, be in ecstasy,' from *entheos* 'divinely inspired, possessed by a god,' from *en* 'in' + *theos* 'god'

Michael Green

BBI – THE AUSTRALIAN INSTITUTE OF THEOLOGICAL EDUCATION
MISSION AND EDUCATION SERIES

Published in Australia by
Vaughan Publishing
32 Glenvale Crescent
Mulgrave, VIC 3170

vaughanpublishing.com.au
A joint imprint of BBI – The Australian Institute
of Theological Education and Garratt Publishing

Text Design by Mike Kuszla, J&M Typesetting
Cover image iStock
The Ascension by Michael Galovich. © Trustees of the Marist Brothers, Province of Australia.
Used by permission.

Printed by Tingleman

ISBN 9780987306098

Nihil Obstat: Reverend Monsignor Peter Kenny STD
               Diocesan Censor

Imprimatur: Monsignor Greg Bennet MS STL VG,
               Vicar General

Date: 19 May 2018

The Nihil Obstat and Imprimatur are official declarations that a book or pamphlet is free of
doctrinal or moral error. No implication is contained therein that those who have granted the
Nihil Obstat and Imprimatur agree with the contents, opinions or statements expressed. They do
not necessarily signify that the work is approved as a basic text for catechetical instruction.

A catalogue record for this
book is available from the
National Library of Australia

NATIONAL
LIBRARY
OF AUSTRALIA

The authors and publisher gratefully acknowledge the permission granted to reproduce the
copyright material in this book. Every effort has been made to trace copyright holders and to
obtain their permission for the use of copyright material.

The publisher apologises for any errors or omissions in the above list and would be grateful if
notified of any corrections that should be incorporated in future reprints or editions of this book.

In *Now with Enthusiasm* Brother Green presents an impassioned and rigorous assessment of challenges and opportunities facing Catholic educators in our secularising and pluralising world. Br Green gathers the most current and authoritative voices on the crisis of identity in the Church which, for Br Green, renders central and futural the role of charismic education for bearing witness to missio Dei in the life of our spiritual communities. The resulting book should be considered exceedingly well-informed and creatively in dialogue with current responses to the widening gap between faith and culture, from which Green summons an original, enculturated and positive voice for the ongoing role of religious education in Australia and beyond. Green's particular emphasis on pedagogical models of recontextualisation and dialogue delineates his challenging and itself enthusiastic contribution for a contextually responsive, confessionally inspired educational community—one that lives in formation of mission, in and through its encounters with the Other.

Prof Dr Didier Pollefeyt
Vice Rector
Onderwijs Katholieke Universiteit Leuven, Belgium

'How can Catholic schools evangelise joyfully, credibly, hopefully, respectfully, and compellingly?' asks Br Michael Green in a book that opens new pathways in Catholic education, spirituality, ecclesiology, and creative discipleship.

To address this question, Green draws on the deep wisdom of the Church's diverse spiritual families, and suggests a 'charismic' approach to cultivating and enhancing incarnational and Spirit-enlivened educational communities, alert to the challenges and opportunities of recontextualisation in ever-changing societies.

Well-designed formation is the key to ensuring the authenticity, accountability, and authority needed to take Catholic schools into the heart of the Church's mission for the life of the world.

Research and teaching in Catholic Education has long awaited a book-length study of the role and distinctive contribution of charism in schooling. This book goes further still, inviting us to reimagine the mission of the Church as a multi-faceted, Spirit-infused responsiveness to the *missio Dei* at work in creation.

Rev Dr Kevin Lenehan
Associate Dean (Postgraduate & Research)
Senior Lecturer in Systematic Theology
Catholic Theological College, Melbourne

BBI – THE AUSTRALIAN INSTITUTE OF THEOLOGICAL EDUCATION MISSION AND EDUCATION SERIES

The Mission and Education publishing project is divided into two series. The *Exploratory Series* seeks to serve leaders in Catholic education. It explores aspects of contemporary Catholic education in the light of the Church's official teaching on mission, and the experience of those who attempt to embrace this mission in their personal and professional lives. The *Educator's Guide Series* is being prepared specifically for teachers in Catholic schools.

The richness of the resources now at the disposal of those who seek to explore education theologically can come as a surprise. Because the faith held by the Catholic community is a living faith, Catholic Church teaching on mission has developed, and continues to develop, in the light of contemporary societal and cultural changes. Similarly, Scripture continues to yield its treasures. Only now, for example, is the Bible being widely recognised as a witness to God's purpose or mission in the created universe, and as an account of human response to the unfolding of that mission.

We live in a period of rapid cultural change driven by global dynamics. This has its impact on how we understand what knowledge is, how it is acquired, and how schools are best led and organised so as to maximise student learning, and the economic and social benefits that are presumed to flow from sound educational policies. Very often the emphasis in such policies shifts from 'the learning student' to the more abstract concept of 'student learning'. This sits uneasily with the concept of a Catholic education.

The consequence of rapid societal change is that, in our time, new areas of mission present themselves with real urgency. It is now clearly necessary to include within the mission agenda both the processes of knowledge construction and meaning-making, and the modes of Christian participation in the new public space created by both globalisation and the communications media. These new areas of mission take their place alongside those fields already familiar to the faith community.

The Mission and Education Series seeks to bring together, in the one conversation, the light that human experience, culture and faith throw on particular topics now central to the future development of Catholic education. It also seeks to honour the significant efforts that Catholic educators make, on behalf of young people, to address the contemporary mission agendas within the total process of education. It provides a forum designed to stimulate further conversation about the 'what' and the 'how' of Catholic education as a work of the gospel in our complex society and culture.

It is the hope of the Mission and Education Editorial Board that Catholic educators, both in Australia and beyond, will view the series as an invitation to contribute their own creativity to this vital conversation.

Prof Therese D'Orsa
Professor of Mission and Culture
BBI – TAITE

FINANCIAL SUPPORT

Since the inception of the program, the Mission and Education series has received financial support from a number of Catholic Education authorities. Their assistance with research and publication costs is gratefully acknowledged:

- *Queensland* – the Catholic Education Offices of Brisbane, Cairns, Rockhampton, Toowoomba and Townsville.
- *New South Wales* – the Catholic Education Offices of Armidale, Bathurst, Broken Bay, Maitland-Newcastle, Parramatta, Sydney and Wagga.
- *Australian Capital Territory* – the Catholic Education Office of Canberra-Goulburn.
- *Victoria* – the Catholic Education Offices of Ballarat, Sale and Sandhurst.
- *South Australia* – Catholic Education South Australia (Archdiocese of Adelaide and Diocese of Port Pirie).
- *Tasmania* – the Catholic Education Office of Hobart.
- *Northern Territory* – the Catholic Education Office of Darwin.
- *Religious Congregations* – the Good Samaritan Sisters, Marist Brothers (Province of Australia), Marist Schools Australia, Edmund Rice Education Australia and De La Salle Brothers.

ALSO IN THIS SERIES

Explorers, Guides and Meaning-makers: Mission Theology for Catholic Educators
Catholic Curriculum: A Mission to the Heart of Young People
Leading for Mission: Integrating Life, Culture and Faith in Catholic Education
New Ways of Living the Gospel, Spiritual Traditions in Catholic Education
Stirring the Soul of Catholic Education: Formation for Mission
Educator's Guide to Catholic Identity
Educator's Guide to Catholic Curriculum: Learning for 'Fullness of Life'

FOREWORD

Thanks largely to the great grace of the Second Vatican Council, this is a charismatic moment in the life of the Church. By that I mean that the prime question is not bureaucratic, such as 'What are the gaps and whom can I find to fill them?' Or, 'What are the tasks and whom can I find to do them?'. To ask only these questions is to settle for what Pope Francis, echoing the Aparecida document of the Latin American bishops, has called 'mere administration' (*Evangelium Gaudium,* 25). The prime question in this charismatic moment is rather: 'What are the gifts that God has given and how can these be allowed to flourish for the building up of the Body of Christ for the sake of mission?'. The answer to that question requires discernment of the ways of the Spirit, which can be tantalising.

In this book, Michael Green interprets Catholic schools in that key, a key which he calls 'charismic'. In Australia, Catholic schools may be the best thing the Church has done in its two centuries on these shores. Those schools take their place in a great story of teaching which looks back to Jesus Christ and even further, given his place in Jewish tradition looking back to Moses. The specifically Christian story took a decisive turn when the monasteries appeared in the West and became centres of teaching and learning. Later the Church saw the rise of charismatic figures like Jean-Baptiste De La Salle and Angela Merici, both of whom founded teaching communities that still exist; and they in turn produced a plethora of other teaching communities founded by charismatic figures such as Marcellin Champagnat, Catherine McCauley and Mary MacKillop. However institutionalised Christian schooling may have become, the charisms of the Church have always been at the heart of its inspiration.

Michael Green argues compellingly that in a time of deep and enduring flux in Catholic education, it is more important than ever to view what is happening through a charismic lens, lest we be left with 'mere administration' or a kind of 'grey pragmatism' (Pope Francis again). He insists on the kind of enthusiasm which comes from a charismic sense of the task. It is a challenge, he proposes, that has its sharpest challenges for the spiritual families of the Church which have inherited its charismatic traditions.

The word enthusiasm has had a long and complex history, regarded at times with favour, but at other times with downright suspicion. Its etymology looks back to the ecstatic effect the act of pagan sacrifice had on some devotees, the word meaning literally 'in the sacrifice'. While that may be a thing of the past, the connection between charism and sacrifice is not. The Lord Jesus who sacrifices himself on the Cross gives the gifts of grace that we call charisms; the gifts pour forth from his wounded side. And it is in receiving and responding to those gifts that the educators are filled with the enthusiasm of Easter, becoming themselves the sacrifice that leads students to life. In that, Michael Green says, educators are called to be like Mary, the mother of Jesus.

The book finishes by turning to joy, and rightly so because the enthusiasm of which it speaks is nothing other than the joy of Easter which has been such a *leitmotif* in the preaching and teaching of Pope Francis. Joyless teaching would leave us with nothing more than 'mere administration' or 'grey pragmatism'.

As I read these pages, I could not help thinking of the journey we are on in Australia to the 2020 Plenary Council and into the future that the Holy Spirit is preparing. We will address many questions in the Council, and Catholic education will surely be among them. It is not that our schools are not doing well: they are. But there is no room for complacency as we find ourselves asking why, for all their achievements, we still have our schools.

Clearly the purpose for which they were founded – the education of young Catholics in an often hostile environment – is no longer the purpose they serve at a time when the enrolment of students other than Catholic is substantial and where religious have given way to lay teachers, many of whom are at best oblique about the Church and its teaching. If the purpose of our Catholic schools is to introduce the young to the life of missionary discipleship (would all agree that it is?) can they be said to be succeeding, whatever else they may achieve? These are the kind of questions that forbid complacency and may well find a place on the agenda of the Plenary Council.

Michael Green is alert to such questions and responds to them here with confidence and creativity. The book is both sharp and dense in the way it addresses the connection between charism, spirituality and culture. It offers a sophisticated treatment of the way in which a crisis of identity is also a crisis of purpose and meaning. It sets a biblical and historical context for typically contemporary reflections. It is theologically very solid but accessible nonetheless.

This is all to say that Michael Green, himself a product and promoter of Marist spirituality and the great tradition of Marist education that has emerged from it, has written a book which is nothing if not timely. In drawing together themes both old and new, it will surely help shed light on our path as we grapple with the large and complex questions prompted by the changing contexts we face in the schools and in the Church.

+ Mark Coleridge
Archbishop of Brisbane
President of the Australian Conference of Catholic Bishops

24 May 2018
Feast of Mary Help of Christians, Patroness of Australia

CONTENTS

CONTENTS

1

INTRODUCTION

And so, the biggest threat of all gradually takes shape: 'the grey pragmatism of the daily life of the Church, in which all appears to proceed normally while, in reality, faith is wearing down and degenerating into small-mindedness'. A tomb psychology thus develops and slowly transforms Christians into mummies in a museum. Disillusioned with reality, with the Church, and with themselves, they experience an ongoing temptation to cling to a faint melancholy, lacking in hope, which seizes the heart like 'the most precious of the devil's potions'. Called to radiate light and communicate life, in the end they are caught up in things that generate only darkness and inner weariness, and slowly consume all zeal for the apostolate. For all this, I repeat: Let us not allow ourselves to be robbed of the joy of evangelisation!

Evangelii Gaudium #83

WHAT ARE WE TALKING ABOUT AND WHY?

Like other terms that colour this book, 'enthusiasm' is a word that attempts to capture something that is profoundly theological – that is, of God and about God. 'Spirituality' is a word of similar provenance and purpose, as is 'mission'. None of these words is to be found in the Christian scriptures – at least, not in the way that they are typically used today. And, of course, there is the much-misconstrued idea of 'charism'. These conceptualisations have appeared relatively recently in the discourses of the Church in general and of Catholic education in particular. Yet they have become defining for those of us who ponder the integrity and vitality of today's Catholic schools, and work for them to be conducive spaces for Christ-life to come alive. 'Enthusiasm' is not commonly employed as frequently as the other three words, but perhaps it should be. In the paragraph of

Evangelii Gaudium cited above,[1] Pope Francis warns of the insidious dangers of greyness, and calls all of us in the Church to hold on to the joy of living and sharing the gospel; a call to go in haste, like Mary, into the hill country to an encounter with the other, with a hope-filled soul magnifying God, and brimming with good news of a faithful, merciful and just God. 'How do we do that?' How to do it in the lived reality of the Catholic school of the twenty-first century?

Neither Benedict nor Scholastica, Francis nor Clare, Teresa of Avila nor Francis de Sales, nor indeed any prompter of a religious renewal movement before the mid-twentieth century, would have described the distinctive paths of Christian discipleship which they inspired as new 'spiritualities'.[2] The word was not around. It is likely, also, that Paul would be somewhat surprised to find the way the Greek word *charis*, which he coined for his Letters, but then lay largely dormant until Vatican II, has been reappropriated in the post-conciliar Church. Ignatius could well be pleasantly surprised that 'mission', a secular word he borrowed from the lexicon of the European traders of his time to describe the foreign outreach of his new Society, has come to be used to plumb the very essence of the life of God. It has been through these words that theologians and missiologists of the last hundred or so years have attempted to understand the human experience of the Divine, and the nature and purpose of the Church. It is interesting, and indeed instructive, that both 'enthusiasm' and 'spirituality' were initially used in a pejorative sense as labels for people whose religious experience was judged to be overly intense, even a little unhinged. Their deep personal sense of the indwelling Spirit of God was suspect.[3] Yet it has been from Christians whose personal encounter with the love of God has been marked by a special intensity and transformative clarity that the most efficacious and enduring paths of discipleship have developed. They have not been grey people. This book explores the spiritual wisdom that has been introduced into the life of the Church as a result, and what it can continue to offer Catholic education.

---

1   Pope Francis (2013) *Evangelii Gaudium, Apostolic Exhortation on the Proclamation of the Gospel in Today's World*. Rome: Libreria Editrice Vaticana, #83. In this paragraph, Pope Francis quotes his predecessor who at the time was Prefect of the Congregation for the Doctrine of the Faith: Ratzinger, J (1996) *The Current Situation of Faith and Theology*. Address at the Conference of Presidents of Latin American Episcopal Commissions for the Doctrine of the Faith. Guadalajara, Mexico, 1996.

2   The concept of Christian 'spirituality' was introduced into theological discourse by French theologians from the late nineteenth century. Now a well-established discipline of scholarship supported by a large body of literature, a key reference work on the subject remains the multi-volume *Dictionnaire de Spiritualité* – www.dictionnairedespiritualite.com – which was compiled under the auspices of the French Jesuits over a sixty-year period between 1932 and 1995, and has continued to be augmented. It is over 60,000 pages and comprises more than 6,500 entries.

3   This suspicion has been more typical of western Christianity, particularly in the modern era. In Eastern traditions, the extolling of *theosis*, or divinisation or union of a person with God, has always been a mainstream theological and spiritual concept.

θεὸς ἀγάπη ἐστίν. Thus wrote John.[4] ***Deus caritas est***. Thus began Benedict XVI in his first and signature encyclical.[5] **God is love**. Thus has been the fundamental experience of all whose lives have been transformed by the gospel of Jesus. It is an experience of a self-giving, self-emptying God, known through encounter with Jesus Christ. And more, as Pope Benedict highlights when he draws his readers' attention to the remaining words of 1 John 4:16: 'Whoever lives in love, lives in God, and God abides in them.' The Spirit of God dwells within. The very life of God which is intrinsically loving and relational, irretrievably and unstoppably yearning for communion, dwells in each of us and in all of us together. It urges us towards love and goodness in all their manifestations, and enables us to practise them – in selflessness, fidelity, forgiveness, altruism, joy, patience, justice, resilience, peace, trust, mercy, vulnerability, truth and hope. How to liberate this inner action of the Spirit is the wrestle of a lifetime. The liberation of the Spirit is the 'life in the Spirit' or spiritual life to which Paul invites us, that Christ may come to life in us.[6] All Christian spirituality has its essence here: in the Latin *spiritualitas* (from *pneuma* in Greek, which tried to capture *ruah* in Hebrew).[7] This is a way of describing the Christian's responsiveness to the indwelling Spirit at work, as God's mission is realised in us and in the world. It is something that is experienced intuitively and through God's gracious favour, as it was for Mary who remains the archetype of Christian spirituality, as the 'First Disciple'.[8]

This is the *missio Dei* to which every Catholic school is called to witness and to nurture in its members, and which underpins the themes of this book. There is no genuine Catholic school without its having an impelling sense of sharing in the mission of God. It is a mission that not only generates theological principles and imperatives for the operation of the school, but also anthropological, sociological, political, liturgical, pedagogical and physical

---

4   1 John 4:8 and, even more powerfully, 1 John 4:16.
5   Pope Benedict XVI (2005) *Deus Caritas Est. Encyclical letter on Christian Love*. Rome: Libreria Editrice Vaticana.
6   Cf. Gal 2:20; 4:6; Rom 8:14-16; 1 Cor 3:16.
7   For further reading on these basic concepts of Christian spirituality see, for example: Sheldrake, P (2013), *Spirituality, A Brief History*, Wiley-Blackwell, Chichester; and Schmidt, RH (2008), *God Seekers, Twenty Centuries of Christian Spiritualities*, William B Erdemans Publishing, Grand Rapids. A useful reference compilation is to be found in: Holder, A (ed.) (2011) *The Blackwell Companion to Christian Spirituality*, Chichester: Wiley-Blackwell. The theology of Karl Rahner is strongly concerned with this idea, that humans are essentially spiritual (whether or not they are cognisant of it) and that it is in 'the mysticism of everyday life' that it is lived out. For a useful introduction, see: Egan, HD (2013), The Mystical Theology of Karl Rahner, *The Way*, 52, 2, 43-62.
8   For an introduction to this concept of Mary as 'First Disciple', see: Francis Moloney SDB, both his 1986 book on the subject and his presentations at the BBI-TAITE e-conference of 2017: Moloney, FJ (1986), *Woman, First Among the Faithful*, IN: Ave Maria Press, Notre Dame; BBI-TAITE (10 August 2017), *Mary, First Disciple*, Third National e-Conference, accessible via the BBI-TAITE website: www.bbi.catholic.edu.au

ones.[9] *Evangelii Nuntiandi*, arguably the most shaping contribution in the post-conciliar period to the Church's understanding of evangelisation,[10] makes clear that the reign of God is evidenced through the whole range of human experience, and that the work of evangelisation is therefore to be cast broadly. There is no dichotomy, in this sense, between the spiritual and the temporal, but, rather, the life of the Spirit is understood to be made manifest in the concrete reality of time and place, people and circumstance. For the concerns of this book, that reality is the day-to-day life and self-understanding of the Catholic school – its students and their families, its faculty and staff, its curriculum and co-curriculum, its policies and practices, its priorities and planning, its campus and resource management, its rituals and meaning-making. Its culture. It is thus that *missio Dei* takes flesh. The working understanding of this mission will be that defined by Jim and Therese D'Orsa in an earlier book in the *Mission and Education* series:

> *God's action in time which begins within the very life of God, flows forth in creation, and is ongoing across the entire universe. The Church's role in the conception is to be the community of Jesus' disciples who are intentionally at the service of God's mission in time.*[11]

This orientation is informed by the approach of Bevans, Sivalon and others, of God-as-mission, that this is the universal principle at work in the cosmos and in the heart of each person, and that it is more helpful to speak of the mission having a Church, rather than the reverse.[12] The same holds for the Catholic school: the mission has a school.

---

9   Thomas Groome has long been a leader in the discourse around the multifaceted dimensions of a Catholic school, and what is distinctive about a school's Catholic character. See, for example: *Educating for Life: A Spiritual Vision for Every Teacher and Parent*, Crossroad, New York; 'What Makes a School Catholic?' in McLaughlin, T et al (eds) (2004), *The Contemporary Catholic School*, Routledge, London.

10   The Encyclical of Paul VI, *Evangelisation in the Modern World* (1975). It remains an indispensable text for anyone exploring the meaning of the Church's participation in the mission of God. A key insight of the document is the sense of God's mission expressed in those human activities that make God's reign present in time and place.

11   D'Orsa, J & D'Orsa T (2013), *Leading for Mission, Integrating Life, Culture and Faith in Catholic Education*, Vaughan Publishing, Mulgrave, p. 8.

12   See, for example, Bevans, S and Schroeder, R (2011), 'The Mission has a Church', *Prophetic Dialogue: Reflections on Christian Mission Today*, Orbis, Maryknoll; Sivalon, J (2012), *God's Mission and Post-Modern Culture*, Orbis, Maryknoll. Sivalon develops at length insights into the mission that is God, most especially as Trinity, and draws implications for how this plays out in a post-modern world through contemplation, self-giving love, conversion, care of creation, inclusion, economic and political systems, and a sense of wonder. Another insightful approach to missiology and the Church's role is found in the body of work of John Fuellenbach SVD. See, for example: Fuellenbach, J (2002), *Church: Community for the Kingdom*, Orbis, Maryknoll; (2006), *The Kingdom of God: The Message of Jesus Today*. Wibf and Stock Publishers, Eugene. Fuellenbach explores the role of the community of Jesus' disciples in sharing in his mission to bring forth the Kingdom in time by influence the meaning and experience of life for people so they can find peace, communion with one another, creation, and God. (He also argues for the use of the term 'Kingdom' as the most appropriate Scriptural word, in preference to 'Reign' or other terminology. While acknowledging the learning and validity of his argument, this book opts to use the terms interchangeably, simply to capture a sense of the living reality of the risen Christ in the hearts of people.)

It is (or should be seen as) a wonderful blessing that it does in fact have a school, for this is one of the few spaces where God's mission can today be explicitly named and strategically pursued. The reality of most Western countries is that it is mostly in its service ministries – in Catholic education, along with Catholic health and aged care, and Catholic social agencies – that many people have any direct and personal contact with the Church. Statistics abound to reveal the small percentage of the general population – tiny, if we are honest – that frequently worships or is active in parochial or diocesan life. There are inspiring and committed people who are exceptions to this, who make up the five per cent of the population who are regular worshippers. Many of them are involved as teachers and administrators in Catholic schools, and in leadership roles in Catholic education. But they are not the norm of all those who have been baptised, let alone of contemporary society. Whatever we might claim, through our faith understanding, about the cosmic and unifying mission of God, or that the basic yearning of all people is an essentially spiritual one, this is not something that has profile or cognisance in the daily lives of the majority of people. They are not ecclesial natives, and God-talk can be a foreign language for them. Esoteric gobbledygook. Some learn to speak it, but without necessarily comprehending its nuances; others do not even get that far. Church is another country, not much understood, and holding waning interest or attraction. People identifying themselves as having 'no religion' are the biggest single group in national censuses. And the figures of active church participants are heading south, alarmingly so. Most prominent among them are the so-called 'Millennials'. We all know this, and it pains us.

But the mission has a school. What a gift!

The mission also has a treasure of accumulated and time-honed wisdom – spiritual wisdom – drawn from millennia of human response to the Divine. It has story, inspiration, language, myth, ritual, knowledge, insight, literature, and music. It has long experience of singing the Lord's song in a strange land. It has all this because, of course, God has always dwelt at the heart of human experience, seeking revelation, seeking incarnation. To the extent that people have allowed glimpses of the Divine to come to light among them, spiritually aligned cultures have developed which have been favourable for Christ-life to take flesh in the contextual circumstances of time, time and actual need. God-friendly cultures. But there is something that opens and drives the development of these cultural traditions that is critical for Catholic education today: it is the fact that all of them grew out of need, a need to represent Jesus and his gospel in new ways. The most enduring of these traditions have never lost this intuition for recontextualising *missio Dei*. They have been able to maintain a perennial and critical engagement with changes in context and need, reimagining and recasting themselves, using fresh language, writing new chapters, reinterpreting old myths, finding credible ways for communion rather than exclusion or alienation, and continuing to make meaning. They have not allowed themselves to become jaded and discredited, nor grey. Today they are found among the Church's most enthusiastic spiritual families.[13]

Here is the kernel of this book. The exploration which follows concerning the concepts of charism, spirituality, culture, and what they can offer Catholic schools, is premised on the primacy of *missio Dei* at the core of the Church, and of expressions of Church such as the Catholic school community. This exploration proposes that there is compelling efficacy in what both the established and the emerging spiritual families of the Church have to offer to those who govern, lead, support, teach and learn in today's Catholic schools, as they go about making disciples of all peoples. This is, nonetheless, not an efficacy that is axiomatic or guaranteed. Every spirituality, to maintain its enthusiasm both theologically and actually, needs to be alert to its context and to be dialogically engaged with it. And spirituality needs to be embedded in communities of faith.

It is not to suggest that these enduring spiritual traditions, and the spiritual families in which they abide, are the only or even the principal means that the Church has to enliven and shape the work of Catholic education. There are many sources of holiness and vitality in the Church, innumerable people of deep spirituality who, as members of vital diocesan and parochial communities, are leading and serving today's Catholic schools with commitment and effect. All of them are expressions of the Spirit alive among God's people. Within that broader context, the focus of this book is threefold: on what the spiritualities that belong to the universal Church can bring to the particular Churches; how they can be received by those Churches; and what the spiritual families themselves need to be in order to ensure their integrity and vitality, and their ecclesial identity.

A CREEPING CRISIS OF PURPOSE AND IDENTITY

From around the turn of the century, 'identity' has emerged with increasing frequency as a hot-button topic in Catholic education. It has done so, evidently enough, because significant numbers of people have been

---

13 The concept of 'spiritual families' will be developed in Chapter 2 and figures centrally to the arguments of this book. It is being used in the sense that it was employed by the Congregation for Catholic Education in its 2007 document *Educating Together in Catholic Schools, A Shared Mission between Consecrated Persons and the Lay Faithful*, Libreria Editrice Vaticana, Rome. (Accessible on the Congregation's website.)

concerned about what they have perceived as a change or diminishment of the integrity of Catholic identity in schools. Some of this concern has been simplistically understood and responses have been likewise naïvely proposed. Other attempts at interpretation of what is happening have been considerably more sophisticated in their analysis and, unsurprisingly, straight-forward responses have not readily emerged. This concern over the identity of schools has grown, of course, within the context of broader and deeper trends in church and society. Catholic schools, however, have often enough been a little more insulated from the impact and urgency of some of these rather fundamental cultural shifts, or late in recognising the significance of them. The principal reason for this is because the schools have remained full. Unlike church congregations, which have become fewer in number and older (and their priests the same) Catholic schools – at least in countries where levels of public funding keep them within the financial reach of most families – have continued to grow, their students the same age they always have been, and teachers not only in good supply but better prepared professionally than ever.[14] Schools are vibrant places. They have also, for the most part, kept the confidence of their communities. They have been and still are good schools. For this reason, the identity crisis with which they are now faced has crept up on them somewhat unsuspectedly. Even in countries such as Belgium or French-speaking Canada, where the collapse of Church life in the 1960s and 1970s was as swift as it was comprehensive, there was not a commensurate exodus from the Catholic schools. In a society that he describes as post–Christian and even post-secular, Lieven Boeve observes that most primary and secondary schools in Flanders, and a majority of tertiary institutions, remain Catholic entities.[15] He makes the critical point, however, that the secularising,

---

14   A country that is experiencing a different trend is the United States of America where there has been a large number of closures of Catholic schools over the last quarter-century, a demise that shows little sign of abating. See: O'Keefe, JM (2012) The Catholic School Leader as Agent of Change, in Robey, PV (ed.) (2012) *Scholarly Essays on Catholic School Leadership Vol. 2. Research and Insights on Attaining the Mission of Catholic Schools*, National Catholic Education Association, Arlington VA.

15   He cites 75% of secondary schools and 62% of primary schools. Boeve, L (2016), *Theology at the Crossroads of University, Church and Society: Dialogue, Difference and Catholic Identity*, Bloomsbury, London, pp. 155ff. Dr Boeve is Director General of Catholic Education in Flanders, Belgium. In his previous roles in the Faculty of Theology at *Katholieke Universiteit Leuven* he was involved in the development of the *Enhancing Catholic School Identity Project* (ECSIP). This longitudinal research project – now taking place in many Australian dioceses, as well as Belgium, the UK and elsewhere – offers a helpful conceptual framework and methodology for interrogating the self-understanding of Catholic school communities, and determining the most legitimate ways for them to proceed as Catholic schools, given the value-bases of their communities and the constitutive dynamics at play in the societies in which they are located. While it is beyond the scope of this book to provide a detailed consideration of ECSIP, reference will be made to its key concepts; a working understanding of these would be helpful for the reader to acquire. For a comprehensive introduction see: Pollefeyt, D & Bouwens, J (2014), *Identity in Dialogue: Assessing and enhancing Catholic school identity. Research methodology and research results in Catholic*

de-traditionalising and pluralising factors that are at play in them today are not forces external to these institutions and their communities; these dynamics are working, rather, from the inside out. They are sourced in the schools' own board members, administrators, teachers, and families.[16] And there is the rub. It raises fundamental questions about the identity of these school communities. What are they, in fact? What are they about? In countries such as Australia where cultural and ecclesial shifts have arguably been slower to emerge, empirical data suggest the very same trends are nonetheless gathering pace.[17] Catholic school communities at all levels are increasingly reflective of the de-traditionalising and pluralising society of which they are part. While the Australian data reveal a far from uniform picture, and a range of experience among schools, the overall directions are unambiguous.

If the questions of alterity[18] that emerge from this development are not constructively addressed, then growing dysfunctionality in identity, or at least a spiritual hollowness, is inevitable. The first risk for a Catholic school is a mission drift or mission softening, so it slips towards becoming indistinguishable for most practical purposes from any fine school, other than for a quiet Catholic heritage that is typically and tamely expressed in terms of 'values'. It will be marked by effective teaching and learning, pro-active instructional and strategic leadership, a safe and cohesive environment, informed strategic directions, sound administration, supported by adequate social capital in its wider community, and with some platitudinous language around its Christian values and Catholic tradition. Nothing too loud to frighten the secular horses. Most of its community

---

schools in Victoria, Australia, LIT Verlag, Berlin. For an accessible introduction to its origins and rationale, see: Sharkey P (2013), Hermeneutics and the Mission of the Church, ECSIP as a case study, in D'Orsa, J & D'Orsa, T (2013), *op. cit.*

16 Richard Rymarz, with others, is one who has researched the religious understandings and practice of teachers in Catholic schools. See: Rymarz, R & Belmonte, A (2014), 'And Now I Find Myself Here': Some Life History Narratives of Religious Education Coordinators', *International Studies in Catholic Education,* Vol. 6, No. 2, pp. 191-201; Franchi, L and Rymarz, R (2017), 'The Education and Formation of Teachers for Catholic Schools: Responding to Changed Cultural Contexts', *International Studies in Catholic Education,* Vol. 9, No. 1, pp. 2-16; Rymarz, R (2018) 'We Need to Keep the Door Open": A Framework for Better Understanding for Formation of Younger Teachers', in Stuart-Buttle, R and Shortt, J (eds), *Christian Faith, Formation and Education,* Palgrave Macmillan, London. He has identified, in particular, the influence of the wider culture in which younger teachers live, the lack of strong religiously-linked networks among friends and family, the more porous boundaries around their religious communities and so their lost association with them.

17 Pollefeyt and Bouwens, *op. cit.* In the concepts used in ECSIP, the data show that Australian Catholic schools have been predominantly in the category of the 'Kerygmatic Dialogue School'. While this has proved effective and still has majority support among those at diocesan level, it appears less aligned with the preferences of school communities which are moving more and more towards being 'Recontextualising Dialogue Schools'. Issues flowing from this are taken up in later chapters.

18 This is the preferred term used in ECSIP, drawn from a concept in philosophy and social anthropology. It is applied to Catholic schools in their becoming something radically other than that which they have been or, in fact, think they still are.

is often content with such quietness regarding evangelisation, with the religious elements of the school's life and identity being kept in a safe space that is not too intrusive or presumptive. Boeve points out, however, that this lower-threshold 'Christian-values basis' for Catholic schooling – at least in his own country of Belgium – has failed. He points to its losing plausibility and even becoming counter-productive as the decline has occurred of the proportion of the population which is at ease with a Christian narrative being attached to what are seen as secular human values.[19] He cites the recent European Values Study to show how well-established is a secular value-base across most countries on the continent.

Have the schools, in fact, drifted into what could be described as the 'grey pragmatism' that *Evangelii Gaudium* fears – at least from the perspective of the role of evangelisation in them? In opting for this softer Christian-values approach as their basis, have they lost their evangelising colour, their enthusiasm? While there can be no naïve wishing away of the de-traditionalising and pluralising that exists among the school community or wider society, and no suggestion that there is going to be anything but alienation resulting from a tub-thumping evangelism that shouts without listening, what is the real place of the gospel of Jesus in the identity and lived daily reality of the school? How can a Catholic school evangelise joyfully, credibly, hopefully, respectfully, and compellingly?

Data from Australian Catholic schools that point to a growing drop in staff and students who describe themselves having a deep personal faith – as people who pray, or have a sense of relationship with Christ – show that there is still a reasonable level of comfort with the stated Christian value-base of the school.[20] While schools may not yet be experiencing the same intensity of overt contestation of the Christian narrative as in Europe, it is beginning to be felt. Such a trend is fuelled by the pervading post-modernist suspicion of any meta-narrative or exclusive truth-claim by an institution, and has only been exacerbated by negative publicity such as the scandal from abuse of minors by Catholic clergy, religious, and teachers and the Church's subsequent management of that. Credibility has been wounded, and with it the moral authority of the institutional Church.

This is not new territory for the Church; it has been here many times over its two millennia. One of the ways it has responded has been through

---

19   Boeve, *op. cit.* p.177. See also, Groome, TH, (2011), *Will There Be Faith? A New Vision for Educating and Growing Disciples* Harper One, San Francisco. Groome draws on the work of philosopher Charles Taylor, cf. Taylor, C (2007), *The Secular Age*, Harvard University Press, Cambridge, Mass. Taylor's view is that western society has moved from socio-cultural conditions that favoured religious belief, even requiring it and ostracising those without it, to a kind of humanism that is exclusive of God.

20   Pollefeyt and Bouwens, *op. cit.*

new spiritual movements. The history of its great renewal movements in the past can be instructive for how to proceed now. The spiritual families of the Church, when they are in touch with what sparked their origins, know this well. It is in their DNA. They know in their bones what Vatican II reclaimed, that the Church is essentially a missionary community, and at its most authentic when it is attuned both to this imperative and to the real situations of people in need of hearing the gospel. It is, on the other hand, at its least authentic and most barren when it becomes self-referential – a recurring theme of Pope Francis.[21] At their best, its spiritual families know intuitively about presenting the gospel of Jesus in language that is accessible, inspirational, and which unifies rather than fractures. If they are, on the other hand, in decline they are more likely to display the introspection and insularity of which Francis warns.

Such a missionary mindset suggests a whole lot more than a simple learning and blind application of an accumulated body of wisdom, such as Benedictine spirituality or Ignatian pedagogical principles, however rich they may be. Critically, it means also a process of contemporaneously understanding the lived reality of people, and the reasons and ways they make their meaning. That is to say, the wisdom of a spiritual family is called continually to be recontextualised and reshaped, a kind of ongoing creative fidelity in light of the signs of the times. Such discernment of the signs of the times and response in the light of them represents, of course, a key teaching of the Second Vatican Council, and a shaping direction of vital church communities for half a century since.[22] The dangers of the sterility and irrelevance stemming from a self-referential Church in general apply with equal validity to particular communities within the Church. A clarity of identity is not sufficient; we need a missionary intuition that continually asks if this or that institutional identity provides a compelling way of evangelising.[23] It is always a trap for any group to get caught up so much in its own rhetoric that it ironically loses touch with its *raison d'être*.

In Catholic anthropology, the importance for a group to revisit

---

21 This was a key point, apparently, in the address of then-Cardinal Bergoglio in his address to his fellow electors during the Conclave of 2012. See: http://en.radiovaticana.va/storico/2013/03/27/bergoglios_intervention_a_diagnosis_of_the_problems_in_the_church/en1-677269

22 Cf. *Gaudium et Spes*, #4. The concepts of 'creative fidelity' and 'discernment' have been used by each of the conciliar and post-conciliar popes, initially addressed to institutes of consecrated life in the main (see, for example, *Vita Consecrata*, #37), but later applied more broadly to wider spiritual movements (see, for example, the development of the concept by Focolare Co-President Jesús Morán, in [2017] *Creative Fidelity, the challenge of the implementation of a charism*, Citta Nuova, Rome).

23 This is the starting point for an exploration of charism and culture by Timothy Cook, drawing especially on US and Australian experience of Catholic schooling. Cook, TJ (2015), *Charism and Culture, Cultivating Catholic Identity in Catholic Schools*, NCEA, Arlington. The themes of the book – especially how to embed and sustain a charism in a school's culture, and to ensure an authenticity in the work of evangelisation – address similar topics that follow in later chapters of this book.

and to be redefined by its founding experience is sometimes addressed through the more radical concept of 'refounding'.[24] This is more than a renewal process, but a process that takes a group creatively and deeply into a re-engagement with its founding experience so that it generates new cultural expressions of itself, ones that don't replicate or restore a past time, but which address contemporary needs in contemporary ways. Restorationists and fundamentalists are far from peculiar to Catholic circles, but many would agree that they have been 'powerful and vociferous in Catholic communities'.[25] Whatever the historical, socio-cultural or simply psychological factors that underlie such forces, the evidence is abundant that they serve only a minority, and lead them towards spiritual, cultural and, often enough, moral bankruptcy. The same holds true for those communities which are involved in education. Rather than becoming defensive or in denial in the face of a crisis of meaning, or the breakdown of old patterns of meaning, an engagement with them can be the best way to reclaim vitality, momentum, and indeed enthusiasm.

And the jury is in. This is indeed a liminal time. Pope Francis has aptly proposed that we are not living in an 'era of change' but a 'change of era'.[26] In earlier books in this *Mission and Education* series the commissioning editors (Jim and Therese D'Orsa) have opened up this concept of 'liminality', which is borrowed from anthropology, and applied it to Catholic education with depth and immediacy.[27] In liminal times, meaning is critical. This provides an important underpinning for the discussions of this book. Any consideration of charism, spirituality and culture needs to take place in light of the needs of the time which is being discussed. If this is a time of paradigmatic cultural shift, then this is the context in which the reign of God seeks to be incarnate.

Paul Sharkey, in his hermeneutical consideration of how the contemporary Catholic school can share effectively in God's mission, provides data on the meaning-making of today's Australian young people.[28] It would be of little surprise to most religious educators to hear that their students do not typically use religious language or employ faith concepts in any deep or

---

24 An advocate of this thinking, since the 1980s, has been anthropologist Gerard Arbuckle. For an application of his ideas to contemporary Catholic schools see: Arbuckle, GA (2016), *Intentional Faith Communities in Catholic Education, Challenge and Response*, St Paul's, Sydney. See also Arbuckle, GA (1993), *Refounding the Church*, St Paul's, Homebush.

25 Arbuckle (2016), *op. cit.*, p. 115.

26 Pope Francis (2015), Address to a Meeting of Representatives of the Fifth National Conference of the Italian Church, Cathedral of Santa Maria Fiore, Florence (November 10). www.associationofcatholicpriests.ie/2015/11/not-an-era-of-change-but-a-change-of-era

27 See especially: D'Orsa, J & T (2013), *op. cit.* From among other sources, they draw on the work of anthropologist Victor Turner for the concept of liminality, and of Gerard Arbuckle for what this means for Christian movements and institutions.

28 Sharkey, P (2013), *op. cit.* Dr Sharkey draws on data from his own doctoral research, and refers to Philip Hughes (2007), *Putting Life Together: Findings from Australian Youth Spirituality Research*, Fairfield Press, Fairfield.

consistent way, but are quite eclectic in their fragmentary grabs of what strikes them as interesting, curious or credible. They are creatures of a liminal time, a post-modernist world. It seems reasonable to extend this observation inter-generationally: it is not only young people who lack sure points of reference, or shy from commitment, but also their teachers' and parents' generation. It is a cultural reality. It is these people who are members of Catholic school communities, who frame the expectations and directions for Catholic schools and who, increasingly, govern and administer them.

The question of identity is therefore upon us: what is a Catholic school today? This question must be posed in the cultural context of today, not that of the 1965 when *Gravissimum Educationis* was promulgated by the Council, nor when *The Catholic School* was published twelve years later by the Congregation for Catholic Education, but now. On the fiftieth anniversary of the conciliar document, the Congregation organised its largest-ever event – an international congress. Its theme? 'A Renewing Passion'.[29] The first of the challenges it identified to be facing Catholic schools today, right across the world? Their identity.[30]

This was a recognition that there was going to be no renewal of passion for Catholic education without the Church being clear on the ends that Catholic schools serve. At the end of the nineteenth century, when the die of Australian Catholic education was cast, there was both considerable passion and clear identity. Catholic schools were filled by and large with Catholics-at-school. The schools served the religious, social, political, economic and cultural ends of a community that was far more homogenous and largely under the hegemony of an Anglican/Protestant ascendancy, or which perceived itself to be. Schools and parishes, and churches of both beauty and strategic prominence, were built in cities and towns across the country. Women – so often it was women – and men did remarkable things with modest resources, through a selfless, inventive and heroic dedication to the cause of Catholic education. They gave their lives to it. It was an extraordinary achievement, and a passion for it was maintained through the first half of the last century. Identity and passion served each other.

The corollary of identity is purpose. To consider the former without the latter is to slip into the self-referential trap. A crisis of identity is always correlated to a crisis of purpose, as much as clarity of identity and intensity

---

29 *Educating Today and Tomorrow, A Renewing Passion*, held in Rome, 18-21 November 2015, attracted tens of thousands of Catholic educators from primary, secondary, tertiary and non-formal sectors. The international Congress's *Instrumentum Laboris,* or working paper, with the same title as the Congress, was published the previous year and the subject of wide consultation, http://www.vatican.va/roman_curia/congregations/ccatheduc/documents/rc_con_ccatheduc_doc_20140407_educare-oggi-e-domani_en.html

30 *Ibid.*, #III, 1(a).

of purpose are inextricably linked. They are two sides of the same coin. For what reason does a Catholic school exist? What are the principal motivations of its governing or sponsoring authority, of its principal and leadership group, of its parent community, of its teachers, of its students, of its supporters, or of its funders (both public and private)?[31] What is the degree of coalescence, both internally within each group and across them? Sometimes the focus is put on one group or another, for example the motivation of parents in sending their children to a Catholic school. It is important, however, to consider all stakeholders because each will influence what the school becomes – where its attention is most directed, where its energies and resources go and do not go, what is or is not honoured, what is or is not challenged, what is or is not symbolised and ritualised, and so on. Whether stated or unstated, cognisant or not, motivation is the shaper of identity. And motivation is an expression of underlying values and meaning-making.

There is, of course, no paucity of literature that seeks to define such purpose. Church documents, government goals and benchmarks, reference texts from canonical authorities, school mission statements and strategic plans abound, not to mention a library of books such as this! They are often rich and comprehensive documents. But it is within the actual human beings – the governors, the administrators, the students, the teachers, the parents, the funders – that understanding and motivation most validly reside and need to be identified. To this end, projects such as the *Enhancing Catholic School Identity Project*, which forensically tap into the meaning-making of the actual people who comprise the school community, have *prima facie* merit. This is a recognition of the primacy of people in the project of the Catholic school, however the school might formally describe itself and its purposes.

The emerging evidence which suggests that there is now drift, inconsistency, and some degree of dysfunctionality within Catholic school communities, is only deepened when their wider stakeholder group (such as government) is taken into account. Catholic schools face a crisis of meaning, and therefore a crisis of purpose. They do so within the crisis of meaning more broadly at play in society in this time of liminality. That is the clear diagnosis. But what do we do with that data? That is where a simply diagnostic approach can stall. It is one thing to describe and to analyse what

---

31   In a study of issues at play in the future mission integrity and authentic Catholic cultures in Catholic higher education in the USA, John Wilcox focuses on *motivation*, especially of faculty. Cf. Wilcox, JR (2013), *Revisioning Mission: The Future of Catholic Higher Education*, CIPP, New York. Dr Wilcox argues for an inclusive and open engagement with the diversity of faith perspectives among faculty as the basis for forming a viable mission community. It is an argument that resonates with the premises of the ECSIP research.

is happening, it is another to ask what can be done. It is another again to ask what *should* be done. And who is it who has authority to introduce the moral weight of 'should' into the question? In order to imagine how *missio Dei* might be fostered it is critical to identify those who carry authority and how they evangelically exercise it in the cultural realities of the Catholic school.

A second potential source of stalling comes from regarding data as prescriptive rather than descriptive. As the result of comprehensive analytical research we may well find ourselves with a set of tables and graphs that show there is a fundamental breakdown in people's secure cultural frameworks and mythologies, a discrediting of the Catholic narrative, a dissolution of their religious faith, a sense of disconnection from institutions, and that their making of meaning is being shaped by pluralising and secularising influences with the result that there is more overt contestation over the *raison d'être* of the Catholic school. It may also be true that this fractured and postmodernist description of a community makes it even conceptually problematic to pursue the 'integration' of 'faith, culture and life' to which Catholic education was called in the last century.[32] But it is a mistake to accept all that as the way it needs to remain. What it provides, rather, is a starting point, a locus of meeting. It is essential to understand it closely, for that is where people must be met. They are not anywhere else and to presume they are is to risk nothing more than a pseudo encounter, certainly not one that will touch them.

Jesus did no other than this: meeting people in the reality of their lives, dialoguing with them, and from there inviting them to new possibilities. He brought about change in their lives, and in their understanding of their lives. That the places of today's encounters are more likely to be Catholic schools, Catholic hospitals, and Catholic social services parallels Jesus' meeting people to teach, to heal, and to empower. It was only a minority of cognoscenti that he met first in the synagogue and the Temple; they were not the main focus of his ministry even though they were part of it. In this sense, people's cultural realities are situations to befriend rather than to fight, because it is in these cultural realities that God seeks incarnation. This is not to imply that that locus of encounter is the end-point of the journey, or that the Catholic school or any other agency of the Church should recast itself as the only place where the Church's ministry should take place. Again, we turn to Jesus: in every first encounter of healing, liberating or teaching, Jesus leads people to something more, something deeper and ongoing. So, also, the experience of belonging, or being taught or made whole in a Catholic

---

32   Sacred Congregation for Catholic Education (1977), *The Catholic School*, Libreria Editrice Vaticana, Rome, #44. This phrase has become an oft-quoted foundational principle for Catholic education.

school should invite a person into the deeper and ongoing life of a vital Church community.

Missio Dei implies the possibility of change; indeed, it requires it. Discipleship is never about leaving things as they are in people's lives; there is no example of this in the scriptures. Rather, it involves *metanoia*. Schools are founded on this conviction. Across the full spectrum of belief and values bases, they exist to be transformative for young people, to educate them. On this, it is not difficult to find common ground among educators. But it is not only young people who are educated in schools. It is also reasonable, in Western education of this century, to assume shared acceptance of the concept of the school's being a 'community of learners' – teachers as well as students. And, to the degree that it is embedded in its community and parents are engaged respectfully and genuinely in the work of the school, then they also will have an expectation of learning. Thus, the very nature of the contemporary school can help to create a climate of openness to change and growth and, more particularly, to evangelisation.

Approaches for going about it – as appropriate to the ages and circumstances and roles of various members of the community – are another matter. The primary principle to recognise is that change and transformation are constitutive of what any good school is about, and it is on this foundation that evangelisation is well undertaken. A critical factor in evangelisation will be, of course, how the organisational culture of the school is constructed and animated. And importantly in these times of liminality it will be the argument of this book that the Church's spiritual families can have vision, resources and intuition with which to do this, and to do so in contexts of jadedness, alienation and disaffection towards the Church. These contexts of jadedness can give the gospel a 'contextual plausibility' because *missio Dei* always requires incarnation in time and place, and in a faith community,[33] and from these the Church's spiritual families attract discipleship. If they are authentic to their founding (including its evangelising impulse and its instinct to understand and embrace contemporary reality[34]), are inspirationally led with integrity and skill, and have members who are influentially active in the school community, they can have a great effect on that community's collective understanding and ownership of an evangelical purpose and identity. On the other hand, if our spiritual families have lost touch with their founding intuitions, if their leadership is neither deeply steeped in the tradition nor highly skilled in educational leadership, or if they have slipped from significant practical influence, then they are unlikely

---

33   Boeve, L, *op.cit.*, p. 2.
34   Cf. *Evangelii Gaudium*, #104

to have much relevance or impact.

So much hinges on the community, and on the self-understanding of the community. When a spiritual family of the Church conducts, sponsors or supports a Catholic school, the degree to which there is going to be a healthy symbiotic relationship between identity and purpose in the school will be a correlate of that same symbiosis within the spiritual family.

OUTLINE AND APPROACH OF THIS BOOK

This book aims to be an academic primer for studying the foundations and character of the spiritual families of the Church, and their potential to contribute to God's mission in the Catholic schools of the twenty-first century. It is about Catholic schools, and it is written for those who teach and learn in them, who lead and govern them, who have pastoral responsibility for them, who hold dreams and fears for them, and who support and challenge them. It is most especially offered to people undertaking post-graduate research in theology and education, and others in leadership who are strategically engaged in shaping directions in Catholic schools. While it draws heavily on the context of Australian Catholic schools, it attempts to situate itself in the discourse of Catholic education and the Church more broadly.

A generic approach to the exploration of charism and spirituality is taken. In one sense, this may seem to be counter-intuitive because the power and grace that emanate from the Church's spiritual families are often appreciated through their distinctiveness, novelty, or uniqueness. From one perspective, this is entirely valid. 'Diversity, plurality, and multiplicity'[35] are characteristic of the Church's spiritualities and essential to their efficacy. Indeed, the individual identity of each spiritual family is paramount. It has been through the nurturing of such cogent identity, typically a *cultural* identity and all that it implies, that they have built community and undertaken their ministries so fruitfully and sustainably, and with evangelical integrity. They have brought forth the Kingdom in time and place; they have given compelling credence to 'now' being the 'favourable time'.[36] In another and more fundamental sense, nonetheless, they are all the same. This sameness is sourced in both their purpose, and the three interconnected ways in which this purpose is pursued. The purpose is *missio Dei* and the Church's service of this; the threefold expression of this purpose is realised through the personal call and faith response of individual disciples, in the forming of

---

35 The phrase is from *Evangelii Gaudium*, #130. See also *Lumen Gentium*, #12; *Christifideles Laici*, #20; *Vita Consecrata*, #5.
36 2 Cor 6:2.

Christian community, and in this community's loving service in the world as it shares in incarnating and fostering the reign of God.

It is to be hoped that the principles, concepts, and challenges proposed in the book will assist the reader to research at greater depth, and in sharper focus, individual spiritual families and their ongoing life in the Church and in the service of Catholic education. This may be, for example, in relation to the history of such an ecclesial community, or its distinctive approach to Christian discipleship, or its characteristic approach to education, or its ways of associating and sustaining its members as a community of faith, or in how it has or has not sought to recontextualise any of these for changing times. This book may help to inform a study of a single school or a group of schools, their cultures, their integrity as communities of faith, their leadership, or their creative fidelity to founding evangelical intuitions. It may guide the generating or evaluating of conceptual or strategic bases for formation, leadership succession, faith development of staff, youth programs, school reviews, or professional appraisal. It may lead to an exploration of issues associated with the fostering of multiple spiritualities in a local diocesan context, or relationships with parochial communities. It may prompt new conceptual discourse and interdisciplinary dialogue. The possibilities are many.

The subjects addressed in the book include those that touch major areas of discourse in theology, spirituality, anthropology, history, and education. While it is necessary to do this, it is readily acknowledged that there is sometimes only passing or brief mention of issues for which there is a large body of literature. Some doctoral dissertations and books are referenced with only a sentence or two of comment. This is not to undervalue or skim over the complexity or depth of such scholarship, but simply to construct a widely cast narrative that gives the reader a context for pursuing more specific lines of enquiry. It is hoped that brevity of treatment does not compromise the richness of the concepts and ideas that are introduced into the discussion. The reader may wish to plumb one or more questions more deeply, or to read one or more writers more extensively. Where possible, advice is offered for doing this. This is frequently done via footnotes so as not to intrude into the principal lines of the narrative.

Chapter 2 begins by introducing the concepts of charism, spirituality, and charismic culture before turning to the challenges associated with ongoing recontextualisation, and the creative tension of the hierarchical and charismatic dimensions of the Church. It is an exploration of the ongoing activity of the Spirit in the life of the Church, especially as this is expressed through its renewal movements and their continued relevance.

In Chapter 3 this is further developed by a viewing of spiritual movements and ecclesial communities through the lens of the ecclesiology that has developed in the light of the Second Vatican Council. It then looks at Catholic schools as expressions of Church and emerging imperatives for the spiritual families associated with these schools. Chapter 4 considers criteria for assessing and fostering the integrity and authenticity of charismic traditions, and the communities which are responsible for them, specifically in the context of schools. It proposes ten factors that are likely to be significant for them, and looks at some specific issues in the context of the organisational culture of schools. Chapter 5 returns to the core questions of purpose and identity, and explores the factors that are likely either to contribute to or compromise the building of a charismic culture in Catholic schools. Chapter 6 turns to the critical element of leadership, and uses the primary Marian principle of the Church as a way to understand what should be the essence of leadership in the context of a spiritual family in a school. It then considers issues associated with the broader whole-of-Church responsibility to foster the spiritualities of the Church, and also the changed role of religious institutes and newer canonical juridic entities and the kind of leadership required of them. In considering the future, Chapter 7 focuses particularly on the centrality of formation. It emphasises the tri-dimensional need for spiritual families to be simultaneously schools of spirituality, schools of community, and schools of mission for their members and those who work alongside them in Catholic schools – and to do so credibly and relevantly in today's school communities.

The spiritual traditions of the Church, and the enduring ecclesial communities that have inherited them and continue to develop and enrich them, are deep and much-studied. Some spiritual traditions have been many centuries in the making, and benefit from wisdom that has accumulated and percolated through countless people of faith, hope and love over that time. The ones that have continued to be fruitful are those which have been able to present the gospel of Jesus with relevance and inspiration to people from quite different periods of history where enormously varying factors have shaped society, epistemology, morality, theology, cosmology, culture – the whole gamut of human experience.

They are traditions, therefore, that offer extensive possibility for commentary and research. Others are less well established, in existence for just a century or two, and are comparatively early in their evolution. Others again are in the process of re-emerging in the present age. All of them have grown out of a felt need, one that called for freshness of evangelical expression. Each has its own profundity of spiritual, ecclesiological and cultural insight. No generalist book such as this can presume to do justice to any one of them. Where passing reference is made to one or other spirituality or one or other founder to exemplify some point, it is recognised that such mention will inevitably lack depth and nuance. It is hoped, nonetheless, that the concepts that are opened and the manner of their treatment will assist readers from any spiritual tradition in gaining further appreciation of their place and potential in the unfolding of God's mission, and specifically in the field of Catholic education today.

2

AN INDWELLING SPIRIT
WHO IRRUPTS

The fruits of the Spirit are different. What the Spirit brings is ...
Gal 5:22

Jesus' promise to his friends that the Spirit of God would continue to abide with them, and would continue to reveal God to them,[1] has sustained the Church in hope.[2] The fulfilling of this promise has renewed the Church and purified it time and again. It has been, as Jesus said it would be, a source of consolation, in the sense of this being the antithesis of fear and despair. With each person and through each community a new aspect of the image of God is revealed. Christ has been formed in these people and these communities,[3] and the life of God has come to be incarnated in them and among them together.[4] And where need has been greatest, where a sense of the absence of God has been most keenly felt, it is there that the Spirit seems to be most active, for the-God-who-is-love yearns to be revealed and to bring life.

There is a basic principle of Christian anthropology here, one that informs the discussion that follows. It is that there is a spiritual way of understanding what it means to be human which is of its very essence, and which is integrally bound up with its physicality and temporality. Religious or spiritual experience is not a tack-on, but part of the nature of being human. To be mystical is not some other-worldly phenomenon, something eerily pursued with Ouija boards or clouds of incense in an attempt to connect with some parallel universe or to be magically transported to some higher realm. It is no out-of-body experience. It is to be in touch with and responsive to the Spirit of God in the here and now. Mary is the archetype of this and, in that sense, the model of Christian discipleship. Without delving into the broad theological discourse around nature and grace, or

---

1 John 14:16-17, 26; 16:13.
2 Rom 5:5.
3 Gal 4:19; Col 1:27-29.
4 John 14: 1-3, 18, 27; 16:20, 33.

debates about metaphysics or neo-Thomistic thought,[5] it is important that we name some key Pauline concepts, since the following discussion on charism and spirituality depends on them.

As incredulous as the early Christians might have been with the proposition, and as well we may we, Paul tells us that God's Spirit dwells in us,[6] prays in us,[7] wants to bring alive the Risen Christ in us.[8] And among us.[9] The signs of this are evident in our ordinary human living, both personally and communally. We see it, Paul tells us, when 'love, joy, peace, patience, kindness, generosity, faithfulness, gentleness and self-control' prevail in our lives, and when 'immorality, impurity, idolatry, sorcery, hatreds, rivalry, jealousy, licentiousness, outbursts of fury, acts of selfishness, dissensions, factions, envy, drunkenness and moral promiscuity' do not.[10] This is the life of the Spirit. It is lived out in the relationships and concrete circumstances of a person's life.

Most fundamentally, the Spirit of God seeks communion, harmony and love, since this is the inner life of God. This life of God seeks to be alive and at work in us. At the start of Part II of his Encyclical *Deus Caritas Est*, as Benedict XVI turns to address the life and work of the Church he draws on this important Pauline understanding and quotes St Augustine: 'If you see charity [caritas], you see the Trinity'[11]. The Pope then goes on to teach:

> *The Spirit, in fact, is that interior power which harmonises [believers'] hearts with Christ's heart and moves them to love their brothers and sisters as Christ loved them.*[12]

God dwells in us, and God reveals Godself in human reality.[13] God's revelation is one of love and in love, and the Church has no other purpose

---

5 While a comprehensive treatment of this huge field of discourse is clearly beyond the scope of this book, the theological questions around the operation of nature and grace, and philosophical questions around essentialism and ontology, are of course germane to what is being considered. From Thomas Aquinas in the thirteenth century to Karl Rahner and Paul Tillich in the twentieth, much ink has been spilt on these subjects. Some entry points for Rahner have been cited in Chapter 1. A helpful introduction to this scholarship, specifically from the perspective of understanding Christian spirituality in its different traditions and expressions, is provided by Michael Downey: Downey, M (1997), *Understanding Christian Spirituality*, Paulist Press, New York.

6 Cf. Rom 8: 9,26; 1 Cor 3:16; Eph 2;18; Gal 4:6.

7 Rom 8:2, 15, 26-27.

8 Gal 2:19-20; 2 Cor 4:11; Phil 1:20-21.

9 1 Cor 12-13; Eph 2:19-22, 4:1-6, 25-32; Col 3:5-17.

10 Gal 5:19-23.

11 *Deus Caritas Est*, #19.

12 *Ibid.*

13 Paul Tillich, the twentieth century Protestant theologian and philosopher, is one who had a highly developed theology around the action of the Spirit being manifested in history, linked to his understanding of the nature of humanity. For an introduction, see: Bullock, VT (1971), *A critical examination of Paul Tillich's doctrine of the Holy Spirit*, Durham University, Master of Letters thesis, http://etheses.dur.ac.uk/9624/

than to serve this end. The Church does this as the 'mystical body of Christ'. The incarnational theology that informs such a concept is captured simply in the statement popular in Catholic devotion:

Christ has no body now but yours. No hands, no feet on earth but yours. Yours are the eyes through which he looks with compassion on this world. Yours are the feet with which he walks to do good. Yours are the hands through which he blesses all the world. Yours are the hands, yours are the feet, yours are the eyes, you are his body. Christ has no body now on earth but yours.[14]

It is not some poetic figure of speech being used here. It is, rather, a profound theological statement that can be seen to align with Paul's understandings. We can apply the word 'yours' both individually and communally to Christians.

This is always a work-in-progress, Paul hastens to add; a glimpse and promise of what will be but is not yet realised.[15] Anyone who has spent time in a Catholic school would understand this readily. They are likely to be able to cite many examples of wonderful moments of grace in the course of their own teaching ministry and in the broader life of the school, but perhaps add many examples to show that things are far from a pure and complete expression of the life of God. It is well, nonetheless, for all of us to lift our heads out of the figurative scrums that the freneticism of school life can induce, and to be in awe of what is at play. God is seeking revelation and the life of God is seeking expression.

The human response to that is often inadequate or misdirected, and the gap between the ideal and the actual can be disheartening for us, sometimes piercingly so. 'But,' encourages Paul, 'the Spirit comes to help us in our weakness', so that despair should not become the fruit of hardship or set-back in ministry.[16] Paul uses powerfully figurative language to describe inadequacies and battles of human experience in this partial unfolding of God, and how the Spirit is at work in it. Childbirth, with its attendant pain, is a rich example.[17] Central to this movement of the Spirit is the Pauline concept of spiritual giftedness. It is from this idea that the term 'charism'

---

14 Although widely attributed to the sixteenth century Carmelite reformer, mystic and Doctor of the Church, Teresa of Avila, the statement is not found in her writings. Its provenance is disputed.

15 Cf. Rom 8:19-22; 2 Cor 1:22; 5:4-6; Eph 1:13-14; Phil 3:12-13. Paul uses the term *sarx* (σάρξ, literally 'flesh', but a more complex concept) in contradistinction to *pneuma* (πνεῦμα, Spirit). See also Rom 8:1-13. He does so not to imply in any sense that the life of the Spirit is a disembodied phenomenon, or that it is inherent evil to be humanly alive in time and place. The theology of the body occupies a considerable body of theological discourse, and was a theme developed particularly by St John Paul II. So, also, is the flesh/spirit antithesis in the Pauline and also Johannine Scriptures a subject of much exegetical commentary.

16 Rom 8:26a. See also Paul's consideration of the trials of apostolic life in 2 Cor 4.

17 Rom 8:22.

has re-emerged in today's Church, in ways that to some extent align well with its Scriptural origins in the Pauline texts, but in other ways that have developed further meanings.

WHAT IS CHARISM?

'Charism' is a term that has come to be applied with both increasing frequency but widening cast in recent decades, including in Catholic education. The resulting imprecision has not always been conducive for understanding the life of the Spirit, which is how the concept is most validly approached. The first point to highlight is that the term is conceptual, and theologically so. Charism is not a commodity, something concrete that can be acquired or deployed. A school cannot go to 'get' a charism from somewhere. Comments like 'We are a charism school' or 'Our school has such-and-such a charism' can be misconceived in this regard. In some circles, the word's meaning has been diminished to become little more than a grab-all, jargon way of labelling a distinctive pedagogical style, a set of characteristic cultural expressions associated with a particular group, a nostalgic or even cult-like attachment to some founder or religious institute, or a circle-the-wagons effort to keep everything as it has been. None of these – in their intuition for self-preservation or individuation or divisiveness – tend to accord easily with the signs of the Spirit that are found in the Christian Scriptures. What did Paul and other writers of the Letters mean by the term, and how has it come to be used in the Church's discourse today, especially in connection to Catholic education? To what extent is it valid to continue to develop new understandings of the original Scriptural sense of the concept?[18]

Paul drew from the Greek word *charis* (χαρις, meaning 'gift' or 'grace') to coin the word *charísma* (χαρισμα) which is usually rendered in English as 'charism', or sometimes more simply as 'gift'. It is not a word that has been found elsewhere in the Greek literature of his time, and one theory is that it was a colloquial term for gift, generous gift, or gracious gift.[19] Paul

---

18 The Congregation for the Doctrine of the Faith has recently treated these questions in some depth. See (2016), *Iuvenescit Ecclesia. Letter to the Bishops of the Catholic Church regarding the relationship between the hierarchical and charismatic gifts in the life and mission of the Church*, http://www.vatican.va/roman_curia/congregations/cfaith/documents/rc_con_cfaith_doc_20160516_iuvenescit-ecclesia_en.html

19 This is the view of Nardoni, E (1993), 'The Concept of Charism in Paul', *The Catholic Biblical Quarterly*, Vol. 55, 1, pp. 68–80; and Hanna, T (2006), *New Ecclesial Movements*, St Paul's, Sydney. For a concise summary of the history of the term in Christian theological discourse, and especially its reclamation and reappropriation in the twentieth century, see, Leahy, B (2011), *Ecclesial Movements and Communities. Origins, Significance and Issues*, New City Press, New York, pp. 81ff. A thorough Scriptural, historical and theological exploration of the concept of charism can be found in a recent study of Yves Congar's approach to the topic by Johnson Mudavassery O.Carm. See Chapter 2 of: Mudavessery, J (2016), *The Role and Function of Charism in the Theology of Yves Congar*, Peter Lang GmbH, Frankfurt am Main.

uses the word fourteen times, mainly in Romans and First Corinthians; it appears elsewhere in the New Testament in another three instances.[20] Charisms are first described in terms of God's gracious initiative towards humanity, including of Christ himself (Rom 5:15-16; 6:23; 11:29; 2 Cor 1:11). Then, and especially in First Corinthians, Paul associates charisms with manifestations of the Spirit, as concrete expressions of the life of God in people. He does not see them as just human talent or generic capacity, but as divinely sourced giftedness. Despite this, they are not portrayed, for the most part, as extraordinary or eccentric gifts, but as expressions of God's grace that are necessary for the full and healthy functioning of the community and for its benefit. Where the gifts are perhaps unusual or individual – such as the gift of tongues (*glossolalia*), to which Paul gives extended attention (1 Cor 14, *passim*) – then he places them in a context of usefulness for the whole community. There is an inherent and characteristic diversity among the *charismata*, but not in any competitive or negatively comparative sense. They are either needed to complete the whole, or to allow the individual to pray, to complement others in the community, or to serve it and its purposes. Paul's analogy to the different parts of the one body, Christ's body, is perhaps his most eloquent statement of this (Rom 12:4-5; 1 Cor 12:12-30; Eph 4:12). In short, the gifts reveal the 'multiform grace of God' (1 Pet 4:10).

The context which Paul uses for his understanding and discerning of the place of the *charismata* is of primary importance. It is an ecclesial context. He describes these gifts as God's way of giving life, fullness and efficacy to God's life in the Church. Complementarity is a central principle, not in the functional sense of there being some advantage in having a balanced organisational chart for the structure of the Church and role allocation within it, but in a more organic sense of full expression of life in the Body of Christ, with people with their diverse giftedness living as members of this Body. Prophecy, governance, teaching, preaching, pastoral ministry, almsgiving and administration are all expressions of this (Rom 12:6-8; 1 Cor 12:8-10; Eph 4:11; 1 Pet 4:10-11). States of life – such as marriage, virginity, widowhood – are understood in a similar fashion (1 Cor 7:7). Paul perceives some natural order of giftedness, judging that apostles, then prophets, then teachers should have prominence, followed by those with gifts of miracles, healing, and languages (1 Cor 12:27-28). Again, this is done

---

20   Rom 1:11; 5:15-16; 6:23; 11:29; 12:6; 1 Cor 1:7; 7:7; 12:4, 9, 28, 30, 31; 2 Cor 1:11; 1 Tim 4:14; 2 Tim 1:6; 1 Pet 4:10. (To describe the two instances in 1 and 2 Timothy as not from Paul is, of course, to favour the argument that these letters, although in Paul's name, were not written by him.)

only as part of the body of Christ and, therefore, for serving God's mission in Christ.

Discernment of gifts is critical for Paul because he sees that not all giftedness is born of the Spirit. Some talents serve evil or idolatrous ends (1 Cor 12:1-3). Paul's concern is for the common good (1 Cor 12:26), for the building up of the Church, and for anything that is conducive to signs of the life of the Spirit. Above all other gifts are faith, hope and love. These are the ultimate signs that the Spirit is active (1 Cor 12:31-13:13). It is most especially love – and the ways that love finds human expression in patience, graciousness, humility, selflessness, gentleness, forbearance, truthfulness, forgiveness, trust, service and endurance – that provides the surest evidence that life in the Spirit is being incarnated. It is to this overriding criterion and this context that Paul most frequently returns in his consideration of the *charismata* (cf. Rom 12:9-13; 1 Cor 14:1; Eph 4:15-16.)[21]

There is, therefore, some underpinning consistency of understanding in the Christian Scriptures on the subject of charisms: they are gracious revelations, in time and place, of the life of God made manifest in and among people; they are sourced in faith, induce hope, and are expressed through love and in pursuit of love; they are diverse but complementary, and always at the service of the Church as it undertakes God's mission. At the same time, however, it needs to be recognised that the New Testament does not offer a fully developed or systematic theology of charisms. The word is used in different ways. It sometimes refers to the appearance and work of Christ directly, to roles and states of life in the Church, or to shared and individual spiritual giftedness. In different instances, charisms are described as coming variously from God (Rom 12:3; 1 Cor 12:28; 2 Tim 1:6; 1 Pet 4:10), from Christ (Eph 4:7) and from the Spirit (1 Cor 12:4-11). It is legitimate, therefore, for the Church to continue to build and refine its understanding of the concept, and to expect that God's Spirit will continue to unfold its expression and meaning in time.[22]

It was in the first half of the twentieth century that the Church began to reflect more explicitly on its inner life in these terms.[23] This paralleled

---

21 For a detailed treatment of each of the occurrences of 'charism' in the New Testament see: Nardoni, *op. cit.* For a succinct but thorough overview, see *Iuvenescit Ecclesia*, #4-8.

22 *Iuvenescit Ecclesia*, #8. See also Nardoni, *op. cit.*, p. 69.

23 The Church's evolving self-understanding throughout its history is a study in itself. Avery Dulles SJ and John Fuellenbach SVD are two scholars of the last century who have led modern thinking in this field, proposing fresh insights for how the Church is most appropriately understood. Dulles' (1974), *Models of the Church*, Doubleday, New York, has been a seminal work. Dulles also posited that Vatican I was not ready to offer any teaching on the Church as the Mystical Body of Christ, judging it to be too ethereal a notion. From that perspective, Pius XII's Encyclical was a significant step in the way the Church understood God's movement within and among its members. Dulles' later preference to see the Church as a community of disciples aligns with emphases within this book.

the contemporaneous opening of a new theological discourse around the concept of 'spirituality'.[24] Neither 'charism' nor 'spirituality' was new in the life of the Church; they were simply new insights for understanding and naming how God's ever-creative and renewing Spirit was active among the Risen Christ's disciples. A catalyst for development in the Church's understanding was provided by Pius XII's Encyclical on the Church as the Mystical Body of Christ, a teaching which carried multiple mentions of the work of the Spirit in the Church through its 'gifts' which are variously described 'charismatic', 'heavenly', 'spiritual' and from 'the Paraclete'.[25] It was, though, the Second Vatican Council which sparked the reappropriation of the term 'charism' in a major way.[26] The sentence that is often regarded as 'most emblematic'[27] in the Council's teaching is found in *Lumen Gentium*:

> *The Church, which the Spirit guides in the way of all truth (John 16:13) and which he unifies in communion and in works of ministry, he both equips and directs with hierarchical and charismatic gifts and adorns with its fruits (Eph 4:11-12; 1 Cor 12:4; Gal 5:22).* [28]

In one of the debates during the drafting stage of this Dogmatic Constitution on the Church, Belgian Cardinal Leo Joseph Suenens rose to make a memorable and influential intervention. This champion of Vatican II argued strongly for the twin dimensions of the Church that came to be included in this paragraph of *Lumen Gentium*, and about which Pius XII had written two decades previously. Without the order and structure from its hierarchy, he acknowledged, the Church would be adrift and without form; but

---

24 This has already been touched on in the previous chapter, and will be discussed in more detail later in this chapter. Leahy (2011), *op. cit.*, pp. 86-87, points to the emergence of 'charism' in German theological discourses in the 1950s, something that had been developing during the previous half-century. It was not a term, however, that had much currency beyond a relatively small number of theologians.

25 *Mystici Corporis Christi* was written in 1943, during some of the darkest days of World War II. It provided a fresh and more balanced perspective for understanding the nature of the Church. Within its teaching is the call to holiness of all the members of the Church, including lay people, and the importance of the Church's charismatic identity to complement its hierarchical one (17). It includes twenty mentions of the 'gifts' of the Holy Spirit. It was indicative of the shift that was occurring away from the Tridentine concept of the Church as the 'perfect society', to use the expression championed by Cardinal Robert Bellarmine SJ in the Catholic Reformation period, to an emphasis that was more concerned with mystery and communion.

26 Belgian theologian Benjamin Wambacq O. Praem made a useful analysis of the term charism as it emerged from the Council: Wambacq, BN (1975), Le Mot Charisme, *Nouvelle revue théologique*, 97, 345-55. John O'Malley is another theologian who has discussed it, seeing 'charism' as a term that became part of the 'lexicon of the Church' that developed after Vatican II. See: O'Malley, JW (2008), *What Happened at Vatican II*, Belkap Press of Harvard University Press, Cambridge MA, p. 56.

27 *Iuvenescit Ecclesia*, #9.

28 *Lumen Gentium* #4, 12, in Flannery, A (ed.) (2008), *Vatican Council II: Constitutions, Decrees, Declarations. The Basic Sixteen Documents* (revised edition), Liturgical Press, Collegeville MN.

without the charismatic giftedness of the Spirit, it would be hollow and sterile.[29]

Lumen Gentium took this a step further in a defining paragraph which described what these 'charismatic gifts' look like in practice:

> *God distributes special graces among the faithful of every rank. By these gifts he makes them fit and ready to undertake various tasks and offices for the renewal and upbuilding of the Church. Whether these charisms[30] be very remarkable or simply and widely diffused, they are to be received with thanksgiving and consolation since they are fitting and useful for the needs of the Church.[31]*

The Pauline concepts are obvious, but the Council's teaching now applied them – and, specifically the term 'charism' – not to the Christian communities of the New Testament age but to the Church of the present time, and indeed of all times. It was a theme that the Council took up elsewhere, including on its decree of the Laity:

> *For the exercise of this apostolate, the Holy Spirit who sanctifies the people of God through ministry and the sacraments gives the faithful special gifts also (cf. 1 Cor 12:7), 'allotting them to everyone according as he wills' (1 Cor 12:11) in order that individuals, administering grace to others just as they have received it, may also be 'good stewards of the manifold grace of God' (1 Pet 4:10), to build up the whole body in charity (cf. Eph 4:16). From the acceptance of these charisms, including those which are more elementary, there arise[s] for each believer the right and duty to use them in the Church and in the world for the good of men and the building up of the Church, in the freedom of the Holy Spirit who 'breathes where He wills' (John 3:8). This should be done by the laity in communion with their brothers [sic] in Christ, especially with their pastors who must make a judgment about the true nature and proper use of these gifts not to extinguish the Spirit but to test all things and hold for what is good (cf. 1 Thess 5:12,19,21).[32]*

Blessed Paul VI, in applying this Vatican II conceptualisation of charism to the consecrated life *per se* as well as to individual founders,[33] helped to expand the way it was to be understood and used theologically. 'Charism'

---

29 Suenens, J (1964), The Charismatic Dimension of the Church, in Y Congar, H Kung, D O'Hanlon (eds.) *Council Speeches of Vatican II*, Sheed & Ward, London. See also: Leahy (2011) *op. cit.*, pp. 53-55, for a commentary on the significance of Cardinal Suenens during and after the Council.

30 Some translators prefer 'charismatic gifts' to 'charisms'; others stay with the Latin word *charismata*.

31 *Lumen Gentium*, #12.

32 *Apostolicam Actuositatem*, #3.

33 See Pope Paul VI (1971), *Evangelica Testificatio, On the renewal of the religious life according to the Second Vatican Council*, #2, 11.

subsequently became a term recurringly used by Saint John Paul II, and which he employed increasingly to refer to founders and movements in the Church, for example:

> *The Holy Spirit, while bestowing diverse ministries in the Church communion, enriches it still further with particular gifts or promptings of grace called charisms. They can take a great variety of forms both as a manifestation of the absolute freedom of the Spirit who abundantly supplies them, and as a response to the varied needs of the Church in history.*[34]

The linking of founders with the concept of charism has turned out to be quite significant, perhaps its most prominent application in the post-conciliar period.[35] It is an understandable and apposite application to make because it has been the founders of religious movements and religious orders who have been so manifestly gifted in their evangelical living and who have contributed most fruitfully to the renewal or upbuilding of the Church at various moments in time.[36] While every Christian has his or her personal charismic giftedness, these women and men have been giants of the Christian story through the ways they have responded to the Spirit dwelling within them. It is for good and abundant reasons that so many of them have been canonised. Typically, they have been people of transparent and intense sanctity who, through choice or circumstance, or a combination of both, have brought vitality, challenge, freshness, urgency, reform, relevance, accessibility or inspiration to how the gospel is lived and witnessed. The Church has been made purer, more credible, and more effective, as a consequence of their witness and work. They have been people that Paul would readily discern to be attuned to the Spirit since they would tick all of his charism boxes: their own personal holiness was evident, their spiritual giftedness was used for others and for the purposes of the Church, and the signs of the Spirit were abundant in them and, where applicable, in those who gathered about them. Their gospel response suited their historical context and the needs in Church and society at that time. Indeed, it was the way that they were able to realise *missio Dei* in the context of their time and place that made them so effective. They were recontextualisers of the gospel.

---

34 *Christifideles Laici,* #24.
35 This is not to suggest that the term is not used usefully in other senses, for example to refer to a general state of life or a particular role in the life of the Church. The theologian and Scripture scholar, Sandra Schneiders IHM, for example, writes of the 'charism of religious life' and links it with the 'charism of prophecy' in the first volume of her trilogy on religious life in the twenty-first century. See: Schneiders, SM (2001), *Finding the Treasure: Locating Religious Life in a New Ecclesial and Cultural Context,* Paulist Press, Mahwah NJ.
36 The term 'religious order' is used generically here to refer to all the various ways the Church categorises people who lived a consecrated life.

The persecutions of empires and rulers, the growth of wealth and the moral laxity in cities, the destruction of culture and learning, the missionary needs of foreign lands, the confusion of heresy and power plays, the jadedness or dulling of existing forms of Christian living, the insidiousness of greed and corruption, the perniciousness of indulgence and greed, the devastation of disease and war, the injustice of ignorance and poverty, the depersonalisation of industrialisation and urbanisation, the challenges of rationalism and secularism, the failed promises of false prophets and religious charlatans, the advances of knowledge and new ways of knowing, have all generated new contexts in different periods of history. And so too have emerged Paul of Thebes, Anthony the Great and the Desert Fathers and Mothers; Benedict of Nursia and his Rule, and growth of western monasticism; Gregory the Great, Bernard of Clairvaux, and the reforms of the medieval Church; Dominic de Guzmán, Francis of Assisi and new ways of living as mendicant friars in cities and towns, and with that the emergence of the great Catholic universities; Julian of Norwich, Teresa of Avila, and the insights of mysticism and the reforms of the spiritual life; Meister Eckhardt, Thomas à Kempis, Thomas Aquinas and the flowering of late medieval theology and spirituality; Ignatius of Loyola, Francis de Sales, Vincent de Paul, and the revitalisation of personal spirituality, scholarship and ministry in the Catholic Reformation; John Bosco, Madelaine Sophie Barat, Marcellin Champagnat, Mary MacKillop and the hundreds of founders of the new apostolic institutes of the nineteenth century to minister in education, health, social services, and missionary work; Dorothy Day, Joseph Cardijn, Andrea Riccardi, Chiara Lubich and the plethora of new ecclesial movements and social justice initiatives of the twentieth century. This short list is, of course, neither representative nor exhaustive, but just a toe-dipping into the vast pool of both need and response that has been and is the Church. The point is the 'multiformity and providentiality'[37] of God's Spirit active in the Church.

It is the unfolding story of God's people, God's revelation of Godself in time. Generation has succeeded generation, and the life of the Spirit has irrupted in innumerable people and communities. Mothers and fathers – countless uncanonised saints among them – have nurtured it in their children. Teachers and pastors – quiet heroes too many to name – have helped it to be learned and discerned. The spiritual wisdom and insights of great renewing movements have flowed and intermingled like spiritual bloodlines through the centuries. This has been how the Spirit's gifting has been mediated. Extraordinary founders have not arrived by spaceship with some magically imbued packet of grace tucked under their arms. This is not their charism. Their charism is they themselves. It is God's reign in them. It

---

37 *Iuvenescit Ecclesia*, #10.

is who they have become through the spiritual accompaniment of family, of educators and of priests, from prayer and learning and received tradition, and, importantly, from the time and place and events of their actual living.

To speak of the 'charism of the founder' has become a familiar phrase in popular Catholic discourse. From one perspective, this is an entirely valid application of the concept, one that finds frequent treatment among theologians and commentators, and one wholly in line with the Magisterium of each of the Popes of the post-conciliar period. It is arguably one of the most authentic ways to use the word 'charism' because the application aligns so readily with the concept's Scriptural origins and with the teachings of Council. There are, however, two qualifications that need to be made, two reasons to be careful with its use. The first springs from the dangers of possible misunderstanding that can come from its lexical first-cousins 'charisma' and 'charismatic'; the second emanates from applying the concept of charism in the same ways to a founder as to the generations of the group or movement which follow the founding period. Let us take each in turn.

Although 'charism' has a quite specifically theological meaning sourced in a graced way of realising *missio Dei* that suits time and circumstance and, in terms of this discussion, a particular person, this is not necessarily the case with the other two words. Charisms can only be authentic in the context of Church, in ways that build up and equip the community of Church to bring timely effect to *missio Dei*. They are always Christocentric. They always bear their fruit through tangible and attestable signs of Christ-life, most tellingly in giving people reason and means for their growth in faith, hope and love. The two words 'charisma' and 'charismatic', which come from the same etymological root, do not carry the same inherently spiritual or ecclesial senses. This can be even more confusing in Latin languages such as Spanish and Italian, where there is only the single word 'charisma'. In English, 'charisma' has more to do with charm, emotional attraction, popularity, and personal magnetism. Its adjective is 'charismatic'. A person can be described as a 'charismatic leader' but in a wholly non-Christian sense, even where the leader's ends' could be malevolent or cultish.[38] In the context

---

38 The German sociologist and philosopher Max Weber (1864-1920), as part of his broader social theories, developed the concept of 'charismatic authority' and 'charismatic social movements'. In Weberian theory, such is exercised through individuals with exceptional personal qualities and character, and always for noble ends. Weber considers how such charismatic elements survive as an organisation continues in the generations after the founding charismatic leader. Weberian and Neo-Weberian theory remains strongly present in the literature of leadership and social theory. One study that explores leadership in Catholic education with Weberian concepts is McMahon, JR (1993), *Educational Vision: A Marist Perspective*, doctoral thesis submitted within the University of London Institute of Education. Another is that done by Sister Michele Aronica RSM on the transition of leadership in the Catholic Worker Movement following the death of Dorothy Day in 1980: Aronica, MT (2017), *Beyond Charismatic Leadership. The New York Catholic Worker Movement*,

of our concerns here, the confusion is exacerbated by founders of spiritual movements also being typically charismatic people in this wider sense. Their personal qualities are compelling for others who are attracted to follow them and learn from them. There is no dichotomy, of course, between the human 'charisma' of the founder, and his or her theologically-understood 'charism', for the former is how the latter is incarnated and made manifest. It is helpful, indeed, when a founder is a humanly charismatic person. At the same time, nonetheless, there is a risk in such cases that later generations can come to distort their image of a founder. This can happen when the spiritual dimension of the founder is overlooked or diminished, in a way that the founder's characteristic way becomes expressed only in terms of human values that are not explicitly named or understood as essentially evangelical. For this reason – at least in the English language where it is possible – there can be advantage in adopting the word 'charismic' to be the adjective that is linked to 'charism', and leave 'charismatic' as that for 'charisma'. This will be the practice mostly adopted in this book, even though it is recognised that 'charismatic' is the more usual descriptor found in Church documents and theological writing.

A second caution addresses a more complex question. It is axiomatic of charismic founders that they are likely to attract around them others who are inspired to follow them in their distinctive path of Christian discipleship and their efficacious means of spreading the gospel. Christian community gathers, sometimes with exponential growth in the time of the founder and for one or two generations that follow the founder. The community might name itself and its way of evangelical living, or come to be named by others in the Church, for example as Jesuit, Benedictine, Franciscan, Lasallian or Salesian. Often the name of the founder is adapted into this name of the group and/or its spiritual and apostolic characteristics. It is common then to extend the application of the term 'charism' to refer to this group or to its distinctive way of Christian living and ministering. Thus, expressions such as 'the Augustinian charism' or 'the charism of the Josephites' are frequently used, proposing that a 'charism' can have a corporate and continuing identity. John Paul II often used the term in this way, for example:

> *The apostolate is always born from that particular gift of your founders, which received from God and approved by the Church, has become a charism for the whole community. That gift corresponds to the different needs of the Church and the world at particular moments of history and, in its turn, it is*

Routledge, New York.

extended and strengthened in the life of religious communities as one of the enduring elements of the Church's life and apostolate.[39]

In *Vita Consecrata*, the Pope uses 'charism' no fewer than eighty-six times, the majority in this collective sense – often referring to the 'charism of the institute'. He calls for each religious institute, as a collective entity, to show a 'creative fidelity' to its charism.[40] He also casts his view beyond the limits of the vowed members of a religious institute to write that:

> *Today, often as a result of new situations, many Institutes have come to the conclusion that their charism can be shared with the laity.*[41]

Thus 'the charism' could be understood as able to be lived out in a variety of ways that suit the states of life of different members of the Christian community. This has been increasingly accepted and affirmed. The Congregation for Catholic Education, for example, addressed the same question a decade later, with specific reference to how this could occur in Catholic schools.[42] More recently, Pope Francis has written with a similar understanding of charism as something corporate, transmissible, and able to be developed:

> *The Holy Spirit also enriches the entire evangelising Church with different charisms. These gifts are meant to renew and build up the Church. They are not an inheritance, safely secured and entrusted to a small group for safe-keeping; rather they are gifts of the Spirit integrated into the body of the Church, drawn to the centre which is Christ and then channelled into an evangelising impulse.*[43]

While the term is able to be applied in this collective and evolving sense is common both in official Church documents and probably even more so in less formal discourse in the Church's different communities, it is also important to recognise some unintended risks in doing so. The first is the commodification of what is understood as 'the charism' and its possible disassociation from a living Christian community. The life of the Spirit, in its Pauline sense, can never be reduced to an idea, philosophy, or set of cultural characteristics. It is not something to be objectified. While a

---

39   John Paul II (1984), *Redemptionis Donum, Apostolic exhortation to Men and Women Religious on the Consecration in the Light of the Mystery of the Redemption*, #15, http://w2.vatican.va/content/john-paul-ii/en/apost_exhortations/documents/hf_jp-ii_exh_25031984_redemptionis-donum.html

40   *Vita Consecrata*, #36-37.

41   *Ibid*, #54.

42   Congregation for Catholic Education (2007), *Educating Together in Catholic Schools, A Shared Mission Between Consecrated Persons and the Lay Faithful*, #27-29, 36.

43   *Evangelii Gaudium*, #130. See also: *Christifideles Laici*, #24, for a similar understanding.

community will want to develop a language, a written and symbolised wisdom, a cultural expression – and needs to do so – it is the life of the Spirit in the community itself that is primary. Commodification risks sucking the life – literally the Spirit – out of a charismic founding, most especially its evangelical life or, to repeat Pope Francis's term above, its evangelising impulse. In the context of Catholic education, what is loosely called 'the school's charism' or the charism of its sponsoring community, can unwittingly drift towards becoming little more than a set of pedagogical principles, cultural traits, generic values named in an idiosyncratic way, or traditional practices and rituals. The degree to which the school's governing body, its leadership team and faculty, and even its students, feel spiritually associated as a Christian community, and to be sharing in God's mission in the Church, may in practice diminish.

In its consideration of how a founder's charism might be more widely appropriated in a community, the Congregation for the Doctrine of the Faith proposes some alternative nomenclature and makes this key point:

> *The relationship between the personal character of the charism and the possibility of sharing it expresses a decisive element in its dynamic, insofar as it touches upon the relationship that, in the ecclesial communion, always links person and community. The charismatic gifts, when exercised, can generate affinities, closeness, and spiritual relationships. Through these, the charismatic patrimony originating in the person of the founder, is shared and deepened, thereby giving life to true spiritual families.*[44]

'Charismatic patrimony' legitimises the bringing together of the spiritual essence of a founder's charism with an ongoing heritage by situating it in a continuing experience of personal relationships in community – in a 'spiritual family'. It is a rich concept and one well suited to the subjects being considered. 'Family' suggests interpersonal bonds of a particular intensity and permanence. People belong to a family; families have homes; they are held together by love. While the term 'community', with its allusions to *communio/koinonia*, may be richer theologically, 'family' has its own figurative strength. Qualifying it with 'spiritual' names its essential identity as a distinctive expression of shared life in the Spirit. The same document is then careful to avoid using the term 'charism' in a collective sense, preferring to associate more with a founder or founding experience. It makes extensive use of the term 'charismatic gifts' which, while arguably a tautology, does place emphasis on the continuing experience of the Spirit among the members of the ongoing group.

---

44   *Iuvenescit Ecclesia*, #16.

So, while it may be a rich concept theologically, the term 'charism' does call for sensitivity in its application. This is especially so when used in relation to groups that trace their origins to a particularly inspirational founder or founding experience, and want to carry on the insights and wisdom that came from that person or that time. This is nowhere more the case than with groups involved in the Church's service ministries — (in traditional language, its corporal works of mercy) —including education. One way to exercise such care in the use of 'charism' is to limit the use of 'charism' to the person of the founder or founding group, and to look for other terms for describing the ways that a community develops and takes forward its founding intuitions.[45] The terms 'spirituality', 'spiritual family', 'charismic tradition', 'ecclesial movements' and 'ecclesial communities' serve this purpose.

FROM PERSONAL CHARISMS TO COMMUNALLY LIVED SPIRITUALITIES

In the Jubilee Year of 2000, the regular meeting of the Union of Superiors General in Rome took as its theme 'Charism and Spirituality'. It was indicative of the degree to which these terms were occupying the thinking of religious institutes at a defining time in the Church's history. Claude Maréchal described the founders of these institutes as people who had some of the 'great gospel ideas' of the Christian story. In an often-quoted expression, the Assumptionist Superior General went on to say that the ways that these ideas had been subsequently taken up by people inspired by those founders had given individual Christians 'a story to join, a community to

---

45   Some writers offer the view that it is never an appropriate application of the concept of charism to use it in relation to the community which continues after a founder. Bernard Lee SM is an example of someone who sees that 'a charism' cannot be transmitted because the all founding conditions are not going to be replicated. He proposes the concept of 'deep story' as what lies at the heart of the continuing group, and discusses principles for how a religious institute can move forward with its defining story. See Lee, BJ (2004), *The Beating of Great Wings: The Challenge of Rebuilding Religious Life for Active Apostolic Communities*, Twenty-Third Publications, Mystic CT. Other writers focus on how a group needs to stay in touch with its founding intuitions, and even needs to enter a conscious process of refounding by reappropriating the founding intuitions for new times and needs. Gerard Arbuckle is an example of someone who has been a leader in this discourse, as mentioned in the previous chapter and taken up later in this one. (See: Arbuckle, *op. cit.*) Other writers are more at ease with use of the term 'charism' in a collective and ongoing sense. In reference to Catholic education, see, for example, Lydon, J (2009), 'Transmission of the charism: a major challenge for Catholic education', *International Studies in Catholic Education*, Vol. 1, No. 1, pp. 42-58. For a less theological consideration see Cook (2015), *op. cit.* Cook writes of 'corporate charism' and 'group charism'. For an earlier work of Cook see: (2010), *Discovering charism: what is it and where can my school get one?* A Presentation at the Fifth International Conference on Catholic Educational Leadership, Australian Catholic University, Sydney, Australia, (August); Cook, TJ and Simonds, TA (2011), 'The Charism of 21st-Century Catholic Schools: Building a Culture of Relationships', *Catholic Education, A Journal of Inquiry and Practice*, Vol. 13, No. 3, pp. 318-33.

which to belong, a work to do, a way to pray, a face of God to see.'[46] He was describing, in accessible language, how the charism of a founder could grow into something that was a good deal more: a story, a community of mission, a distinctive way of Christian discipleship, and a recognised place in sharing in God's mission in the Church. It was in and from these spiritual families that inspirational paths of gospel living and evangelising have stood the test of time and have proved perennially fruitful. these founders have graced successive generations of Christ's disciples to recognise and to love their God, and to share in God's mission. They have made the gospel present and accessible for them, offering people a 'doable discipleship'. They have become the spiritualities of the Church, lived and developed by its spiritual families.

Each has grown in answer to an evangelical need – an absence or dimness in the Reign of God – for this is where the Spirit seeks most earnestly to bring Christ-life to birth. People have felt anointed personally by God to bring effect to *missio Dei* and, with the indwelling Spirit of God irrupting in them, good news has been heard by the poor, captives have found release, the blind new sight, and the downtrodden justice.[47] Some movements have lasted for a relatively short period, serving a time and circumstance; others have gone on for two or three centuries, and some for many. They are the multi-faceted story of the Church, and God's revealing of Godself in it.

A conceptual framework for charism and spirituality therefore suggests itself – at least in relation to the genesis, the character, and the place of the Church's spiritual families. A founder (or founding group) is charismically gifted to respond personally to a profound encounter both with God's Spirit within and with evangelical need. Such need is in the founder himself or herself, in others, and more broadly in church or society. The concrete expression of the founder's graced response, in time and place, is inspired and inspiring. It opens the way for the life of the Spirit to irrupt not only in the founder, but in resonant ways also in others who find the founder's way of gospel living to be attractive and accessible. A like-hearted community gathers. A characteristic way of Christian living and evangelising develops. For those who feel drawn to it, it is compelling. That is to say, it is more than simply a clear lens on the gospel for them; it has the effect of fanning their own giftedness into a flame.[48] As the founding experience unfolds and as a community develops and grows, its ways of living and sharing the

---

46   Maréchal, C (2000), 'Toward an Effective Partnership between Religious and Laity in Fulfilment of Charism and Responsibility for Mission', in *Charism and Spirituality, Proceedings of the 56th Conference of the Unione di Superiore Generale*, USG, Rome.

47   Cf. Luke 4:14, 18-19.

48   Cf. 2 Tim 1:6

gospel develop characteristics that are spoken about, written down, and symbolised. A language for their way of gospel living follows, and with it an accumulating wisdom and a discerned expertise.[49] A literature grows, both formal and informal. Perhaps it comes directly from the insight and pen of the founder, perhaps from the community of the first generation as it reflects on the founding. As more time passes, the wealth of experience and wisdom expands, to the stage where it can be faithfully passed on within the community. At some point it must be taken up by a generation which has had no direct experience of the founder(s) or the founding time. It begins to be taught as well as being caught. When and if that happens, the community crosses a bridge towards being the custodians and co-creators of a school of Christian spirituality. It is recognised as such by the Church's pastors. There has been a progress from a *charism* associated with a person, to a *spirituality* of the Church.[50]

The *Catechism of the Catholic Church* puts it this way:

> In the communion of saints, many and varied spiritualities have developed through the history of the churches. The personal charism of some witnesses to God's love for humanity has been handed on, like 'the spirit' of Elijah to Elisha and John the Baptist, so that their followers may have a share in this spirit. A distinct spirituality can also arise at the point of convergence of liturgical and theological currents, bearing witness to the integration of the faith into a particular human environment and its history. The different schools of Christian spirituality share in the living tradition of prayer and are essential guides for the faithful. In their rich diversity, they are refractions of the one pure light of the Holy Spirit.[51]

---

49 As part of a widely-cast compendium on Christian approaches to prayer, Robert Wicks has selected eight authors to write about praying in several spiritual traditions – the Franciscan, Carmelite, Dominican, Benedictine, Salesian, Augustinian, Ignatian and Mercy traditions. Each author draws on the accumulated wisdom of his or her tradition, showing how prayer in that tradition began with the distinctive emphases or insight of a founder or foundress, but has evolved as others have followed in that tradition of contributed their own wisdom and experience. Methods or orientations to prayer represent one of the most helpful and fruitful elements that spiritualities of the Church offer people to assist them to come into the presence of the indwelling God and to respond to this presence. These eight chapters of this handbook provide a rich window in the novelty, diversity and wisdom that have entered the spiritual life of the Church through its various traditions. See: Wicks, RJ (ed.), (2016), *Prayer in the Catholic Tradition. A Handbook of Practical Approaches,* Franciscan Media, Cincinnati:

50 Various writers on the growth of the Church's spiritualities understand their origin and growth in similar ways. One of the most influential in modern time has been Peruvian theologian and philosopher Gustavo Gutiérrez OP. Gutiérrez proposes that growth is a three-stage process: the powerful religious experience which gives an individual a new insight into Christian living; the gathering of a group that reflects on this and expresses it in writing, art, formation processes, prayer and evangelising so that it becomes a new school of spirituality; and finally its entry into broader ecclesial life, and its continued development. See: Gutiérrez, G (1983), *We Drink From Our Own Wells,* Orbis, Maryknoll, pp. 52-53.

51 *Catechism of the Catholic Church* (Edition for Australia and New Zealand), St Paul's, Sydney, #2684.

There are, in this conceptualisation, both personal and communal dimensions. And from them comes the third essential dimension for any Christian spirituality: its expression in selfless and loving service of others. Let us turn first to the personal, for this is the core of any spirituality. Mystics of all ages typically use evocative language to capture their experience of human seeking for the Divine. For the Psalmist it was a panting,[52] for Augustine it was a restlessness,[53] for others a thirst, a hunger, a yearning, or a burning. It is a primal urge within us. Ronald Rolheiser has famously written of all longing being a 'holy longing' in this sense.[54] Its sating is a profoundly satisfying and fulfilling experience. Spiritual masters such as Bernard of Clairvaux, Teresa of Avila and Francis de Sales have put it in ecstatic terms, intuitively drawn to the love poetry of the Song of Songs to find Scriptural resonance for it. There is a twin dynamic of yearning at work here: the deep passion for communion in each person, that can only be satisfied divinely, is met by a prior yearning of the Spirit within the person to irrupt in the person's lived experience. This irruption occurs in prayer, in personal relationships, in values and the principles of life, in a commitment to truth and a vision of beauty, and ultimately in an impulsion to concrete love and service.

The initiative is God's. This is not in any magical, paranormal sense as if an alien God visits from some otherworldly heaven. No, the driving urge to integrity, communion, and love that springs up from within is the very life of God within us, seeking incarnation. When the word 'spirituality' first appeared in the seventeenth century it was used pejoratively to describe the questionable intensity of individuals' 'spiritual' experiences. It was, nonetheless, an apt coinage for it was taken from the Latin *spiritus*, translating the *pneuma* of the Christian Scriptures – the Spirit which blows where it will.[55] By the early twentieth century writers were beginning to use the term more universally for human experience of the Divine.[56]

---

52 Ps. 42.

53 St Augustine's oft-quoted sentence comes from his *Confessions* (Book 1, #1). 'You have made us for yourself, O God, and our heart is restless until it rests in you.' The sense of restlessness, longing and yearning is a central theme in Augustinian spirituality.

54 See: Rolheiser, R (1999), *The Holy Longing: the Search for a Christian Spirituality*, Doubleday, New York; (2014), *Sacred Fire, A Vision for a Deeper Human and Christian Spirituality* Crown Publishing, New York. The considerable popularity that Rolheiser's insights have achieved, as may also be the case for Henri Nouwen's, is arguably due to the way that this basic restlessness of the human condition is described in a grounded and contemporary way. Both draw on the experiences and wisdom of the great mystics, such as John of the Cross, and re-present these in accessible language and imagery.

55 Cf. John 3:8.

56 Influential Lutheran theologian Rudolph Otto was, for example, proposing the idea of the 'numinous' at the core of all human spiritual experience. Otto's 1917 book was one of the most impactful publications of the last century in this field: Otto, R (1917; 1950), *The Idea of the Holy: An Inquiry into the Non-Rational Factor in the Idea of the Divine and its Relation to the Rational,* (J W Harvey, trans.) Oxford University Press, New York. While Otto's ideas regarding spiritual experience have been much critiqued, and do not sit comfortably with some of the incarnational theology and

From this emerging strand of scholarship, the Christian story could be seen through a new lens, and interpreted through a fresh conceptual framework – that of multiple spiritualities, often linked to a founding figure or time. Scholars began to write, for example, of Origen and Alexandrian spirituality, Anthony and the spirituality of the desert, Gregory of Nissa and Cappadocian spirituality, Columba and Brigit and Celtic spirituality, medieval spirituality, monastic and apostolic spiritualities, mystical and ascetical spiritualities, eastern and western spiritualities, spiritualities named after saints and founders – Augustinian, Benedictine, Dominican, Franciscan and Ignatian, for example. With the growing diversification of Christianity came spiritualities associated with new denominations – Lutheran spirituality, Anglican, Calvinist, Methodist, Baptist, Mennonite, and so on. The list is long, and growing. The bloodlines that flow through the various strands of Christian spirituality have mixed, mingled, and been mutually enriching. One major strand – and the one from which emerged many of the apostolic religious institutes associated today with Catholic education around the world – is collectively known as the 'French school of spirituality'. More accurately understood as western European rather than exclusively French, it emerged as part of the Catholic reformation. The French school gave rise to a range of spiritual families, which have developed spiritualities that although varied and distinctive in their own ways, all tend to emphasise a mystical and personal encounter with Christ. It is a theology that captures both the immanence and majesty of God and is notable for quite affective and relational styles, generosity in service and mission to the marginalised. These spiritualities stood in contrast to more rigorist, moralist and ascetical spiritualities of the time. [57]

The term 'spirituality' has come to be applied – like 'charism' – with increasing breadth and, arguably, growing imprecision and ambiguity. For example, terms such as liberation spirituality, feminist spirituality, earth

---

Catholic doctrine that informs the exploration of charism and spirituality in this book, they do align with the proposition that there is an inescapably spiritual dimension and explanation to all human maturity. His sense of the awe that is attendant on spiritual experience matches the place of humility as the essential spiritual disposition of the Catholic mystical tradition. Another early an influential writer was Pierre Pourrat. Like others of the French-associated thinking on spirituality – for example the editorial group behind the definitive *Dictionnaire de Spiritualité* mentioned in Chapter 1 – Pourrat places emphasis on tension between the mystical and ascetical dimensions of spirituality. See: Pourrat, P (1918), *La Spiritualité Chrétienne* (4 Vols.), J Gabalda, Paris. Most of the early discourse was premised on the idea of a single Christian spirituality.

57 A comprehensive survey of Christian spiritualities, their origins and essence, from a number of perspectives can be found in: Holder, A (ed.) (2011), *The Blackwell Companion to Christian Spirituality*, Wiley-Blackwell, Chichester. For an introduction to the field, see also: Sheldrake, P (2013) *Spirituality, A Brief History*, Wiley-Blackwell, Chichester; Schmidt, RH (2008), *op. cit.*; Downey, M .(1997), *op. cit.*; Cunningham, LS & KJ Egan, (1996), *Christian Spirituality: Themes from the Tradition*, Paulist Press, New York. For a consideration of historical, theological and anthropological approaches to the study of spirituality, one the leading writers of the present time is Catholic theologian Sandra Schneiders IHM.

spirituality, or post-modern spirituality are contentious in some quarters.[58] While each of them, and many others, have a validity in that they refer to insights that can reveal another of the innumerable faces of God, and bring relevance and spark to the gospel, they may also be more ideological or hermeneutical in their substance. That does not diminish their evangelical authenticity nor the insights they provide, but they may be better labelled as theology or philosophy in some instances. A Christian spirituality, like a charism, is not essentially about ideas or a system of meaning. While it is likely to be a richer and more enduring spirituality if it has indeed developed an extensive wisdom literature that is the fruit of reflection on experience, and if it has fostered ongoing dialogue and scholarship, and from this has developed an effective method for undertaking its particular field of ministry, these are not its essence. A Christian spirituality is, rather, about personal encounter with and response to the life of God, as revealed in Jesus Christ and experienced in his indwelling Spirit. Additionally, a Christian spirituality has a communal expression, and a spiritual family in which the spirituality is lived out and continually developed. This community shares responsibility for living the tradition, for inducting and forming others in it, and for keeping it intuitively in touch with its founding. Thirdly, it expresses itself in concrete evangelical outreach and service. It is about love realised. If a narrative – even a deeply theological one – is dissociated in practice from these three constitutive elements then it is not rightly regarded as a Christian spirituality.

Additionally, 'spirituality' is a word that has currency outside Christian and even religious discourse. While Christian people have no copyright on the term and no control over its etymological development, it is important that they themselves are clear on what they mean by it. For example, a 'new age spirituality' that is focused on pursuing self-actualisation, leading a stress-free lifestyle, and achieving personal satisfaction, is something different from a Christian spirituality which is concerned intentionally with fostering a discipleship of Jesus Christ and all that that implies in self-giving love and service of other people. That the word μαθητης (*mathetes*, 'disciple') occurs more than 250 times in the Gospels and in Acts, highlights the centrality of this concept for any path of gospel living. From those scriptures, some clear elements of this discipleship present themselves: a sense of conversion, a choice to follow Jesus in a way of life that is lived according to evangelical imperatives, relationally, joyfully, celebrated sacramentally, and with a

---

58   Such breadth is partly informed by the conceptual orientation that is being taken. See Sandra Schneiders for a discussion of historical, theological and anthropological approaches to studying spirituality. Schneiders, S (2011), 'Approaches to the Study of Christian Spirituality', in Holder, *op. cit.*

commitment to carry to the world news of Christ risen.

When a school draws on one of the charismic traditions of the Church to shape its identity, this is done most authentically at a spiritual level. It is for spiritual reasons that the tradition came into the life of the Church, to allow the life of the Spirit to become manifest in people, the reign of God to prevail, so that the Risen Christ is at the heart of the Church, its communities, and its work. Christian discipleship is the purpose and fruit of this. Because Christian spiritualities are found primarily in living spiritual families – and only vicariously in books and manuals, symbols and labels – it follows that these spiritual families needs to be present in an influential even defining way within the school community – in its governance, in its leadership, in the people who in practice shape its identity.

BUILDING AND SUSTAINING A 'CHARISMIC CULTURE'

Much of the foregoing discussion has considered personal charism and its growth into spirituality theologically, with some historical references. Another way to approach this conceptualisation of the life of the Spirit is to do so anthropologically. This can be especially relevant and helpful in a school context. There is both validity and risk in doing so. The validity is sourced in the principle that there is no dichotomy between the life of faith and the physicality and temporality of human existence. Christian faith always needs a context of time and place, a cultural context; the Word of God has taken flesh and come to dwell in our midst, and in this we have seen the glory of God.[59] At the same time, a focus on human behaviours, human values and human meaning-making and rituals, risks neglecting or even omitting spiritual awareness.

As spiritual families grow, they inevitably develop cultural expression, as do the sub-strands, the individual communities, and the works of those spiritual families, such as schools. This is not a dangerous by-product to be handled with care. It may indeed carry some dangers, and care is certainly required, but the development of a culture is necessary if a spirituality is to grow from a personal charism. In the context of the Catholic school, this is something that has long been recognised:

---

59 1 John 14. Alongside the Pauline sense of the indwelling Spirit of God is the Johannine sense of humanity, and the disciple of Christ, as the figurative 'Temple' where God dwells, replacing the literal temple in Jerusalem. For an introduction to the concept of Temple in John's Gospel see: Coloe, ML (2001), *God Dwells With Us: Temple Symbolism in the Fourth Gospel,* Michael Glazier Inc., Wilmington.

... faith which does not become culture is faith which is not fully received, not assimilated entirely, not lived faithfully.[60]

In fact, it is in entities such as individual schools, networks of schools, and teams and central offices which support such networks, that culture is likely to be most significant and therefore most worthy of scrutiny. In large and diverse international spiritual families, it is their local cultural expression that is likely to be most salient. But whether local, regional or global, a culture is necessary for a spirituality to be lived. In Chapters 4 and 5 there will be further consideration of how cultures operate in individual schools. Here, let us approach the matter more conceptually.

The application of the anthropologically-derived term 'culture' to individual human organisations such as corporations, non–government agencies, and schools – rather than to societies, ethnic groups or religions which had been its more normal use since the nineteenth century – has been common since at least the 1980s. It is now well enough established that the concept of 'organisational culture' is a recognised sub-field of cultural anthropology, with its own extensive body of literature.[61] Close on the academic heels of this was a parallel and partly-related application of the concept of culture to schools, and linked closely to the school effectiveness and school leadership discourse that was beginning to grow.[62]

---

60 'Sacred Congregation for Catholic Education' (1977), in *The Catholic School*, Libreria Editrice Vaticana, Rome, #33.

61 Peters and Waterman were prominent in the 1980s as the field of organisational culture was being empirically developed. See, for example: Peters, TJ & Waterman, RH (1982), *In Search of Excellence, Lessons from America's Best Run Companies*, Harper & Row, New York; (1985), *The Passion for Excellence: the leadership difference*, Fontana, London. From the perspective of Catholic cultural anthropology, Gerard Arbuckle has long written and researched in this field. See, for example: Arbuckle, GA (2010), *Culture, Inculturation, and Theologians: A Postmodern Critique*, Liturgical Press, Collegeville: (2013), *Catholic Identity or Identities?: Refounding Ministries in Chaotic Times*, Liturgical Press, Collegeville.

62 This has been a rich field of scholarship for forty years. Two researchers who had a shaping influence on discourse during the 1980s and 1990s were Deal and Kennedy. See, for example: Deal, TE (1985), 'The Symbolism of Effective Schools', in *The Elementary School Journal*, Vol. 85, No. 5, pp. 601-20; (1993), 'The Culture of Schools', in Sashkin, M and Walberg, HJ (eds), *Educational Leadership and School Culture*, McCutchan Publishing, Berkeley; Deal, TE & Kennedy, AA (1991), 'Culture and School Performance', *Journal of Educational Administration*, 29, 2, 72-82; (1992), *Corporate Cultures: The Rites and Rituals of Corporate Life*, Addison-Wesley, Reading MA. Tom Sergiovanni became influential in the field at the same time, especially in terms of cultural leadership in schools. See, for example: Sergiovanni, TJ (1984), 'Leadership and Excellence in Schooling: Excellent schools need freedom with boundaries', *Educational Leadership*, 41, 5, 4-13; (1990), *Value-Added Leadership: How to get Extraordinary Performance in Schools*, Harcourt Brace Jovanovich, San Diego; (1992), *Moral Leadership: Getting to the Heart of School Improvement*, Jossey Bass Publishers, San Francisco; (1994), *Building Community in Schools*, Jossey-Bass Publishers, San Francisco; (1996), *Leadership for the Schoolhouse*, Jossey-Bass, San Francisco; (2004), *Strengthening the Heartbeat*, Jossey Bass Publishers, San Francisco. In Australia: Headley Beare (University of Melbourne) and Patrick Duignan (Australian Catholic University) were among those leading discourse in school culture and leadership. See, for example: Beare, H (1987), Metaphors About Schools: The principal as a Cultural Leader', in WS Simpkins, AR Thomas, EB Thomas (eds) *Principal and Change: The Australian Experience*, University of New England Press, Armidale; Beare, H, Caldwell, BJ & Millikan, RH (1989), *Creating An Excellent School*, Routledge, London;

How has the term been used? The first thing to recognise, as for other terms already considered, is that 'culture' is a theoretical construct, a way for conceptualising and coming to an integrated understanding of the binding beliefs, meaning-making, defining myths, shared values, and normative behaviours and ritualising of an identifiable group of people. While these elements are all real – in their being observable or inferable – the unifying and integrating of them as 'a culture' is essentially conceptual. 'Culture' is like 'charism' and 'spirituality' in this sense. It is not something to be commodified, nor can it be acquired or adopted in ways that are independent of the lived context of a group, or only tenuously connected to it. This is a criticism of the rather instrumentalist or utilitarian ways the term has sometimes been purloined in the commercial and sporting spheres, or indeed in education, in the interests of maximising effectiveness or fostering excellence. While the achievement of desired outcomes is a correlate of cultural factors, and there is an inevitably a functional relationship at work, the primary emphasis must be on the community itself, the people in all their complexity.[63] There is, additionally, some degree of metaphor in the application of a term sourced from anthropology to a group such as an organisation or spiritual movement. It is, nonetheless, a metaphorical application that has proven to be useful.

Especially from the perspective of incarnational theology, the concept of culture does provide a way of describing the human reality in which the spiritual life is incarnated. Thus, identity and values, myths and legends, sagas and heroes, symbols and rituals, language and art, music and sacred sites, and accepted ways of knowing, acting, relating, ordering, responding, judging, rewarding and punishing, and choosing and ostracising members, and generating meaning, are all typically understood to be constitutive of culture – and they can all be understood as the defining cultural characteristics of a living spirituality.

Culture is always deeper than a simplistic *how* 'we do things around here'. It is, before that, *who* is doing these things, *with whom* and *for whom*, *why* are they doing them, *what* do they understand themselves to be doing, and *when* and *where*. The *how* is expressive of deeper identity, belief, purpose, and world view.[64] Cultural and even spiritual traditions are sometimes

Duignan, PA (1987), 'Leaders as Culture Builders, in *Unicorn*, 13, 4, 208-213; Duignan, PA (1997), *The Dance of Leadership: At the Still Point of the Turning World*, Australian Council for Education Administration Monograph. Subsequent developments in understanding school culture is well treated in the early book in this BBI-AITE *Mission and Education* Series, D'Orsa, J & T (2013), *op. cit.*

63   Commentators such as Sergiovanni (see above) increasingly came to this emphasis on the primacy and priority of community.

64   In the context of Catholic education, and its essential characteristics, Tom Groome has described this another way, but perhaps with the same essential meaning. He writes of a characteristically Catholic anthropology, cosmology, sociology, epistemology, historicity, politics, spirituality and universality that makes Catholic schools Catholic. See Groome (2001), *op. cit.* This is further discussed in Chapter 5.

simplistically and erroneously understood at the expressive level, the *how*. While the *how* is an integral and important dimension of culture, it is not its core. To observe or to take part in a ritual, for example, but not to have a grasp of what it is that is being ritualised, is to miss its purpose and significance, and not to be affected by it. If such a person is a member of the group which is undertaking the ritual, then it will be nothing more than a set of actions. Similarly, for such people, the core myths of the group – which figuratively carry its core-identity, beliefs and values – are likely to be little more than folk stories. Its sacred sites would be visited as tourism rather than pilgrimage. Its language might be known, but with the head and not the heart.

All groups and communities have cultures. These cultures will all find themselves somewhere on the spectra of functional to dysfunctional, strong to weak, mature to underdeveloped, and sustainable to disintegrating. Members of a group will relate to its culture in ways that range from meaningful to irrelevant, inspiring to alienating, fully engaged to observational. In a strong and functional culture, the core beliefs, values and purposes, and the chosen means for nurturing and expressing these, will have higher degrees of homogeneity and resonance among members of the group, so that people make meaning and define their world in largely resonant, though not necessarily identical ways. A mature culture will have developed rich and wise ways to mythologise, ritualise, articulate, symbolise, dialogue, self-critique, induct, form, nurture, bond, and witness. The relationship between these expressive elements and the members of the cultural group will be reciprocal: people will shape the culture, and the culture will shape people. It all comes back to the people, the community.

At the heart of any personal charism is a deep experience of the Spirit which yearns to bring Christ-life to birth, and a graced response to this. A charismically gifted person, such as a founder, is someone who is graced to respond with effect, simultaneously and co-relationally, to a deep encounter both with the Spirit and with concrete human need. The revelation of God in Jesus Christ and the coming of the Reign of God, in real people and real time, are the essence of what it is about. As a personal charism moves towards becoming a spirituality, and this spirituality is expressed culturally in a living and self-identifying spiritual family, as it must be if the Kingdom is to be incarnated, then the challenge is to keep Christ at its heart. Christ-life, in all the human manifestations that St Paul uses to describe it, must remain the heartbeat of all its mythology, its symbols, its language, its values, its community-building, its formation, and its work. To the degree that it does so, its culture may be called charismic. To the degree, on the other hand, that members of the community lose touch with that heart of their founding story, then their shared spirituality will dissipate, and their culture − irrespective of any apparent strength or functionality − will fade from being authentically charismic.

AS CONTEXTS CHANGE

A telling sign of the evangelical robustness and durability of a spiritual family is found in how it responds to changes in its context. One common reason that some movements last only a short time is that their cultures are quite context-specific − developed to work evangelically in particular times and places, to respond to particular needs, to be suited to particular lifestyles or states of life, and ritualised and articulated in the Beguines or the Knights Templar of medieval times, or many of the apostolic foundations of the eighteenth and nineteenth centuries. That such groups flowered for a time and then either died out or continued only minimally is not to devalue their evangelical authenticity or effectiveness. We need to recognise, however, that their vitality was connected in a defining way by the circumstances of their founding. They gave people a way of living the gospel for a time and served well the needs of God's people during this time − inspired and enlivened by the same Spirit that always brings life to the gospel of Jesus. But that time passed. Indeed, this has been the fate of the great majority of spiritual movements in the Church's story. Only a minority has lasted more than several generations, and a small fraction for more than two or three centuries.[65] Similarly, specific strands of a spiritual tradition or styles of living out that spirituality may cease or diminish. Examples include medieval-style monasticism, the lay penitent movement that flowered after the Gregorian reforms of the eleventh century, and the kind of lay confraternities established in the sixteenth century by the Jesuits. While charismic intuitions that prompted such developments continued − spiritualities such as Benedictine or Augustinian or Ignatian − needed to find continually fresh means of expression or else risk fading relevance.

Europe is dotted with the ruins of medieval abbeys and monasteries. Some had a violent end, but many others just gradually emptied. An illustration is provided by the ruins of the Abbey of La Chaise-Dieu in south-central

---

65   One influential theorist on this topic, specifically in relation to religious institutes during the sharp decline in the consecrated life in the 1960s and 1970s in many parts of the Western world, was the French Jesuit Raymond Hostie. See: Hostie, R (1972), *Vie Et Mort Des Ordres Religieux,* Desclee de Brouwer, Paris. Hostie posited that most religious institutes lived through a predictable life-cycle that involved a founding period of 10-20 years, followed by consolidation lasting a similar time, then an expansion during the subsequent century. Most then stabilised for a time or began to decline. Few lasted more than 250-300 years.

France. As for many other monastic communities, this eight-hundred-year-old centre of spiritual life was completely ransacked in the ecclesiastical purges of the French Revolution, its monks expelled and the buildings looted. It had been one of the most significant centres of Benedictine life in Europe – with hundreds of monks in community at La Chaise-Dieu itself at any one time, and countless others in almost three hundred dependent monasteries and priories across Europe. It had produced scholars, artists, abbots, bishops and even a pope. While it is tempting to shoot the blame for its destruction at the secularist and perhaps greedy revolutionaries who destroyed it, the truth is elsewhere: by the late eighteenth century, this Abbey was already in terminal decline. There was only a handful of old monks still living there in 1790 when the militants of the Revolution threw them out. Only a shadow of what it had been at its height, the Abbey's demise had been happening for some time. What had gone wrong? What had led to this once-vibrant hub of the gospel of Jesus to diminish and become an anachronism that had long since ceased attracting young men to embrace its way of life? 'La Chaise-Dieu' meant 'the House of God,'[66] originally a fitting name for such a centre of the Christian spiritual life, but ironically by the time of its demise it was a place of empty choir stalls and the cold void of an abbey church. What had caused this spiritual death?

With a touch of extra irony, the answer hides in a three-panel fresco that survives in the old abbey church – *La Danse Macabre* ('the Dance of Death'). The fresco depicts twenty-three figures from medieval church and society – a pope, a prince, a preaching monk, a merchant, a peasant, and so on.[67] Each is dancing with a skeleton, as a chilling reminder of their mortality: their rank, power, prestige and wealth, or lack of them, are all transitory. The fresco was probably painted in the late fifteenth century, but by the eve of the nineteenth, it portrayed a society that no longer existed. And therein was also the problem for the monks of La Chaise-Dieu: they were living in ways that addressed the context and need of another time. Their abbey had been founded and thrived on Benedictine spirituality – one of the richest spiritual traditions of the Church, one that has provided and continues to provide countless people with a richly effective way to embrace the gospel of Jesus. There was and is nothing anachronistic about the essence of Benedictine spirituality. Where the Chaise-Dieu monks went wrong was their failure to bring it into dialogue with the spirit of their age. They continued in a medieval time warp, inattentive to the liberating movements of thought and profound societal realignment that

---

66 From medieval Occitan or *lengua d'oc*, 'Chasa Dieu'.
67 This genre of art occurs in other churches across Europe, and dates from the time of Black Death.

marked the Enlightenment. It was a liminal time, and they neither read its signs nor made an attempt to reinterpret their tradition for a new era. Their ruin was not so much at the hands of external adversaries, but the result of their own lack of readiness to renew and to reimagine their spiritual heritage for their own times. It offers a salutary lesson for any spiritual family.

All spiritualities grow out of a need to recontextualise the gospel for a new time. At their origin, they are inherently disruptive in their novelty. They emerge from their time and present the gospel in ways that are prophetic, relevant and compelling for the people of that time. They speak with cogency, and for that reason they take root and grow. They provide 'providential answers' for specific circumstances.[68] As these circumstances inevitably change over time, or as a spirituality is taken by members of its family to different geographical locations and social situations, it needs to continue to recast itself in ways that address these new contexts. There is the need for the spiritual family to show creative fidelity to its founding spiritual intuitions – maintaining the essence of the founding insights, but developing new language, rituals and symbolism that are influenced by dialogue with the new ways of knowing and interpreting that are abroad. In this way, the spirituality retains accessibility, relevance and engagement for people. Where such a transition – sometimes through a more radical reform – does not occur, the spirituality loses the vital edge that created its original appeal. But more: it is essential that a spirituality not only recontextualises time and again, but that it retains an intuition to do so, to be disruptive, to be prophetic. More colloquially put, a spirituality that is robust and enduring will be one that continues 'to cut through'. In saying this, it is critical to understand that 'the spirituality' is not an objective commodity, but is the lived gospel experience of a community of people. It is the members of the spiritual family who need to remain intuitively agile and adaptive, deeply attentive and responsive to the reality of their world, as were their founders.

For example, mendicant orders were able to recontextualise monasticism for emerging urban environments; the Cistercians renewed Benedictine life for their times; Teresa of Avila and John of the Cross revisioned eremitical Carmelite life and recast it in ways that internalised the spiritual journey and revitalised their communal expression of it; Ignatius was one of a number who took the consecrated life out of its conventual restrictions and into the school and the missionary field; in the early-modern and modern eras, many of the centuries-old religious orders adapted their monastic

---

68   Cf. *Iuvenescit Ecclesia* (quoting John Paul II), #2

ways in the light of new forms of apostolic life that emerged during these times.[69] While foundational literature and wisdom are kept, new patterns of living and praying are developed, and new documents are written – for new times. Recent decades have seen new scholarship and new publications, for example, on Jesuit education or Marist education, or many other Catholic educational traditions that have emanated from various spiritual families. If such fresh thinking and writing were not occurring within a spiritual family, one would need to question if its members had lost their collective intuition to recontextualise. It is likely to be one sign that they were in decline.

Another telling sign of when a spiritual family's culture has lost its charismic heartbeat is when its rituals, symbols, behaviours, and other expressive elements of its culture are tenaciously protected and preserved, but with little or no reference among its members to the core Christocentric beliefs and values that are supposed to be being represented. If the evangelising impact of such ritual and meaning-making is dulled by other factors such as simple nostalgia, tradition, circle-the-wagons insularity, hero-worship, gimmickry, or other plays on emotion, then the culture is unlikely to be one that is alert enough to the gospel to be able to recontextualise it with much effect.

It is one that will more likely be ossifying or insulating, each a process that is antithetical to the free movement and influence of the Spirit. These do not need to be negative factors. Schools, for example, may have strong academic, emotional intelligence, leadership, arts, community service, or sporting emphases that are justifiably pursued and ritualised accordingly. Yet the community may lose a sense of evangelical imperative in them. The critical element is the degree to which the purpose for doing all of this is understood by the community – *missio Dei*.[70]

Spiritual families – and nowhere more so than in Catholic schools – can find that their tradition is a double-edged sword. One of the strengths and riches of a spiritual tradition is just that: it is a tradition. Tradition is a function of history. It is by drawing from the story of the spiritual family that cultures are built – the heroes who are honoured, the sacred places that are visited, the events that are recounted, the literature that is studied, practices that are handed on, and so on. But when a spirituality becomes anchored by its history, even defined for the most part by it, then it risks not living the gospel

---

69   Many historians of Christian spirituality trace these and other adaptations and reformations. See, for example: Maas, R & O'Donnell, G (eds) (1990), *Spiritual Traditions for the Contemporary Church*, Abingdon Press, Nashville. See also Sheldrake, *op. cit.* for a comprehensive treatment of this.

70   Cultural anthropologist Gerard Arbuckle, for whom mythology is a key element of a culture, points to 'myth drift'. He claims that this can happen unknowingly in a school as it drifts to make life intelligible for its members in ways other than spiritual ones: Arbuckle, G (2016) *op. cit.* pp. 10 ff. Jim and Therese D'Orsa, while recognising that apparently secular purposes and explicitly evangelical ones can serve the same ends – such as justice or social inclusion – state that the enduring challenge for Catholic schools is 'securing the quality of mission thinking' (2013) *op. cit.* p. 228.

but preserving an artefact of it. Thus a measure of the 'evangelising impulse' of a community is likely to be found in how it treats its prophets.

Doing things in new ways is not straightforward, especially in places or communities with strong cultural norms. School communities can be stubbornly resistant to change, students as well as staff. There are various reasons for this, ranging from psychological insecurities to change-fatigue, but many of these can be addressed through skilled change-management processes. If the source of change-resistance is, however, a subtler disconnection with the living of the gospel of Jesus, then the influence of what has culturally developed in the school may be working against evangelical vitality and responsiveness rather than for it. At its worst, it can become toxic to a promotion of the Reign of God. School cultures that exploit, negligently tolerate, or simply fail to address anti-evangelical practices such as abuse of power, pursuit of achievement for self-serving or inequitable ends, rivalry, shouting, envy, petty bickering, deceit, emotional bullying, immoral conduct, or exclusion, are working against the Spirit – whatever results are being achieved academically or otherwise. Read Galatians 5:19-20. Any culture needs ongoing critiquing and purifying through the lens of the gospel.

Robust Christian spiritualities are those that remain strong because of their historical and cultural circumstances, not despite them. The members of their spiritual families have a disposition towards attentiveness, engagement, and creativity. They want to understand their world, and to meet people where they are. They seek to be alert to what is shaping people's values and leading them to make meaning. For example, the post-modernist distrust of institutional narratives and ambit truth claims, the curious counterpoint between xenophobia and the promotion of inclusion that plays out in many Western countries, the discrediting of organised religion and the normalising of secularism, the way the digital revolution is transforming ways of knowing and relating – these are all cultural influences that a spiritual family needs to attempt to comprehend. A genuinely charismatic one will feel the impulse to do so. For those spiritual families which share in the Church's ministry of education, this becomes even more immediate since so much of the *raison d'être* of the Catholic school is about attempting integration of faith, culture and life.[71]

---

71 Bishop Michael Putney is one commentator who has provided some insights into the changing context in which the Catholic school finds itself, and how the Church needs to reorient itself in the light of this. See: Putney, M (2005), 'The Catholic School and the Future', *Australasian Catholic Record*, Vol. 82, No. 4, pp. 387-398; (2008), 'A New Ecclesial Context for Catholic Schools, in Benjamin, A and Riley, D (eds), *Catholic Schools, Hope in Uncertain Times,* John Garratt Publishing, Melbourne. The New South Wales Bishops also addressed the changing context in which schools operate and the Church's preferred response to this in their 2007 document *Catholic Schools at a Crossroad,* Catholic Education Commissions of NSW and the ACT and (2007) *Catholic Schools at a Crossroad, Pastoral Letter of the Bishops of NSW and the ACT.*

Empirical studies, such as the *Enhancing Catholic Schools Identity Project* (ECSIP), are useful for serving such intuition.[72] The data that have emerged from ECSIP, specifically in Belgium and Australia, demonstrate just how much the secularising, pluralising and detraditionalising trends in those societies are inexorably impacting on those who comprise Catholic school communities. The prevailing interpretation of the data, and the trends evident from them, is that the traditional assumptions that have underpinned the identity of the Catholic school, and have shaped its life and work, have changed radically or are in the process of so doing. Catholic schools which once served largely homogenous Catholic communities now find themselves working in a growingly post-Christian and quite heterogenous context. To march on in denial of this change is likely to be at best ineffective for the work of evangelisation, and probably quite counter-productive.[73] ECSIP proponents argue for dialogue and recontextualisation, but also underline the value for the Catholic community itself of being educated comprehensively and having the opportunity for effective catechesis so that its members can engage meaningfully in such dialogue. There does not need to be any undervaluing of the power of *kerygma*, or any commitment to bringing young people to the fullness of the gospel, but there is the recognition that the soil needs to be readied for good sowing.

In many Western countries, those responsible for Catholic schooling are finding themselves in situations that in some ways parallel Catholic schools in most Asian countries: serving a minority Catholic community, but predominantly providing a service to society by an approach marked by integral education and the promotion of social harmony. All this with a view to building a readiness for young people to make a critically aware and responsible contribution to building a society marked by fairness, compassion, equity, ecological care, and peace. Such is an authentic participation in *missio Dei*. Indeed, the 2017 document from the Congregation for Catholic Education, *Educating for Fraternal Humanism*, recognises this as the core of the purpose of the Catholic school.[74] This document focuses on the

---

72 In Australia, a perennially useful source of data is the National Church Life Survey: www.ncls.org.au. Census data is also always revealing: www.abs.gov.au/census. Similar research bodies operate in other countries, e.g. the Pew Research Center in the USA: www.pewforum.org. And Faith Survey in the UK (also with Irish and continental European data and trends): faithsurvey.co.uk.

73 Boeve (2016), *op. cit.* and Sharkey (2013), *op. cit.* argue this way. Each writer considers at length the implications of the data from the ECSIP research and other related material, in the context of Catholic schools in Flanders (Belgium) and Victoria (Australia) respectively. He argues for recognising who it is who make up Catholic school communities, what are and are not sources of meaning for them, what this might mean for who is enrolled and employed in Catholic schools, and how the life of the gospel and the Church is expressed. Both favour inclusivity and dialogue as key elements of any future approach.

74 Congregation for Catholic Education (2017), *Educating for Fraternal Humanism, Building a Civilisation of Love Fifty Years after Populorum Progressio*, Libreria Edictrice Vaticana, Rome.

'humanising' purposes of education, and the promotion of inclusivity in schools and genuine dialogue. In doing so, it restates orientations for Catholic education that have been important to the Church's hopes for it since *Gravissimus Educationatis* and *The Catholic School*.[75] At the same time, while such documents have understood the role of the Catholic school in society in quite broad ways, in some countries there has been a more narrowly conceived catechetical emphasis in Catholic schools.

This is a recognition that evangelisation and secularism are not necessarily oppositional concepts. The proposition that the concepts can be more integrated, and that the Catholic school can be a catalyst for this coming together, is the kind of thinking that underpinned the support that Benedict XVI gave to the 'Courtyard of the Gentiles' initiative by the Pontifical Council for Culture in 2011. In his message to the launch of this forum, he wrote:

> *Dear young people, it is up to you, in your own countries and in Europe as a whole, to help believers and nonbelievers to rediscover the path of dialogue. Religions have nothing to fear from a just secularity, one that is open and allows individuals to live in accordance with what they believe in their own consciences.*
>
> *If we are to build a world of liberty, equality and fraternity, then believers and nonbelievers must feel free to be just that, equal in their right to live as individuals and in community in accord with their convictions; and fraternal in their relations with one another. One of the reasons for this Court of the Gentiles is to encourage such feelings of fraternity, over and above our individual convictions yet not denying our differences.*[76]

'New Evangelisation' is a term that has, at least since John Paul II's first Encyclical *Redemptoris Missio*, taken on a narrower Eurocentric focus than its original conceptualisation in Latin America. The latter-day meaning, which has in some quarters led to some degree of restorationist thinking and acting, is captured by this extract from the Encyclical:

> *… countries with ancient Christian roots, and occasionally in the younger Churches as well, where entire groups of the baptised have lost a sense of the faith, or even no longer consider themselves members of the Church, and live*

---

75 *Gravissimus Educationis, Declaration on Christian Education proclaimed by His Holiness Paul VI, 28 October 1965,* Libreria Editrice Vaticana, Rome; Sacred Congregation for Catholic Education (1977), *The Catholic School,* Libreria Editrice Vaticana, Rome.

76 Benedict XVI (2011), *Message to Courtyard of the Gentiles,* 26 March, Libreria Editrice Vaticana, Rome.

a life far removed from Christ and his gospel. In this case what is needed is a 'new evangelisation' or a 're-evangelisation'.[77]

The source of the term is, however, in another continent and another context – the watershed meeting of the Latin American Catholic Bishops' Conference (CELAM) in Medellín in 1968. The Medellín meeting was influenced by various thinkers and theologians, not least the Jesuits, and among them Pedro Arrupe SJ, their new Superior General. From Arrupe, CELAM took the phrase 'preferential option for the poor' and gave it to the whole Church of Latin America, along with the term 'new evangelisation'. This meeting, which sought to liberate the people from the preventable 'institutionalised violence' of poverty and hunger, also introduced the concept of 'basic Christian communities' (BECs) as the locus for the empowerment of poor people, especially through programs of literacy. This was the beginning of what came to be called 'liberation theology', developed by theologians such as Gustavo Gutiérrez OP. Paul VI took all of this up in *Evangelii Nuntiandi* (1975).

The original sense of the 'new evangelisation' was more rooted in interpreting the implications of the gospel for the lived reality of people, particularly marginalised people that the Church was neglecting. It was, in essence, the kind of recontextualising that has needed to happen time and again in the story of the Church, and the kind of process in which every ecclesial community has needed to enter for its relevance and vitality to continue. It is always marked by engagement with the needs and aspirations of people, rather than the language and idealism of a past time.

SPIRITUALITIES AND INSTITUTIONALISATION: A CREATIVE TENSION

Ideally, the Church will be a space where 'charism and institution are always complementary',[78] but the reality is frequently enough something else. Leo Joseph Suenens' intervention during the drafting of *Lumen Gentium*, mentioned above, named a tension that is always present in the Church. This tension is not a case of the white-hats against the black-hats, right against wrong. The extensive prescriptions in Canon Law regulating the power of bishops with respect to religious institutes and similar entities, and vice

---

77 John Paul II (1990), *Redemptoris missio, On the permanent validity of the Church's missionary mandate,* Libreria Editrice Vaticana, Rome, #33.
78 Benedict XVI (2009), *Attract to Christ Men and Women of All Ages,* address at Castel Gandolfo to Members of the Franciscan Family participating in the 'Chapter of Mats', 20 April, Libreria Editrice Vaticana.

versa, and the need for a document such as *Mutuae Relationes*,[79] are evidence that it is not always plain-sailing when it comes to the Church's acceptance of both its 'hierarchical and charismatic gifts'.[80] There is a creative tension that exists not only between the institution of the Church and the groups which have care of its charismic traditions, but it is a tension that arises within these groups themselves. It is not a simplistic dualism.[81]

Over the centuries, the Church's hierarchy has responded in mixed ways to new irruptions of the Spirit among the Church's members. Some founders of new ways of living the gospel have met with ready acceptance and have been immediately welcomed as providential. Others have come up against more suspicion and resistance. While Ignatius of Loyola's new form of religious life for men quickly gained acceptance, Mary Ward's for women did not. Angela Merici, Mary MacKillop and many others – women perhaps disproportionately among them – found less-than-favourable responses to what they were proposing, at least initially. Similarly, some apostolic institutes founded in the eighteenth and nineteenth centuries felt that the Church forced them into paradigms of religious life that were ill-suited for what their founders had in mind. The pastors of the Church do have a legitimate and necessary role to discern authenticity and value in new ways of gospel living – as did St Paul and the early churches – and need criteria for doing so.[82] They also have the responsibility of enabling these new ways to become part of the life and organisation of the Church, and indeed to ensure that they do. If they are genuine irruptions of the Spirit then, *de facto*, they cannot be outside the Mystical Body of Christ

> *A sure sign of the authenticity of a charism is its ecclesial character, its ability to be integrated harmoniously into the life of God's holy and faithful people for the good of all. Something truly new brought about by the Spirit need not overshadow other gifts and spiritualities in making itself felt. To the extent that a charism is better directed to the heart of the Gospel, its exercise will be more ecclesial. It is in communion, even when this proves painful, that a charism is seen to be authentic and mysteriously fruitful.*[83]

---

79 This document, the English title of which is *Directives for the Mutual Relations between Bishops and Religious in the Church*, was jointly promulgated in 1978 by what was then known as the Sacred Congregation for Religious and for Secular Institutes and the Sacred Congregation for Bishops.

80 *Lumen Gentium*, #4.

81 Indeed, the CELAM Declaration of 1968 and the growth of liberation theology to which it gave impetus through the 1970s is a stand-out example of how such complementarity of charism and institution can play out fruitfully. This all stemmed from the hierarchy of the Latin American Church taking the lead by being responsive to what the bishops discerned to be genuinely evangelical in the work of theologians and pastors close to the lived reality of the poor. It was the Church working with its institutional and charismatic dimension in sync.

82 This will be developed further in Chapter 4.

83 *Evangelii Gaudium*, #130.

Enabling these new ways is a responsibility that belongs to both the pastors of the Church and to the spiritual families themselves. *Iuvenescit Ecclesia* is almost entirely concerned with addressing this question, prompted mainly by the exponential growth of new ecclesial movements. Welcomed and championed by John Paul II, these movements, in their structures, exercising of authority, and ways of Christian living particularly in local church situations, have generated some questions and created tensions, particularly at parochial and diocesan levels. In addressing such issues, *Iuvenescit Ecclesia* names two 'fundamental' and 'inseparable' criteria for how the relationship between hierarchical and charismatic gifts should be developed: (a) the avoidance of 'juridical straight-jackets that deaden the novelty' that emerges from specific spiritual experiences, and (b) respect for 'ecclesial regimen' that allows the new charismatic entities to work as part of both the local and universal Church.[84]

Whatever the noble theological rhetoric that may be used to describe the co-essentiality and complementarity of the hierarchical and charismatic giftedness of the Church, this can be compromised by the very human behaviours that play out in structures and bureaucracies. Bureaucracies, at least unhealthy ones, tend to favour uniformity, confusing it with unity. Similarly, they can confuse management with leadership, and control with authority. They can tend to avoid diversity and heterogeneity, misreading it as disunity or disloyalty. Nor are collegiality and subsidiarity their natural habitat. 'Blue-sky' thinkers and whistle-blowers are kept in check or, worse, ostracised. The literature of organisational culture is replete with such tendencies. At its best, the Church should not be marked by this kind of culture, but the experience of the centuries has shown that it has sometimes fallen well short of the ideal. The risk applies just as much within spiritual families themselves as it does to diocesan offices and agencies.

Charismic movements are not immune from the downsides of bureaucratisation in their own life.[85] As a movement grows, so does its management and infrastructure, its rules of life, its general body of texts, along with its customs and accepted practices. For example, by the end of the sixteenth century, the spiritual and educational intuitions and insights of Ignatius had grown into the Spiritual Exercises, Constitutions and a *Ratio Studiorum*, and its educational institutions had begun to be associated with a particular stratum of society. Other groups with long histories in education, for example the Benedictines and Augustinians, had previously developed their pedagogical principles, sourced in Rules and their founding insights.

---

84 *Iuvenescit Ecclesia*, #23. See also #8–10, and *Lumen Gentium*, #12.
85 Weberian and Neo-Weberian theory (see above) deals extensively with the development of bureaucratisation in organisations following the charismatic leadership of a founder.

These days, charismic traditions involved in education typically have reference texts that distil the characteristics of their approach, and which are often used as touchstones for school communities. Such documenting of method, expectation, characteristics, and general ways of proceeding are all necessary, and potentially very helpful for capturing and building wisdom, and maintaining integrity of purpose and method in a group. But they can also freeze it. And they can insulate it from its original sharpness. Vatican II's call to religious institutes to 'renew and adapt'[86] sprang from a recognition that many of them had become barnacled, anachronistic and petty in their ways of life, and this was often reflected also in their approaches to their educational ministries. A spiritual family that is not continually looking for fresh expression and resourcing may be one that is being unhealthily institutionalised.

As the members of religious institutes – because of ageing or lower numbers – become less directly connected with the schools and other ministries with which they have been associated, there needs to be care that the people who succeed them are attuned spiritually to the evangelical heartbeat of the spiritual family. The Church cannot afford to see echoed in the spiritual families twenty-first century the sclerotic state that so much of religious life had found itself in before Vatican II. Institutional paralysis needs to be eschewed. The Church may head in that direction, however, if those at all levels in schools – governance, leadership or direct service of young people – are people whose hearts and minds are shaped by priorities that are different from the founding evangelical impulse of the movement. Both for their own charismic integrity, as well as for the prophetic role they are called to play in and for the Church more broadly, spiritual families need to develop self-critiquing strategies, and to be open to external critiquing from the Church.

THE SPIRIT BRINGS LIFE

The life of the Spirit is the spirit of life. 'Charisms' and 'spiritualities' are no magical-mystery phenomena like kryptonite from a parallel universe in the back-pockets of super-founders. They are conceptual constructs that the Church has developed for integrating its understanding of the vivifying triune God that continually seeks to create, to reconcile, and to bring all into communion, and to do so in the here and now, in and among people. All people are gifted with this indwelling God by their very nature, but some have been extraordinarily sensitive and responsive, literally *enthused*.

---

86   Cf. *Perfectae Caritatis*, #2, 4, 18, 25.

Around such people, others have been inspired to gather, and providentially novel ways of Christian discipleship have developed, ways that have catalysed the coming of the Kingdom in particular temporal contexts. It is God being God. The inner life of God has continued to be incarnated. In quintessentially human ways — in culture — this Christ-life has become manifest and new spiritual families have emerged. In and through these communities the Church's spiritualities have been developed and lived. They have given people accessible and effective ways for sharing in *missio Dei* in and from the Church. They have helped to enrich, enliven and renew the Church, especially when it has been most in need. A Christian spirituality has no existence without a continuing spiritual family whose members are inspired and formed by its evangelical intuitions, and impelled into mission from them. Those spiritual families that have been able to adapt and renew their spiritualities for fresh and emerging contexts have endured. Among them have emerged some of the Church's most efficacious educational traditions.

3

NEW ECCLESIAL PARADIGMS

Now, you are Christ's body

1 Cor 12:27

Two of the signature teachings of the Second Vatican Council – the universal call to holiness and the essentially missionary nature of the Church – have provided spiritualities of the Church with considerable opportunity and challenge. More than that, they have helped to generate significantly changed contexts with which both old and new spiritual families have been called to engage. The reorienting of the Church's self-understanding of its being in the contemporary world rather than in reactionary resistance against it – as captured most profoundly in *Gaudium et Spes*[1] – has provided impetus to the need for spiritual families to renew, if not to reimagine themselves, perhaps to refound. This revitalised understanding of the role and place of the laity in the Church, and of the role and place of the Church in the socio-economic and political realities of the world, has provided the conditions for ecclesial communities to recontextualise Christian discipleship for themselves and for those to whom they minister.

It was not, of course, that these ideas emerged from nowhere between 1962 and 1965. Various lay movements from medieval and early modern times were mentioned in the previous chapter. In the late nineteenth century, lay involvement began to take new directions. Catholic social teaching, for example, had been gathering momentum since Leo XIII's Encyclical *Rerum Novarum* in 1891, and had been prompting participation of the laity quite broadly. The Young Christian Worker (YCW) movement began in 1924 in Belgium and received Papal approval almost immediately; the Catholic Worker Movement started nine years later in New York. Yves Congar, a close associate of YCW's founder Joseph Cardijn and appointed

---

1 *Gaudium et Spes, The Pastoral Constitution on the Church in the Modern World* is frequently seen as the most genuine fruit of the Council in that it was not envisaged at the start of the Council in 1962 but emerged from the spirit of the Council, being symbolically adopted on the Council's final day in 1965. Although somewhat dated now in much of its language and concepts – for example 'modernity' and 'man' – it helped to confirm the Church unambiguously on the trajectory of its growing social teaching. Paul VI was a strong advocate and helped to shape it. developed its themes himself in *Evangelii Nuntiandi*.

by Pope John XXIII on the preparatory committee for the Vatican Council, was teaching new ideas in ecclesiology from the 1930s. By the early 1950s he was publishing to a widening readership on reclaiming the proper role of the laity as the normative group in the Church.[2] Similarly, not everything changed overnight at the end of the Council in 1965. There is the view that the Church is still in a process of receiving the fullness of its teaching, something that could play itself out for another half-century or so.[3] The Council does, nonetheless, provide the usually recognised milestone for marking a substantially new, or more accurately *renewed*, ecclesiology.[4] Any emerging or continuing spirituality of the Church can be validly critiqued through a Vatican II lens, and needs to be.[5] Of special significance for the Church's spiritual families has been the post-conciliar fostering of the rights and responsibilities of all who have been baptised into the priesthood of Christ – including those who had come to be called, misleadingly enough, the 'laity'.

LAY DISCIPLESHIP – A FLAWED CONCEPT

It is likely that all the writers of the books of the New Testament, if not Jesus himself, would have had a problem with the concept of 'lay' disciples. The word *laikos* does not appear in the Christian Scriptures. Saint Paul would have shied from the proposition that there are degrees of spirituality that presume that some of us are the professional, full-time, holy Christians, while others of us are only part-timers, with serviceable enough spiritual lives but having no serious claim to a developed spiritual expertise. Paul, rather, taught the Christians at Colossae, as he teaches us: 'You [that is, all

---

2   His 1953 book *Jalons pour une Théologie du Laïcat,* Les Editions de Cerf, Paris, was influential in pre-conciliar theological discourse, see pp. 79ff.

3   See, for example: Faggioli, M (2012), *Vatican II. The Battle for Meaning,* Paulist Press, New York. Faggioli examines the differential reception of the Council by various schools of theology and communities of the Church.

4   Faggioli describes ecclesiology as the 'macro issue' of Vatican II. See: Faggioli, M (2016), *The Rising Laity. Ecclesial Movements since Vatican II,* Paulist Press, New York, chapter 2. A key point for Faggioli was the transition during the mid to late twentieth century of lay movements that were essentially of Papal or episcopal initiatives, to new movements that emerged more organically, and often outside of traditional diocesan or local church parameters.

5   There has been a sometimes intense theological debate, one in which Benedict XVI personally involved himself, contesting whether Vatican II should be understood in terms of a 'reforming continuity' or as a 'rupture'. Rupture is a word that carries some pejorative connotations, along with other words that share its Latin etymological roots – disrupt, erupt, corrupt and even the word that we have used for the action of the Spirit, irrupt. Such negative allusion has not been helpful for assessing the hermeneutics of the Council. Whichever conceptual orientation is preferred, it cannot be denied that the ecclesiology promoted before, during and after the Council was, first, markedly different in its emphases from that which had prevailed in the Latin Church between medieval and modern times but, second, was demonstrably more aligned with early Christian ecclesiology. This will be considered later in this chapter, and also in Chapter 6, through the lens of the traditional icon of the Ascension.

of you] are God's chosen ones, his saints.'[6] In the first letter of Peter we read that we, all of us, are 'a chosen race, a royal priesthood, a holy nation, a people set apart.'[7] The four evangelists would have similarly been intrigued by a notion of a 'lay' spirituality. In each of the four Gospels, the so-called 'hard-sayings' of Jesus are not directed at a special elite, or just to the Twelve, but to everyone who is listening.[8] They did not pen the Gospels for monks and nuns. The core concept is that of discipleship, and that this discipleship is for all who respond to the invitation of Jesus to follow him. In all that has happened and has been written in the two millennia since, nothing has altered this basic truth. Each person is called to be a disciple of Jesus. There are no grades of discipleship, no business-class and economy-class Christians, no full and associate members of the Church.

The development of a clergy/laity dichotomy in the Church is an interesting and complex theological story, not least from the perspective of ontology.[9] It is sufficient here to recognise that a ministerial priesthood was defined clearly enough in the first centuries after Christ and that a concept of laity therefore emerged by a kind of default. Over the course of the Church's history, and in its various rites and geographical regions, there have been considerable differences and development in how the clergy and the laity – and additionally those in the various forms of eremitical, monastic, mendicant and apostolic religious life – have understood their respective places and purposes in the life of the Church, and how they have related to one other. Social and cultural factors have influenced this as well as theological and ecclesiological understandings, one example of which is the cultural 'clericalism' that continues to dog the Church.[10] By the end of the Middle Ages, there had developed a marked clerical ascendancy, additionally influenced by a certain *fuga mundi* emphasis in spirituality which, by implication, was exclusive of most lay people in their normal worldly lives. Mandatory clerical celibacy in the second Christian millennium exacerbated this lived understanding, helping to sustain a perception that

---

6   Col 3:12.
7   1 Pet 2:9.
8   For example, Matt 4:18-22; Mark 1:16-20; John 1:38-50; Luke 5:1-11. This idea is developed well by Donna Orsuto, Director of the Lay Center at Foyer Unitas (Rome), and Professor at the Institute of Spirituality at the Gregorian University. See: Orsuto, D (1992), 'Spirituality of the Laity', in De Cea, E, *Compendium of Spirituality* (Trans. J Aumann), Alba House, New York; (1997) 'The challenge of lay spirituality', in *Faith in the Home*; (2007), *Holiness*, Bloomsbury Publishing, London.
9   For a good analysis of this see: Faivre, A (1990), *The Emergence of the Laity in the Early Church*, Paulist Press, Mahevah NJ Tony Hanna also considers the question well: (2006), *New Ecclesial Movements*, St Paul Publications, Sydney.
10 Condemnation of this has been a recurring theme of Pope Francis. See, for example, his 2014 Christmas address to the Curia: https://w2.vatican.va/content/francesco/en/speeches/2014/december/documents/papa-francesco_20141222_curia-romana.html. For an exploration of the historical and current role of the laity in the Church, especially factors that impede its full expression, see: Shaw, R (2013) *Catholic Laity in the Mission of the Church*, The Chartwell Press, Langley BC.

clergy were removed if not above the normal concerns of ordinary people. The sidelining of lay people was challenged from time to time by popularly based spiritual renewal movements in the Church, often enough led by lay people or certainly accessible to them, such as that begun by Francis and Clare of Assisi, or spiritual schools such as that developed by Francis de Sales and his contemporaries as part of the Catholic Reformation after the Council of Trent. But the institutional face of the Church, rather than its charismatic one, came to be a largely clerical or monastic one. The concerns and documents of the Council of Trent, for example, were occupied almost entirely with the ordained priesthood, something that set a pattern for the succeeding centuries. As late as the time when, in the nineteenth century, John Henry Newman was pioneering some reclamation of the legitimate role of lay people in the life of the Church,[11] his views were infamously dismissed by Monsignor Talbot in a letter to Cardinal Manning:

What is the province of the laity? To hunt, to shoot, to entertain. These matters they understand, but to meddle with ecclesiastical matters, they have no right at all.[12]

In the post-war period, Congar and other theologians such as Hans Urs von Balthasar and Karl Rahner, began to challenge such misconceptions. Already grass-root, lay-led movements such as Focolare and the Cursillos had been growing, these particular ones starting in 1943 and 1944 respectively. The Council caught this spirit and formalised it by teaching unambiguously that the call to holiness was for everyone, and that the responsibility to share in God's mission in the Church, and to share in the priesthood of Christ, belonged to all as a fundamental consequence of their Baptism. It was a paradigm shift. It was, as hoped for by Pope John XXIII, an *aggiornamento*. The notion of the Church as the People of God was reclaimed and developed. All of us, pilgrims and disciples. All called to be holy.[13] The ways in which people respond to that call, in relationship with others and for the mission of the gospel, can be understood as their spirituality.

---

11 John Henry Newman published his ideas in 1859 in a journal article (in *The Rambler*) entitled: 'On Consulting the Faithful in Matters of Doctrine'. Although sparking controversy in clerical circles, the article, ironically enough, had limited circulation among lay Catholics and was not further published.

12 Quoted in Hanna, *op. cit.*, p. 129. Russell Shaw uses the statement for a longer study of its underlying assumptions. See: Shaw, RB (1993), *To Hunt, To Shoot, To Entertain: Clericalism and the Catholic Laity.* Ignatius Press, San Francisco.

13 See Donna Orsuto (2007), *op. cit.* for a comprehensive treatment of the concept of holiness. Ron Rolheiser is a theologian who has written accessibly about the call to radical discipleship that pertains to all Christians. See: (2014), *op. cit.*

Today, at least in most Western countries, the pastoral ministry of the Church – in its schools and universities, catechetical programs, hospitals, health and aged care facilities, social services agencies, liturgical support, spiritual direction, and even parochial services – is largely undertaken by lay people, and led and administered by them. They comprise women and men – with probably more women than men – of all ages, of diverse backgrounds, with a range of connections with parishes and the life of the institutional Church, and with an even greater range of faith experience and maturity in the spiritual life. Experience suggests that they are people of enormous good will, generosity and professional skill, fired by their genuine love of the people they are serving. Their discipleship of Jesus is expressed first in their marriages and family life – with all its joys and complexities – and then in their wider employment and involvements.

Clergy and religious are generally few and becoming fewer and older. It needs be emphasised that this was not the vision of Vatican II. When Congar and others were writing of the coming age of the laity back in the 1950s, and when the Council captured many of these hopes in documents such as *Gaudium et Spes* and *Apostolicam Actuositatem,* no one envisaged that lay people would or should replace an ageing clergy or a vanishing band of religious. Indeed, the new thinking was formulated at a time when numbers of clergy and religious were at their height. It was not anticipated that this would change, that there would be what is often called a 'vocations crisis'. It was not an ecclesiology that was born out of a context clerical diminishment. There was not a sense that lay people needed to step up to the plate because the innings of the nuns and brothers were over. So, also, in pivotal gatherings such as the Synod on the Laity in 1987,[14] and the landmark Apostolic Exhortation *Christifideles Laici,* that came from it, there is no sense of a church or a mission that was to be the remit of lay people alone. Other documents – and, particularly for the concerns of this book, those published by the Congregation for Catholic Education – are written within a similar conceptual framework. The first part of *Educating Together in Catholic Schools, A Shared Mission between Consecrated Persons and the Lay Faithful*[15] locates this mission in the context of *communio,* an important theme of today's Church. *Communio* is not a sociological concept but a theological and ecclesiological one, founded on the complementary, reciprocal and unified states of life in the Church – the laity, the ordained

---

14 Or, to give it its full title: 'A Synod on the Vocation and the Mission of the Lay Faithful in the Church and in the World.'

15 Congregation for Catholic Education (2007), *Educating Together in Catholic Schools, A Shared Mission between Consecrated Persons and the Lay Faithful,* Libreria Editrice Vaticana, Rome.

priesthood, and the consecrated life – and their all being sharers in the life of the Risen Christ.[16]

Vatican II can be misrepresented in this regard, and a misconceived ecclesiology can develop as a result. It is not good theology or ecclesiology to speak of a 'lay church'. This is not what John Paul II meant when he envisaged the twenty-first century as the century of the laity. Nor does a sound or viable understanding of 'lay spirituality' emerge if we consider this spirituality to be a phenomenon that is independent from priests and those in consecrated life (or equivalent forms of life where the primary commitment of people is to an ecclesial community). This would be a diminished and incomplete understanding of spirituality, because it is a diminished and incomplete understanding of church. From this perspective at least, 'lay spirituality' or 'lay discipleship' are flawed concepts. In the context of the charismic spiritual traditions of the Church it is similarly misconceived to understand that lay people are the successors to the spiritualities of the religious institutes that are now so limited in their presence and activity. A challenge for all spiritualities of the Church is that they find ways to build community and go about ministry that reflect and nurture inclusivity, mutual respect and co-responsibility, both in their inner life and mission and across the life and mission of the wider Church.

KOINONIA – AN IMPERATIVE FOR MOVEMENTS NEW AND OLD

Communio has emerged as one of the hermeneutical keys to Vatican II and the post-conciliar period. It is perhaps the most useful key.[17] It is a twin-dimensional concept. First, it carries the spiritual sense of communion with Christ, of being caught up in the inner life of God-who-is-mission. The Church is essentially sacramental. Second, it is simultaneously a communion for the sake of God's mission – the diversity of charisms united and complementary in order to realise the Reign of God in the world. This is more than simply 'community'. *Koinonia* (κοινωνία) carries a sense of co-responsibility, full participation, reciprocity, bonding, sharing,

---

16 See then-Cardinal Ratzinger's editorial piece for the twentieth anniversary of the theological journal *Communio* of which he was one of the co-founders. Ratzinger, J (1992), 'Communio: A Program', in *Communio*, Fall issue, pp. 435-449.

17 This was the conclusion of the Extraordinary Synod of 1985 marking two decades after the Council, cf., *The Church, in the Word of God, celebrates the Mysteries of Christ for the Salvation of the World, Final Report of the Synod*: 'The ecclesiology of communion is the central and fundamental idea of the documents of the Council', #II C,I. See Cardinal Marc Oullet's reflections on this almost another two decades later: (2013), *Communio, the Key to Vatican II's Ecclesiology*, an address to the 'Great Grace receiving Vatican II' Conference, Sydney, 21 May. Among others who see *communio* as the 'leitmotif' of the Council's understanding of Church is John Fuellenbach. See (2006) *op. cit.*, p. 259-60.

contributing, fellowship, and even intimacy. It is a strong word. In its nineteen appearances in the Acts and in the Letters *koinonia* is employed variously to convey these meanings, in relation to communion with both Christ and fellow Christians. Since the Council, the concept has helped to give direction to the universal call to holiness, to episcopal collegiality, to ecumenism, and more lately at the prompting of Pope Francis, to a culture of synodality.[18] It has provided a charter for how and why church comes to be – church in all its multiform expression. It is always about communion in mission and for mission; through Christ, with Christ and in Christ.

All ecclesial communities, and the living spiritualities for which they have shared responsibility on behalf of the entire Church, have a twin challenge as a consequence. First, they are called to be radically spiritual, literally rooted in the Spirit. They are to be schools of holiness. They are to be more than people coming together simply to pursue some worthwhile purpose, such as a school. They must be able, as *Iuvenescit Ecclesia* puts it, to prompt 'a particular attraction to the gospel' and to offer a 'proposal for the Christian life'.[19] Second, ecclesial communities are called to be inclusive of the charismic giftedness of all their members in ways that maximise people's engagement, their sense of co-responsibility, and their collaboration. It is equally incumbent upon them to ensure that the engagement, responsibility, and collaboration that define them internally are also extended to their relations with other ecclesial communities in particular church contexts, and to the Church as a whole.

A litmus test for how well the charismic families are responding to these calls are the roles that lay people are able to take within them. There are two common ways in which lay people are able to develop *communio* through the spiritualities of the Church: first, through what are often called the 'new ecclesial movements', and second, through movements associated with longer-established religious orders and institutes. This parallel but not unconnected development experienced some serendipity near the turn of the last century when two quite separate convened gatherings occurred around the same time in Rome. One was the regular meeting of the Union of Superiors General, referred to in the previous chapter. This meeting was devoted to examining the myriad of ways that lay people were seeking, and were being invited, to associate themselves in one way or another with the spiritualities that had long given life to religious orders and religious

---

18 Pope Francis's address on 17 October 2015 to mark the 50th Anniversary of the Synod of Bishops is often seen as a defining moment in his efforts to foster a 'synodal Church' at all levels. http://w2.vatican.va/content/francesco/en/speeches/2015/october/documents/papa-francesco_20151017_50-anniversario-sinodo.html

19 *Iuvenescit Ecclesia*, #2.

institutes. Some of these orders had had tertiary branches or had supported lay sodalities for centuries, while for others it was a new challenge. It was their common experience, however, that lay people were being attracted in unprecedented numbers to share in the spirituality and the mission of the different traditions. There was a broadly felt call that they needed to widen the space of their tents.[20]

The other gathering, which preceded the first by two years, was the first World Congress of Ecclesial Movements, a plenary gathering of invited leaders of fifty-six new ecclesial communities. Over 400,000 people gathered, at Pentecost. Many saw it as a watershed moment in the history of the Church.[21] Much promoted by John Paul II during his pontificate, these movements had grown to such an extent that many in the Church were beginning to see them as the most providential way that the Church of the post-conciliar period was being prompted by the Spirit to be renewed and reformed.[22]

Among such movements are ones who conduct or sponsor Catholic schools and universities. Although they comprise a range of style, structure and emphasis, most of these share a number of characteristics: they are predominantly lay in their membership but also have ordained members, and often a small number who make a deeper, life commitment (in some cases as consecrated people, in some cases not); they have a quite radical way of living the gospel in daily life; they emphasise fellowship and community

---

20   Cf. Isa 54:2.
21   Scholars of the ecclesial movements phenomenon, for example Brendan Leahy (*op. cit.*, 2011) often see the 1998 Congress in this light. The four people chosen to provide testimonies to Pope John Paul II at the Papal Audience, and a fifth chosen to offer a vote of thanks, represented the flagship movements that had grown so exponentially over the preceding decades: Chiara Lubich of Focolare, Luigi Giussani of Communion and Liberation, Kiko Argüello of The Neocatechumenal Way, Jean Vanier of L'Arche, and Charles Whitehead of Catholic Charismatic Renewal. Two further World Congresses have been held: 31 May – 3 June 2006, and 20-22 November 2014.
22   *Iuvenescit Ecclesia* recurringly affirms this. Archbishop Julian Porteous has critiqued the new movements from historical, theological and pastoral perspectives, seeing them optimistically in a similar vein to the timely great movements of other times such as monasticism and the mendicants, but cautioning against any exclusivity and insularity: (2010), *A New Wine and Fresh Skins: Ecclesial Movements in the Church,* Connor Court Publishing, Redland Bay. Tony Hanna (2006, *op. cit.*) offers a comprehensive, critical and well-balanced analysis of the new ecclesial movements in general, with a specific focus on three of them: Communion and Liberation, The Neo-Catechumenate, and The Charismatic Renewal. Another useful exploration of the new movements, and their development under the patronage of John Paul II, can be found in: Leahy, B (1999) 'Charism and Institution: a new ecclesial maturity', in *The Furrow,* Vol. 50, No. 5, pp. 278-285. Leahy later developed into a book his survey of various movements and their significance in the charismatic dimension of the Church, *op. cit.* (2011). A Church historian who has devoted significant attention over the last two decades to study of the new movements is Massimo Faggoli. He traces them back to the industrial, political, social and financial movements of the late nineteenth century. See: *op. cit.* (2016) where he considers the movements from the various perspectives – theological, canonical, sociological, political and ethnographical. He sees that they have moved from being agencies of the hierarchy (including the Papacy) in their earlier years through to the 1930s and 1940s, through to the later twentieth/twenty-first century emergence of movements that are no longer run by bishops and clergy but which are more genuinely participatory and animated by a theologically educated laity.

experience rather than private spirituality; they are zealous in catechesis and evangelisation; and they are attractive to young people in particular by proposing Christ in compelling and fresh ways. They are typical, therefore, of how the Spirit has always renewed the Church.

The growth and the vitality of the new ecclesial movements can teach something quite important to the whole Church.[23] Almost without exception – whether they appeared before or after the Council – they have typically a structure that is consistent with Vatican II's emphases: they are a majority lay, with lay people unambiguously embracing their baptismal responsibilities to grow in holiness and share together in the *missio Dei*; they value lay ecclesial leadership; they also have a strong sacramental life with the ordained pastors of the Church actively exercising their sacerdotal ministry within the movement's life; and mostly they allow for a relatively small number of members to make a more intense, long-term or permanent commitment usually as celibates, and to live a common life in ways not dissimilar to older forms of the consecrated life. They exist to provide a means for their members to deepen their own sense of baptismal vocation and holiness, to form community, and to take part in the mission of the Church.[24]

In this they provide a new paradigm for the traditional spiritualities to continue to be relevant and engaging for the contemporary Church. These 'older' spiritualities, and the spiritual families in which these are lived, are similarly called to be largely but not exclusively lay; to be conceived around charismic giftedness rather than hierarchy; to be eucharistic; to be able to integrate their inherent distinctiveness into the institutional and pastoral life of the Church globally and locally; and to inspire their members to a holiness that gathers community and impels them to mission. Indeed, it may be argued that these spiritual traditions will have a considerably diminished presence and relevance in the Church of the twenty-first century unless they can be lived and developed by communities that reflect a post-conciliar ecclesiology.

Yet it is the change to this meaningful inclusion of lay people – as a numerical majority, from their actual life situations, and with genuine authority – that can offer the most significant cultural challenge for many of the traditional spiritualities that have for so long been defined

---

23 Hanna, *op. cit.* considers these features and supports them by a comprehensive survey of relevant research.

24 This is not to suggest that the NEMs have not attracted justifiable criticism and caution from various quarters of the Church, including from Popes Benedict XVI and Francis. Indeed, *Iuvenescit Ecclesia* was prompted by concerns especially about examples of exclusivity, cultism, revisionism, insufficient personal freedoms, and inadequate transparency. Faggioli (*op. cit.* 2016) offers a more nuanced critique on these and other issues that have emerged.

primarily in terms of clergy and religious, with lay people often seen only as associates. Even those with long histories of take-up of their spiritualities by tertiaries, oblates, and members of confraternities, are faced with the question of whether they can or should reimagine themselves to allow for the full participation of all rather than to retain what are, in effect, grades of membership. Some of these communities are structured along the lines of the classical three-tier order. While this may have proved enduring and fruitful for centuries, it is germane to acknowledge that it is a creature of the medieval church. Remember the lessons of the Abbey of La Chaise-Dieu – eight hundred years of Benedictine life, just to fizzle out anachronistically within a generation. It was not a problem with Benedictine spirituality *per se*, but with the non-engagement of the community with the signs of the times. For example, women religious in such orders remain under male clerical oversight, something that may be judged to be out of sync with the understandings of the present times. Other lay groups and religious institutes of women religious have taken up spiritualities from existing clerical institutes but have developed structures that are independent of them, or interdependently related. For example, a number of groups of religious sisters such as The Institute of the Blessed Virgin Mary (the 'Loreto Sisters'), the Sisters of Charity, the Faithful Companions of Jesus and the Society of the Sacred Heart, are all Ignatian in their spiritualities and identities but are not institutional appendages of the Society of Jesus. But groups such as this, now with their own strands of the spiritual traditions and their own spiritual families, are faced with the same predicament.

Antonio Sicari offers an interesting measure for gauging how genuinely reflective of *communio* a spiritual family is in its membership and its self-understanding. Commenting on his own Order, he suggests that the term 'Carmelite' is used as a noun for a friar, but as an adjective for a lay person.[25] This implies a kind of 'ecclesial caste system'; even using the term 'ordo' for the clerical, conventual and lay expressions of Carmelite life can imply some hierarchy of holiness.[26] He suggests that the model of the typical new ecclesial movement offers a better paradigm for the older spiritualities of the Church, one closer to the Church's hopes that are expressed in *Christifideles Laici*. He wonders if older religious orders can reimagine themselves along these lines. By embedding authority and responsibility for the continued development of a spiritual tradition among the people attracted to the spirituality, and immersed in the reality of their lived situations rather than in the rarefied environment or reflected glow of a monastery, the spiritual family is going to

25   See Sicari, AM (2002), 'Ecclesial Movements: A New Framework for Ancient Charisms', *Communio*, Vol. 29, Summer, pp. 286–308.
26   *Ibid*, p. 392.

be better positioned to continue to recontextualise it. His proposal is a radical one because it calls for nothing short of a refounding. But that has happened more than once for some of the richest spiritualities of the Church.

The challenge for spiritual families to develop such a post-conciliar model of *communio* is not a one-way street. While it can be confronting for the members of a religious institute to surrender their sole authority and control of the spiritual tradition, and indeed of the family itself, there can also be hurdles or even reluctance on the part of lay people to accept roles of responsibility for leadership, formation, and on-going development.

The 2015 document *The Identity and Mission of the Religious Brother in the Church* takes up this theme, defining the essential role that religious can and should have in a wider spiritual family. While the subject of the document is specifically the religious brother, its principles can be applied also to religious sisters and ordained religious:

> *The founding charisms ... now take the form of rivers watering the surface of the Church and extending far beyond it. The faithful come to their shores from different states of life to drink from their waters and to participate in the mission of the Church from the constantly renewed inspiration and vigour of such charisms.*

> *Laity and religious ... and priests unite together in a charismatic family to revive the charism that has given rise to this family, to incarnate together the Gospel face that the charism reveals, and to serve together in the same Church mission, which is no longer the mission of a particular Institute.*

> *The religious brother finds in this charismatic family an environment conducive to the development of his identity. In such an environment, the brothers share the experience of communion and promote a <u>spirituality of communion</u>, being the true blood which gives life to the family members and which extends to the whole Church from them. In the charismatic family, religious brothers place themselves together with other Christians and in accord with them. It is <u>with them</u> that the brothers build a fraternity for the mission, motivated by the foundational charism; <u>for them</u> they are signs of that same brotherhood that they are called to live in the consecrated life.*[27]

Here was new language for the primary contribution of consecrated members within a spiritual family: to be its 'true blood' but as part of the family. It was not about being in charge or in control of the family; that

---

27   Congregation for Institutes of Religious Life and Societies of Apostolic Life (2015), *Identity and Mission of the Religious Brother in the Church*, Rome: Libreria Editrice Vaticana, #38.

was not the charismic essence of religious life. The locus of the authority of religious should lie elsewhere. Their role within a spiritual family was the same as their role within the Church: to be a 'living memory' of Jesus in the community.[28] Not from any sense of spiritual or ecclesial superiority – either actual or perceived – but by the humble witness of their lives, and their respectful dialogue, their focus was to help the People of God be mindful of the heart of gospel.[29] It was also to be a living memory of particular incarnation of the gospel that came from their founding charism.[30] Within their own charismic family, they were to be 'as leaven in the dough.'[31] Being a 'living memory' of the gospel and of their founding charism was the 'first ministry' of the religious.[32] In fact, the paradigm of being in a wider spiritual family allowed religious to live out more effectively the essence of their state of life, rather than – in their relatively small numbers – to be caught up in responsibilities of governance and administration.

There has been a variety of ways that these imperatives have played out in Catholic education, and not always helpfully or generatively. Sometimes it has been a sole religious who has been left in a school as its principal, or as the designated representative of the spiritual tradition on a school board, or in charge of running formation programs in that spirituality for a school or a network of schools. There are, similarly, instances of governance structures set up to retain actual or reserved powers for the council of a religious institute, even when there is little practical connection of the religious with the school or the network of schools. Leaving religious in these positions of organisational authority or control is out of alignment with where the Church is calling them to be. Such situations are changing rapidly, either as the result of strategic vision and choice, or simply by default of circumstance. In the United States, Australia and Ireland – these three countries more than elsewhere – there have been a range of initiatives since the turn of the century in the establishing of new entities that have taken over the administration of Catholic schools from religious institutes, either civilly or both civilly and canonically. Groups such as Edmund Rice Education Australia, Mary Aikenhead Ministries and Mercy Partners are examples of a growing number of new public juridic persons (PJPs) that have been incorporated to operate Catholic schools and other ministries previously conducted by religious institutes.[33] In other cases, entities – both

---

28   *Identity and Mission of the Religious Brother,* #7.
29   *Vita Consecrata,* #33, 84.
30   *Ibid.* #9.
31   *Ibid.* #10.
32   *Ibid.* #7.
33   This is a term which Canon Law uses to describe one or more persons who form a canonical legal entity that can act in the name of the Church and own property in the name of the Church; it gives the entity legal status that is recognised by the Church. This is analogous to terms such as

civilly incorporated and not – have been established but under the delegated authority of the religious institutes who retain ultimate canonical oversight.

Not all the new PJPs have an understanding of being (or being part of) spiritual families or ecclesial communities themselves but, rather, they act as stewards or trustees *on behalf of* a spiritual family and/or a religious institute. Or, simply, they act generically in the name 'of the Church' and as part of the Church. Most frequently, both the members of the PJP and its board(s) of trustees – are relatively few in number. Others, such as the Marist Association of St Marcellin Champagnat, have a broadly-based membership with elected leadership, and are closer in concept to the new ecclesial movements discussed above. In whichever ways they may be conceived and operate, however, they all have the challenge of building themselves and their ministries in a spirit of *communio* – in both its theological and anthropological dimensions. Part of this challenge is the imperative for any board, council or group of trustees to have a real and enduring relationship with a real and enduring community of the Church. Trusteeship and stewardship needs always to be undertaken on behalf of a community of faith – not as a tradition or philosophy. A critical question for any governing group is to ask itself on behalf of *whom* it is exercising its canonical authority, rather than on behalf of *what*.

SPIRITUAL FAMILIES AS IMAGES OF THE MARIAN PRINCIPLE OF THE CHURCH

As the concept of *communio* has emerged as a way of receiving Vatican II's ecclesiology over the past half-century, it has been augmented by another perspective, one that emerged especially from the theology of Hans Urs Von Balthasar and came to find a central place in the magisterium of John Paul II. It is the Marian principle or Marian dimension of the Church.[34] It is a conceptualisation intimately linked to that of *communio*. Benedict XVI who, as a theologian, was a champion of *communio*, emphasised both the horizontal and vertical dimensions of it: its complementary union of the states of Christian life, united in the holiness to which all are called and

---

'incorporated entity' or 'corporation' in civil law. Dioceses, parishes and religious institutes are all PJPs. A new PJP may be approved by a local bishop, a bishops' conference, or by the Holy See – the approving authority being the person/body to which the PJP is accountable.

34   There is a large library of commentary on themes in the theology and ecclesiology of von Balthasar, and the interest of John Paul II in it. Bishop and theologian Brendan Leahy offers a considered, accessibly written and comprehensive study of this particular aspect of Balthasarian ecclesiology, drawing from his own doctoral studies on the subject, and preferring the expression 'the Marian *profile*' of the Church. See: Leahy, B (2000), *The Marian Profile in the Ecclesiology of Hans Urs von Balthasar,* New City Press, London, pp. 62-64. Leahy argues that, along with communio, the theologising of this Marian profile is another of the keys for a reading of Vatican II. See also: Leahy *op. cit.* (2011), p. 119.

focused on Christ. This holiness and Christ-centredness is represented archetypically in Mary.[35] Balthasar wrote extensively of what he described as principles or dimensions of the Church – the Petrine, the Pauline and Joahnnine, and also the Jacobean. The primary principle of the Church was, however, the Marian – a teaching that came to be included in the *Catechism of the Catholic Church*:

> *In the Church, this communion of men [sic] with God, in the 'love [that] never ends,' is the purpose which governs everything in her that is a sacramental means, tied to this passing world* (1 Cor 13:8; <u>Lumen Gentium</u>, 48). '[The Church's] structure is totally ordered to the holiness of Christ's members. And holiness is measured according to the 'great mystery' in which the Bride responds with the gift of love to the gift of the Bridegroom' (<u>Mulieris Dignitatem</u>, 27). Mary goes before us all in the holiness that is the Church's mystery as 'the bride without spot or wrinkle' (Eph 5:27). This is why the 'Marian' dimension of the Church precedes the 'Petrine' (cf. <u>Mulieris Dignitatem</u>, 27). [36]

These concepts are perhaps most effectively approached through the visual theology of the traditional icon of the Ascension:

---

35 See, for example: Joseph Card. Ratzinger, *The Ecclesiology of the Constitution on the Life of Church, Lumen Gentium,* an address at a symposium on the reception of the Council, Rome, November 2000, reported in *L'Osservatore Romano,* 19 September 2001, p. 5.

36 *Catechism,* #773.

The icon of the Ascension is an icon of the Church. It represents an ecclesiology that recognises the Church's fundamental Marian principle: that the disciples of Christ assemble in all their giftedness around Mary, First Disciple, who, like them, is centred on and enlivened by the Risen Christ. Flanked by Peter in gold at her right hand and an active Paul in the blood-red of witness at her left, with John cloaked in brilliant red on her far left, and James, the brother of the Lord, holding the Scriptures, the breadth and purpose of ecclesial life is held in unity in Mary. With one hand Mary symbolises witness; with the other, prayer. Discipleship and the full reign of Christ on earth and in heaven are the two defining themes. Heaven has come to earth and earth has come to heaven, with heavenly angels alongside Mary, and angels in earthly colours alongside Christ. The figures in the icon reflect the different dimensions of the life of the Church, its poles of reference – the Petrine, the Pauline and the Johannine, the Jacobean, unified in the Marian. The hierarchical/pastoral, the apostolic/missionary, the mystical/sacramental, the Scriptural/traditional, are all gathered and centred on holiness and communion personified in Mary. Although Mary is prominent in the icon, providing something of a pivot and a unity, the visual flow of the image is towards the ascended Christ figure. Mary is no-one's object of devotion, yet she is there at the heart of the Church, as a kind of model and archetype of Christ-life on earth. It is she who has a halo, a symbol of holiness. She is *Theotokos*: the bearer of God, as all the Church is called to be.

The ecclesiology of this ancient icon is very much a post-conciliar one. This is the people of God, in all its charismatic diversity, and in communion with one another, with God, and with the eternal cosmos. It is a visual theology that could be applied not only to the universal Church, but to each manifestation of church – whether this manifestation be diocesan, parochial, or within one of the ecclesial movements or spiritual families of the Church. The same poles of reference apply and the same universal call to holiness. The lives of all the Church's members lead to and from Jesus, forming a community of disciples, on mission. Any ecclesial community is at its richest when it is inclusive of all people and states of life, centred on Christ, nourished by Word and Sacrament. The whole image is defined by *communio*, a communion of holiness. At the end of the Jubilee Year in 2000, it was to this that John Paul II called the Church:

> To make the Church the home and the school of communion: that is the great challenge facing us in the millennium which is now beginning, if we wish to be faithful to God's plan and respond to the world's deepest yearnings.

But what does this mean in practice? Here too, our thoughts could run immediately to the action to be undertaken, but that would not be the right impulse to follow. Before making practical plans, we need <u>to promote a spirituality of communion</u>, making it the guiding principle of education wherever individuals and Christians are formed, wherever ministers of the altar, consecrated persons, and pastoral workers are trained, wherever families and communities are being built up. A spirituality of communion indicates above all the heart's contemplation of the mystery of the Trinity dwelling in us, and whose light we must also be able to see shining on the face of the brothers and sisters around us. A spirituality of communion also means an ability to think of our brothers and sisters in faith within the profound unity of the Mystical Body, and therefore as 'those who are a part of me'. This makes us able to share their joys and sufferings, to sense their desires and attend to their needs, to offer them deep and genuine friendship. A spirituality of communion implies also the ability to see what is positive in others, to welcome it and prize it as a gift from God: not only as a gift for the brother or sister who has received it directly, but also as a 'gift for me'. A spirituality of communion means, finally, to know how to 'make room' for our brothers and sisters, bearing 'each other's burdens' (<u>Gal</u> 6:2) and resisting the selfish temptations which constantly beset us and provoke competition, careerism, distrust and jealousy. Let us have no illusions: unless we follow this spiritual path, external structures of communion will serve very little purpose. They would become mechanisms without a soul, 'masks' of communion rather than its means of expression and growth.[37]

Then, with reference to the Church's communities, he added:

Along these same lines, another important aspect of communion is the promotion of forms of association, whether of the more traditional kind or the newer ecclesial movements, which continue to give the Church a vitality that is God's gift and a true 'springtime of the Spirit'. Obviously, associations and movements need to work in full harmony within both the universal Church and the particular Churches, and in obedience to the authoritative directives of the Pastors. But the Apostle's exacting and decisive warning applies to all: 'Do not quench the Spirit, do not despise prophesying, but test everything and hold fast what is good' (1 Thess 5:19-21).[38]

John Paul II saw the growth of the new ecclesial movements in the Church as a flowering of its Marian principle, linking this to a reclaiming of the

---

37 John Paul II (2000,) *Novo Millennio Ineunte*, Libreria Editrice Vaticana, Rome, #43.
38 *Ibid.* #46.

rightful place of its charismatic dimension.[39] It is Mary who is the model *par excellence* of attentive openness and dialogical responsiveness to the Spirit, that Christ-life may come to birth. The spiritual families of the Church are called to this basic orientation: that of spiritual communion and spiritual fruitfulness. They are born from the charismatic dimension of the Church, rather than its hierarchical one, and they remain vital for the Church for as long as they can be 'schools of communion' for their members and for the Church more broadly, bringing about the Reign of God in their time and place. While the necessarily new ecclesial movements must also have structures and an inner politic, these cannot come to define or dominate them. Before all else, they will be schools of Christian discipleship for their members and for those who are served by their members.

SPIRITUAL FAMILIES AND CATHOLIC SCHOOLS

Not all religious institutes can be understood to have introduced a new spiritual tradition of the Church or to have been part of one. Some had a much more functional origin and development – responding in practical ways to a pressing need for Catholic schooling, for example, in a concrete time or place. These religious institutes began as the consequence of a serious pastoral need of the Church, and often developed in such a way that their primary orientation was to serve the pastoral imperatives of a local church. This is more commonly the case for national, diocesan and parochial foundations. Sometimes this has led to a demeaning view of these religious women and men as little more than a cheap labour-force for the local church. Without in any way accepting the pejorative and utilitarian senses of that labelling, there is, nonetheless, some degree of legitimacy in its intended meaning: the identity and purpose of such a religious institute (and, now, the PJP that may have succeeded it) are shaped by the pastoral program of a local Church situation, to enable that program to be pursued by the Church. The institute becomes a canonically recognised Catholic entity that acts in the name of the Church, and derives its identity from that context. It may have developed some characteristic pedagogical approaches, a community story, and a distinctive *modus operandi*, but it would be an overreach to describe it as a spirituality. In concept, it is more analogous to how a parish operates within a diocese. These religious institutes are a valid, even normal way for church communities to share in the life and mission of the Church, and for the life of the Spirit to be expressed in them.

---

39   Tony Hanna is one who has examined John Paul II's approach in these terms. See, Hanna, T (2005) 'New Church Movements: Friends or Foes?' *The Furrow*, Vol. 56, No. 2, pp. 83–93.

The enduring spiritualities of the universal Church – those of both older and newer origin – have typically emerged differently. While they have certainly grown in response to evangelical need, their founding has been more typically sparked by an intense spiritual experience of a person or persons which has resulted in fresh and compelling insights for embracing Christian discipleship, for forming Christian community, and for bringing about the Reign of God. A community has gathered; spiritual and apostolic wisdom has accumulated. The first purpose of the community has been the nurturing of the faith of its own members. When a ministry of education grew from this, it may not have been the only work of the community. Indeed, more usually it has not been. So, for example, the traditions of Augustinian, Benedictine or Dominican education have emerged from living communities of Augustinians, Benedictines and Dominicans. Communities originating later during the great phase of founding of institutes of apostolic life, such as the Salesians or the Marists, although younger in the accumulation of their spiritual wisdom, can be nonetheless similarly conceptualised as living communities through which distinctive apostolic approaches have developed. The respective approaches to Catholic education of all spiritual families are best understood as the expression of their spiritualities in their work of evangelisation through education, rather than as any objective philosophies or pedagogies. So, 'Franciscan education', for example, becomes most validly understood as how, why, where and with whom Franciscans go about education. It will develop its ways of being articulated, and needs to do so, but this language and methodology will change over time. The necessary constant is the community itself. If the nexus is broken or weakened between the community and its apostolic methodology, then it will lose its vitality and authenticity. Lasallian education will only exist where and if there are Lasallians to sustain it, to develop it, and to form the next generation in it. So the question arises as to who will be the Lasallians of tomorrow, or the Josephites, or the members of whichever spiritual family? How will they be formed? How will they be associated? How will they find their due place in the Church, and the Church its rightful place in them?

If these spiritual families reimagine and recast themselves more inclusively in ways that align with a post-conciliar ecclesiology, then this could give them a way forward.[40] If, on the other hand, the people who are recognised

---

40   This idea is extensively developed in the Congregation for Catholic Education's (2007) document *Educating Together in Catholic Schools, A Shared Mission of Consecrated Persons and the Lay Faithful.* The document emphasises that a 'spirituality of communion' is lived out in the Catholic school, as a 'special expression of Church', when all states of life are included as part of the individual community of a spiritual family in the school. Cf. #16.

as the 'real' Ignatians, or Carmelites, or whatever, are a decreasing and ageing group of religious, with less and less direct involvement in the day-to-day reality of their schools, then it is unlikely that the spirituality which is at the heart of their apostolic works will retain its integrity or its salience. If they delegate the conduct of their works to another body – however professionally competent and strategically astute its members may be – if the members of this body do not feel the same spiritual intuitions and sense of belonging to the spiritual family in their 'bones' and marrow, their and hearts and souls, then the nexus will be broken. If staff in a school, or in a schools' network, have a self-understanding as mostly working *on behalf of* a group, or simply *employed by* it, rather than being full members of the spiritual family which is conducting the schools, then the educational approach which is an expression of a community's spirituality is not likely to have much longevity. The same caution applies to a newer ecclesial movement whose members may be younger and more directly engaged in the school, but who have a culture of exclusivity. This is not a comment on the individual commitment, professionalism or indeed the personal holiness of these people, but simply a statement about self-identity and alignment.

The Church continues to place great store in the capacity of religious institutes and new ecclesial movements to offer 'great hope for the future of the Catholic educational mission',[41] sourced in the ways that large numbers of lay people seem to be attracted to being in dialogue with 'the spiritual and apostolic fruitfulness [of] the original charism' of the institutes and movements which are reimagining themselves as inclusive 'spiritual families'.[42] This points to a rationale for Catholic schools that is essentially evangelical and ecclesial, and depends on gospel-inspired people to form community:

> The project of the Catholic school is convincing only if carried out by people who are deeply motivated, because they witness to a living encounter with Christ, in whom alone 'the mystery of man [sic] becomes clear'.[43]

At their best, at their most vital, this is the strength of the Church's spiritualities and spiritual families: their perennial facility for inviting people into accessible and compelling ways that lead to Christ, to Christian discipleship, and to a Christian community of mission. Perhaps their greatest contribution, at this time in the story of Catholic schools in Western countries, is to do this among the faculty and staff of Catholic schools. The first apostolate of the Catholic school is its educators.

---

41 *Ibid.* #28.
42 *Ibid.* #28.
43 *Ibid.* #4.

Arguably, the greatest risk that is posed to the integrity and effectiveness of Catholic schools as agents of evangelisation is the depth of Christian spirituality in those who teach and work in these schools and the nature of their ecclesial engagement. Let us consider the example of the Australian experience of Catholic education which has some unique characteristics but, in most ways, parallels what is occurring in other Western countries. In world terms, Australian Catholic schools are built and resourced outstandingly. They are led and staffed by well-educated professionals, indeed people who, in the history of Catholic education in Australia, have never been more highly qualified. While more public funding is always sought, and can never be taken for granted, present levels of funding have provided resources that are the envy of most countries. The schools are serviced by diocesan, state, and national offices that provide high level curricular, financial, legal, and personnel support for policies, programs and governance. These offices allow parishes, dioceses, religious institutes, and other PJPs to conduct a world-class network of schools, and to be able offer these to virtually anyone who is seeking a Catholic education. In the secularising and pluralising context that such professionalism and resourcing exists, however, there are other issues that have to be addressed. To what extent is it still a Catholic education that is being offered? Or, to put it more pointedly, to what extent are the school communities places where the Christian gospel is proclaimed unambiguously and received openly, where Jesus is known and loved personally, where the reign of God pervades all that is done there – and how it is done? Are they places that satisfy the God-thirst in people and promote Christian discipleship? The answers to these questions are likely to fall across a range. The degree to which they can be answered affirmatively in any individual school is likely to largely be a reflection of the depth to which the school staff can personally answer yes to each of the questions.

Other questions present themselves. What are the staff's personal senses of being disciples of Jesus, or their being Christian educators? What is their understanding of the Church's purposes in Catholic education and their own role as evangelisers? How many have daily consciousness or commitment to a religious faith, specifically a Catholic one? What is their working knowledge of scripture and of the teachings and traditions of the Church? What is their parish connection? What are their social justice involvements? These are not unreasonable questions to ask. The world of young Australian people, including younger teachers, is for the most part a post-Christian and pluralising one. There are quite notable and inspiring exceptions, and there are certainly variances among ethnic communities across the country, but most people aged under fifty live quite secular lives. The Census statistics speak for themselves. Not being the 'ecclesial natives' that their grandparents were, they may not intuitively identify with the Church, or understand its language. They have witnessed twenty years of discrediting of the Church. As the next generation of teachers moves into middle-management and senior leadership – a larger number of whom have grown up in families that have not been active in their practice of the faith in the traditional sense – this is likely to become more the norm.[44]

'Mission drift' can happen subtly.[45] It may be seen first in little ways, such as the staff briefing starting with a 'reflection' rather than a 'prayer', so as to be more inclusive and not to offend anyone's religious sensibilities; or images and posters to do with caring for the planet taking the place of more overtly religious figures or images. Then the rhetoric of the school may shift ever so imperceptibly from talking about faith in God and a personal relationship with Jesus, to more generally espousing the Christian values that underpin the school. Masses may begin to be replaced with non-eucharistic liturgies, and gradually the celebration of the sacraments in the school community does not happen any longer. The danger? It moves towards becoming just a low-fee private school – albeit one that may be quite professionally run and with a solid value base that is not in conflict with the gospel – but with little capacity for explicit evangelisation or catechesis, or much understanding of it or vision for it. As far as connection with the life of the Church goes, the main point of connection may be through a diocesan education office or board rather than through a parish or pastor. That is not a pejorative comment on such an office which has, of course, an intrinsically ecclesial identity as an arm of the bishop's pastoral office, and its personnel may be quite active in Church life. It is a comment, rather, on how the faculty of a school are or are not personally involved in the Church beyond their professional work at the school. If the people who comprise the school community do not personally identify and connect with the Church as its members, it can be a pretence to claim that the school somehow has one corporately. Not everyone will be uncomfortable with such a scenario. That a school would have a sense of itself as a good educational institution with a quiet Catholic heritage may be an identity that sits well with the majority.

---

44 Trends such as these are evident in the ECSIP data from Victorian schools. See: Pollefeyt & Bouwens, (2014), *op. cit.*

45 See Nicholson, P (2009*), PJPs: Issues in Formation,* for a discussion of this phenomenon. Gerald Grace writes about 'mission integrity' in the context of two decades of research into the mission in Catholic schools. See, for example: Grace, G (2002b), 'Contemporary challenges for Catholic school leaders: beyond the stereotypes of Catholic schooling', in Leithwood, K and Hollinger, P (eds), *International Handbook of Educational Leadership and Administration,* Kluwer Academic Publishers, Dordrecht.

It is in such contexts of spiritual tepidity and ecclesial disconnection that many spiritualities have had their origins, either recently or in past centuries. Their growth was a function of the effectiveness of the founding generation to engage with such contexts. The degree to which those spiritual and apostolic intuitions remain alert and agile among the members of the spiritual family will be a major determinant for how well they are able to effect meaningful connection with members of staff and build an inclusive sense of community among them, a community underpinned by evangelical values. Closeness to people in their actual situations, language that they understand, vision that lifts their eyes and hearts, purpose that girds them – these are what spiritual families can offer. Their instinct will be to reach out, to dialogue, to understand, to reframe meaning. There is, however, no guarantee that they will. If they have become jaded or old – even by as little as a single generation – and speak or judge in anachronistic or cynical ways, then they will have diminished capacity to connect. If they smack of elitism, exclusivity or clericalism, then they are likely to meet a similar fate. And clericalism, it needs be noted, is not a malaise reserved solely for clergy.

It is no accident that programs of social justice frequently figure prominently in educational institutions with vibrant Christian spiritualities. It is indicative of a disposition of sensitivity to need and engagement with the marginalised, and provides a telling barometric reading on the vitality of the gospel. Jesus went about his ministry this way: he healed, he forgave, he reconciled, he fed, he liberated, he conversed, he dined with, he washed feet, he loved, he offered signs and means of hope and wholeness. It was because of this that he is described by the Evangelists as teaching 'with authority', in contrast to the Scribes and Pharisees.[46] The ways that the 'new evangelisation' is sometimes pursued can be criticised from this perspective. If there is mainly an emphasis on clarity or security of Catholic identity and teaching, with less attention to its being lived out in a spirit of service, then the credibility and effect of the evangelising efforts will be softened. A document such as *Catholic Schools at a Crossroad*, which seeks unambiguously to make Catholic schools 'centres of the new evangelisation' may draw some comment on this score. While it opts for Catholic schools to be open to a broad range of families and clearly rejects exclusivity and elitism, its two principal means for building them as 'truly Catholic schools' comprise the ensuring that students would have 'high levels of Catholic literacy' and that they would be led and staffed by people who can achieve that.[47] Among

---

46   Cf. Matt 7:29; Luke 4:32.
47   Catholic Education Commissions of NSW and the ACT (2007), *Catholic Schools at a Crossroads, Pastoral Letter of the Bishops of NSW and the ACT,* CEC, Sydney, p. 5.

its 'critical indicators of progress' for monitoring this, there is little overt mention of criteria that are drawn from the Church's social teaching.

In the pontificate of Pope Francis, through initiatives such as the Extraordinary Jubilee Year of Mercy in 2016 and his calls for the Church to refind itself on the existential peripheries of society, a different orientation has been presented. It is helpful to recall that it was with such contexts in mind that the term 'new evangelisation' was first coined in the 1960s. Similarly, it is where the great spiritualities of the Church have had their genesis. It will be through creative fidelity to such founding experiences that they are more likely to be open to new possibilities for how they build credibility and engagement with a new generation.

SOME PRACTICAL IMPLICATIONS

The story of Catholic education in a country such as Australia has been historically one that has involved pastors, Catholic communities, and spiritual families working in complementary ways. It has had its share of tensions and misunderstandings, and not been without rivalries and internal Church politics, but each of these three elements has been important for shaping what has developed. Among the pastors have been bishops who have acted with decision and vision to create a Catholic schools sector, and have striven in various ways to secure its viability, as well as developing an ordering of the sector that is cognisant of whole-of-church collaboration and integrity. Among them also have been many parish priests who have led the planning and building of schools, coalesced energies, and done so often with scarce resources and in unlikely places. They have ensured that Word and Sacrament have come into the ordinary life of schools. Parish and diocesan communities have been generous in their endeavours to support, to finance and to sustain these schools and school systems. From the late nineteenth century until the latter part of the twentieth, the third element of this story was the religious institutes. It was they who not only conducted almost all the schools and taught in them, but they also brought with them the depth and diversity of their spiritualities, the wisdom and experience of their apostolic traditions, and the communitarian essence of their consecrated lives. However things have changed. The practical oversight of existing and new Catholic schools, and indeed most of the pastoral care of those who lead and teach in them, is now largely done by professional lay people rather than ordained pastors. Religious institutes – or, at least, the vowed members of religious institutes – constitute around one per cent of people who are engaged in the ministry of Catholic education. What has been lost and what has been gained?

There is much about the present that is better than the past. Lay people have assumed a rightful place in sharing fully in the missionary activity of the Church. Through one of its most esteemed ministries, they are now able to exercise the responsibility of their baptism. They have brought with them an enhanced professionalism and expertise. They have been additionally able to undertake theological studies, and to develop competence and confidence as religious leaders, to an extent not previously possible. Lay people have helpfully brought into schools their experience of living their Christian discipleship in normal family and societal milieus, a broader witness to students than religious and clergy. Schools and school systems are now governed more robustly, transparently and accountably than before. The levels of tertiary qualifications of teachers have never been higher; specialist knowledge has never been greater; ongoing professional learning has never been more targeted. Strategic planning, appraisal of performance, and matching of resources to need have never been more rigorously undertaken. All of this and more are worthy of the strongest affirmation. It is right and appropriate; the Church is stronger for it.

There are other developments that may be seen less favourably. First, the place of the pastors in Catholic school life is diminishing in many places. That is not a uniform situation; there remain many other places where clergy are intimately involved in schools, not only parochial primary schools where there is a natural and close connection, but also in secondary schools. This has occurred because of the pastoral emphases of the priests themselves and/or because of structural arrangements concerning civil and canonical governance. Where there has been, on the other hand, a reducing role, it appears to have several causes. The ageing and falling numbers of parish clergy, and a five-per-cent engagement of Catholic families with active parish life, are obvious ones. Priests can also feel that they are out of their professional comfort zones when dealing with full-time educationalists, when working with youth, or when in the classroom environment. Some, because of their own cultural or ethnic origins, can find it difficult to adapt to a milieu with which they have limited familiarity.

Second, the higher and justifiable community expectations around school governance can mean that clergy are coming to have a less influential role in it, or may even be excluded entirely other than in token ways. It is not unusual that a secondary school student, or even a teacher, would not feel known personally by a priest, or would ever converse with one. At least at the level of the secondary school, and especially in some larger urban settings, there can be less meaningful overlap between parish life and that of the school than has been the case, even as recently as a decade or two ago.

Again, there are many heartening exceptions to this, but the trends are clear enough. If the chief means of connection of school with the wider Church comes to be through a diocesan education office rather than a parish or other ecclesial community, then a key link is broken. Much of the life of school, again more especially at the secondary level, can fall outside the normal ministry of the pastors of the Church. It is not only that Sacramental worship can prove to be a challenge in consequence, but that the members of the school community can have only a vague sense of being part of Church, an expression of Church. There can grow a disconnect between the Catholic school community and the community of the Church.

It is the third element, however, that is of special concern for our purposes here. In the discussion above it was proposed to challenge religious institutes – as well as the newer ecclesial communities –to imagine how the spiritualities that came into the life of the Church through them can be appropriated in fresh ways by more inclusively-conceived spiritual families. This, indeed, is the hope of the Church.[48] But why? What have these groups to offer Catholic education that it would be poorer for losing? The answer to that is not found in the loss of professional skill of religious, notwithstanding how valuable this may have been in the past through the wonderful scholarship, vision and competence of numerous religious women and men who have served especially in leadership roles. The Church is blest, fortunately, at this time in its history with no lack of competence among those it employs professionally – in universities, in sector-level administration, and in school contexts. The absence of religious would, however, mean the loss of the witness and leaven of the consecrated life – in its threefold role of being a 'sign', a 'living memory' and a 'prophecy' of the gospel of Jesus.[49] While that is certainly to be lamented, and the Church community poorer for it, there is something arguably more significant at risk of being lost in Catholic education if religious institutes are not involved. Partly it is a function of this sign–memorial–prophet function, but more it is the potential loss of an aspect of the charismatic dimension of Church life that their leaving could bring. This could lead to what may be described as a homogenising of the intrinsically multiform expression of the Spirit in the Church.[50]

The 'co-essentiality' of the charismatic and the hierarchical giftedness in the identity and mission of the Church, and the need for the Church

---

48   Cf. *Educating Together in Catholic Schools*, #16-17; 28.

49   Congregation for Catholic Education (2002), *Consecrated Persons and their Mission in Schools,* Libreria Editrice Vaticana, Rome, #19. This document, drafted at the time of the Jubilee Year of 2000, takes up the themes of *Vita Consecrata* and applies them more specifically to religious who are in school situations. It strongly affirms the continuing role of religious institutes in the service of Catholic education at all levels.

50   Cf. *Iuvenescit Ecclesia*, #1-2, 4, 8-9; 1, Pet 4:10.

to include both, has been a recurring theme in Church documents.[51] Religious institutes do not have a monopoly on the charismatic, of course, but most of them have emerged from that dimension, as have the new ecclesial movements and other renewal movements. It is of their essence when they are at their most vital and integral. It has been in the Church's spiritual families that its charismatic dimension has often found expression through its history, and continues to do so. If the Catholic education sector of today is to be a genuine expression of Church, as it is called to be, then it is incumbent on it to nurture both the charismatic and hierarchical in its life and mission. As religious institutes fade in number and position – a sad reality, but a reality all the same – then the challenge for the Church as a whole is to look for how to maintain its spiritual multiformity. It is a twofold challenge: first, for the spiritual families themselves to develop new ways of being and, second, for the hierarchy of the Church to welcome and to integrate this development.

To meet this dual challenge, both the institutional arms of the Church and its various spiritual families have their roles to play, and neither can effectively usurp the role of the other. For example, a diocese cannot unilaterally attempt to impose a spirituality on its people generally, or even within individual school communities. It may try, of course, but it is almost guaranteed not to find traction, notwithstanding how rich the spiritual tradition might be. Archbishop Polding tried this in nineteenth century Sydney only to meet with spectacular failure,[52] just as much as a diocesan education office would fail today. The reason is that spiritualities abide in relational communities. Without such real and living spiritual families, the spiritualities of the Church will dissipate and dry up. While a spirituality can be taught and learnt, and needs to be, it is more profoundly a living reality that needs to be intuited and inspired. What a diocese can do, rather, is to invite recognised and vital spiritual families into its life, and integrate and support them. Similarly, no spiritual family carries either the fullness of the gospel or the entirety of the Church. It is called to be a genuine and living expression of both, but it is only part of the Body as St Paul might point out. It needs the whole, as much as the whole needs it. It has no mandate to try to live as a community apart, somehow in parallel to the rest of the Church.

It is the reality that the great majority of parish primary schools, and an increasing number of secondary schools, are no longer actively connected

---

51   Cf. *Ibid.*, #10, 1.3.
52   In the so-called 'Benedictine experiment', the first archbishop of Sydney, John Bede Polding OSB, an Englishman, attempted to shape Sydney as an Abbey-Diocese. The largely Irish clergy and people resisted both the English and the monastic overlay to their own faith and community expressions.

with spiritual families of the Church. Most newer ones never have been. At the level of diocesan, state and national Catholic education boards and commissions, it is also increasingly rare for spiritual families to have the influential voice they once did through major superiors of religious institutes. Often enough in these bodies, it is one or two religious who may be members, and they are not always closely involved in schools. In diocesan education offices which are, necessarily, arms of the bishop's curia, the focus is understandably on diocesan business. Has this Church picture become too monochrome? Have structure and culture become too monolithic? It is timely for the Church to ask if it is doing enough to foster the multiformity of the spiritualities of the Church. To what extent is it pro-active in inviting and supporting spiritual families to conduct Catholic schools? And to what extent is it welcoming their presence and voice in State and National bodies, and inclusive in their embrace of all entities who are called to act in the name of the Church? Similarly, it is timely to ask spiritual families if they are allowing lay people to step into positions of real authority, and if lay people are fulfilling their responsibility to do so. Are these communities looking to contribute co-responsibly to the present and to future of Catholic education as much as they contributed to its past? Do their new structures foster this? Are the canonical structures that are being developed likely to sustain enduring and bonded ecclesial communities, communities that can continue to take responsibility for the development of spiritualities and for the apostolic traditions to which they give expression? Do they attend adequately to the spiritual formation and the spiritual accompaniment of their members?

These questions come into focus for spiritual families, and indeed for the Church generally, in the structures and methods that spiritual families decide to develop for the governing of their ministries, including their schools, and equally the governance approaches that are in place at the level of the wider Church. Governance arrangements constitute an issue for both because the vitality and integrity of a spiritual family is not only an internal matter for itself, but is at once a responsibility for the whole Church, and specifically for the hierarchical leadership of the Church. It is such because of the basic principle that the charismic giftedness that the Spirit brings is for the work of the Church. In the context of Catholic education, the governance question will be twofold: the governance that each spiritual family uses for its educational ministries, and the governance that the Church uses for overseeing and supporting all the canonically erected entities that provide Catholic education in the name of the Church.

There are civil as well as canonical governance implications to consider when designing governance frameworks for the ministries of religious institutes and of spiritual families more generally. There are also ecclesial and spiritual ones. There is a range of models and various permutations of models that religious institutes and newer PJPs are choosing to use. For some, the decision has been to separate the bodies which exercise canonical oversight from those which are the civil governing authority, while in others these have remained the same body. For example, a religious institute may retain canonical governance, but civilly incorporate each school or its group of schools collectively. For a newer PJP, the members of the PJP who are the canonical entity may appoint a board of directors which has civil responsibility in ways that are common in the not-for-profit sector. In others, the council of the members of the PJP may opt also to be the governing body of its works in civil law. In many cases, schools are individually incorporated, each with its own board of governance. Whatever the model that is developed, and whatever may be the legal and administrative strengths of its civil and canonical arrangements, it is equally important that it is likely to operate in ways that, first, ensure the spiritual and apostolic vitality and integrity of the tradition and, second, foster a sense of being a co-responsible part of Church. Each of these considerations is critical, but they are not always served by the structures that are developed. Legal advice for developing canonical and civil governance structures is usually not wanting. A trap for a spiritual family – one not without irony – can be not to look more deeply than that which the lawyers and the canonists recommend. A religious institute or other PJP, if it sees itself as part of a recognised spiritual family of the Church, has a concomitant responsibility to ensure that a community-sourced charismic vitality is nurtured in and through its governance arrangements. It also has responsibility to ensure that there will be a culture of critical engagement with church, and identification with church, among those who discharge governance. At the level of the wider Church – whether this be diocesan, province or national – there are reciprocal questions.

In former times, when canonical entities associated with Catholic schools comprised mainly dioceses/parishes and religious institutes, much of this was taken for granted, and played out largely as a matter of course. The life of religious institutes was integrally bound up with the regular life of the Church – the profession of members was made in the presence of bishops; religious communities typically lived together in the parish where they ministered and were closely involved in its day-to-day life; accountability relationships between bishops and major superiors were clear. But new ecclesial paradigms are developing in this time of liminality. *Ekklesia* is being renewed and reimagined, and nowhere more so than in Catholic education. There is a call for the newly sophisticated governance and management to be matched by alertness and receptivity to new ways that spiritual families can grow their communities and contribute to Catholic education.

At their worst, the spiritual families of the Church can become trapped in heritage-thinking and/or effectively sidelined from the practical control of their schools, with less and less capacity to build community, so that their spiritualities are left to drift or wither as a result. Their spiritual and apostolic wisdom become the stuff of text-books and manuals rather than a compelling and distinctive path of Christian discipleship, embedded in living communities. Their school communities – and those who govern them – would have ever-lessening integration with church life, and an inevitably fading sense of shared responsibility for the whole Catholic education sector. At its worst, the Church-level bureaucracy that governs and manages Catholic education could become characterised by the kind of grey pragmatism that Pope Francis fears in *Evangelii Gaudium*. There would be little invitation or welcome of difference or diversity. At its best, on the other hand, the leadership of the Church would, as one of its ways of enhancing mission vitality, seek out and encourage a range of spiritual families to be active in local churches, and ensure structures and cultures in Catholic education bureaucracies that value and support such spiritualities. They would see them as manifestations of the one Spirit which is inherently multi-faceted and which exists to give life and effect to the work of the Church. The leadership of the Church would call these spiritual families to fulfil this purpose and to play their part in the Church. At their best, spiritual families would foster communities that are schools of Christian spirituality and schools of *communio* for their members. They would seek out new members and new ways of belonging and acting. They would know that their charismatic giftedness belongs not to them, but to the whole Church, for the Church's participation in *missio Dei*. There is never a want of impulse and gifting from the Spirit of God.

4

AUTHENTICITY, INTEGRITY AND VITALITY

By their fruits you shall know them.

Mt. 7:16

Saint Paul faced the problem. It remains with the Church to this day. And well that it does. It is the recognition that not all that lives and moves in the Church is of the Spirit, and that there is a consequent need to discern. Testing of spirits is always necessary, counsels the First Letter of John.[1] Some apparent prophecy, despite the strength of its attraction, is false. More usually, it is not a dichotomous question of something being wholly true or false, good or bad, useful or not. While such oppositional figurative imagery is characteristic of the Semitic literary style in which the Christian Scriptures are written, lived experience is more complex. What needs to be discerned are, often enough, parts of the whole: what is it specifically about an initiative, decision, project, or way of living that suggests that it is born of the Spirit, and what suggests otherwise? Criteria are needed. The central task for any discernment is, of course, to identify a compelling sign of the presence and will of God. To discern is to look for indications of God, signals of Christ alive. It is seeking God in the first place, looking for God, wanting what God wants. Discernment is an imperative that is ongoing for the Church and for each expression of the Church. For the Church's spiritual families, this is a duty that falls both to the pastors of the Church and to the leaders of the ecclesial communities themselves, an interplay of external and internal critique, sourced in faith, trust, detachment, listening, thoroughness, and review.

Every new movement in the Church needs to be discerned in this way. Existing movements need to be discerned time and again, to take the pulse on their charismic heartbeat. Ironically enough, it is perhaps those movements with the strongest attraction and tightest adherence which need to be discerned most carefully, because such groups can tend unwittingly towards exclusivity and self-righteousness. The publication of *Iuvenescit*

---

1   1 John 4:1. See also: 2 Pet 2:1-10, Matt 7:15-20, and Gal 5:16-25.

Ecclesia by the Congregation for the Doctrine of the Faith is an effort to explore the implications of this in today's Church, prompted mostly by the explosion of new ecclesial movements in the Church, but also with the wider purview of how the charismatic and hierarchical dimensions of the Church should complement one another.

Such alertness to the discernment of spiritual movements was present during Vatican II and has been a recurring theme both in the Magisterium of the Church and in theological discourse throughout the post-conciliar period during which the terms 'charism' and 'spirituality' have grown in usage. For example, in *Christifideles Laici*, John Paul II named 'five criteria of ecclesiality' for new lay movements. For him, it was essential that they:

- gave first place to the call of every Christian to holiness;
- discharged their responsibility to profess the fullness of the Catholic faith;
- witnessed to a strong and authentic communion with the leadership and entities of the Church;
- conformed to and participated in the Church's apostolic goals, and
- were committed to active service in society, in the interests of justice and peace.[2]

These points and others are included in the eight markers of authenticity that are named in *Iuvenescit Ecclesia* and which are distilled from several key Church documents, relevant elements of the orientations given by the post-conciliar popes,[3] and, importantly, from lived experience. Each criterion captures some important learned wisdom of the Church that has emerged from its receiving of the teaching of the Council for over half a century. It is the fruit of the wrestle of the hierarchical and the charismatic, at a time when the Church has been buffeted by many challenges but also graced with new forms of ecclesial life that have sprung up in abundance.

The first three criteria of *Iuvenescit Ecclesia* align exactly with those of *Christifideles Laici,* and in fact include four of the five from the earlier document. First, *the primacy of the vocation of every Christian to holiness,* and, second, a *commitment to spreading the gospel,* name two central emphases of the Council and the post-conciliar period. There is the additional imperative that both are pursued as part of the community of the Church,

---

2 *Christifideles Laici*, #30. These criteria are reflective of the Council documents *Lumen Gentium* (#23, 39) and *Apostolicam Acuositatem* (#19-20; 23).

3 See *Iuvenescit Ecclesia*, #18. The eight criteria are drawn from: *Lumen Gentium* #39-42; *Evangelii Nuntiandi* #58; *Mutuae Relationes* #12; *Christifideles Laici* #30; *Evangelii Gaudium* #58, 130, 174-75, 177, 184, 186; and several addresses and homilies.

and in fidelity to the *profession of the Catholic Faith* in its entirety. Each of the next three criteria amplifies the integration of the charismatic in the frameworks of authority, accountability, collaboration, and mutuality of the Church, rather than in any way living or acting apart from it: a *witness to a real communion with the whole Church;* the *recognition of and esteem for the reciprocal complementarity of other charismatic elements in the Church;* and an *acceptance of moments of trial in the discernment of charisms.* This emphasis on the importance of inclusion of ecclesial communities into the life and mission of the wider Church, and their acceptance of the hierarchical authority of the Church, reflects a major concern that the document seeks to address. The final two criteria relate to the lived reality and practical expressions of a particular tradition – the degree to which the reign of God is evident both within the members of the tradition itself, and in their evangelical impact on society: the *presence of spiritual fruits* such as charity, joy, peace; and the *social dimension of evangelisation.* The former is concerned with both personal and spiritual well-being: 'human maturity'; the 'desire to live the Church's life more intensely; a more intense desire of listening to and meditating on the Word; the renewed appreciation for prayer, contemplation, liturgical and sacramental life, the reawakening of vocations to Christian marriage, the ministerial priesthood and the consecrated life'. The latter explicitly uses the social teaching of the Church as a measure of authenticity and draws on *Evangelii Gaudium* to do so: 'at the very heart of the gospel is life in community and engagement with others … Our faith in Christ, who became poor, and was always close to the poor and the outcast, is the basis of our concern for the integral development of society's most neglected members'.

Theologians and historians of Christian spirituality have proposed a range of psychological, sociological, ecclesial, scriptural, doctrinal, liturgical, phenomenological and ministerial criteria which align in various ways with these eight from the Congregation for evaluating the authenticity of Christian spiritualities.[4] But there is more to consider than these. Just as necessary as determining the degree to which a particular community is living out an authentically Christian spirituality, there is the attendant need to ensure that its spirituality remains internally faithful – and creatively so – to the charism that prompted its founding. This is something that

---

4   One early but useful approach was developed by D. Tracy who proposed 'criteria of adequacy' (concerning healthiness of human life) and 'criteria of appropriateness (concerning fidelity to Christian fundamentals – elements such as the Triune God, both Scripture and tradition, the fullness of the gospel, eschatology.) See: Tracy, D (1975), *Blessed Rage for Order*, New York: Seabury Press, pp. 64-79. Sandra Schneiders is another theologian who has considered these matters. For a comprehensive overview with an historical perspective, see Cunningham and Egan, *op. cit.* who name six premises that all authentically Christian spiritualities share. This has also been a focus of the theology of Sandra Schneiders. See, for example, Schneiders (2011), *op. cit.* pp. 15-18.

can be regarded as its charismic integrity. It is a measure of its continuing alignment with the ever-gifting Spirit.

The third of the criteria of *Iuvenescit Ecclesia* is that it is necessary for the spirituality to keep a vitality that is sourced in its continuing credibility for its present time and place, and its being lived out and developed in a sustaining faith community of the Church. These three inter-related and mutually-enriching elements – authenticity, integrity and vitality – are of indispensable importance for any spiritual tradition of the Church if it is to continue to be a genuine and relevant expression of the charismatic giftedness of the Church, and helpful for the Church's sharing in *missio Dei*.

THE THREE CONSTITUTIVE ELEMENTS OF ALL CHRISTIAN SPIRITUALITIES

When 'spirituality' first emerged in Christian theological discourse, it was typically considered as a uniform concept.[5] If there was an adjective used to qualify it, there was only one that seemed to be needed: 'Christian'. The inherently 'multiform' character of the life of the Spirit in the Church, as defined by Vatican II, sits comfortably with the more usual way that the term 'spirituality' has come to be used – as a descriptor of ways in which various Christian traditions, families, denominations, movements and communities are gifted by the Spirit to participate in God's mission within and among themselves, and in the world at large. There remain, nonetheless, three interrelated dimensions to all Christian spiritualities. In this sense they have an essential commonality. Their authenticity, integrity and vitality of all Christian spiritualities depend on their attending to all three dimensions. While it can be tempting to describe a Christian spirituality by its distinctiveness, this can misrepresent or skew its essence which will be the very same essence of every other Christian spirituality. The charismic giftedness in any tradition is only ever a means to an end rather an end in itself. This end will be the trifold living of the Christian life in its personal, communal and ministerial dimensions. Every Christian is created, baptised, and is called to live, as an icon of the Triune God.[6]

---

5   Examples of French theologians reflective of this thinking were Pierre Pourrat and Louis Bouyer. See Pourrat, P (1918), *op. cit.*; Bouyer, L (1968), *A History of Christian Spirituality (3 Volumes)*, Burns and Oates: London.

6   For an introduction to this theology and for how the three elements of mystery, communion and mission permeate the documents of Vatican II, see: Markey, J (2003), *Creating Communion: The Theology of the Constitutions of the Church*, New City Press, New York. Von Balthasar wrote of the 'Trinitarian logic' of God in the same terms as mystery, communion and mission. See Leahy, (2000), *op. cit.* pp.33–66.

A Christian has, first, a personal life of faith: his or her own experience of the Divine, and an ongoing *metanoia* that is about the heart and which is the project of a lifetime. This is the mystical dimension of Christian discipleship, the individual journey inwards to relationship with the indwelling God, nurtured in prayer, contemplation, and the harnessing of all a person's senses, awareness, and will to come to know the love of God and grow in holiness and compassion. Second, the disciple's response can be only to witness to this knowledge and love, impelled to bring the mind and heart of God to the world. This is the prophetic dimension of every Christian's life, that person's fulfilling of his or her baptismal responsibility to evangelise. Third, this Christian life and mission are lived out relationally and communally. Each person will have one or several key personal relationships, and will belong to one or several wider ecclesial communities in which the life of faith is shared, deepened, sacramentalised, and from which mission is engaged. In these relationships and communities, there is a range of ways in which people live out their Baptismal vocation complementarily.

To be mystically attentive, prophetically active, and communally co-responsible – this is the tridimensional life of the Christian disciple in the Church. It is a life archetypically personified in the Lucan image of Mary, First Disciple. Mary was the receptive virgin who was alert to God's Spirit, who let it touch and unsettle her, and who said yes to the growth of Christ-life within her; the one pregnant with promise who set out in haste and in joy into the hill country, with good news of the faithfulness, justice and mercy of God, the woman of faith who was one with the disciples as the Church came to be born at Pentecost. Mary of the Annunciation, of the Magnificat, and of the Upper Room – this is the Church's Marian way of evangelisation.[7]

Mystical, prophetic, and in communion. Prayer, ministry and community. *Mysterion/Didache, Diakonia, Koinonia/Ekklesia*. There are different ways to approach an understanding of Christian discipleship. *Christifideles Laici* framed it in three Scriptural images from John. Its three Chapters on the essence of the Christian life were titled:

- *I am the vine and you are the branches* – the dignity of the lay faithful in the Church as **Mystery.**
- *All branches of a single vine* – the participation of the lay faithful in the life of the Church as **Communion.**
- *I have appointed you to go forth and bear fruit* – the co-responsibility of the lay faithful in the Church as **Mission.**[8]

---

7   Cf. *Evangelii Gaudium*, 288.
8   *Christfideles Laici* – titles of Chapters 1, 2 and 3.

Vita Consecrata used a similar mystery-communion-mission structure:

- *Confessio Trinitatis*, the origins of the consecrated life in the mystery of Christ and the Trinity.
- *Signum fraternitatis* – the consecrated as a sign of communion in the Church.
- *Servitium caritatis* – consecrated life as a manifestation of God's love in the world.[9]

Variations on the same theme have appeared in other documents about the essentials of Christian discipleship in individual states of life. For example, *The Identity and Mission of the Religious Brother* applies the conceptual framework to the life of male religious in describing 'brotherhood' as a threefold giftedness:

- *Mystery*: Brotherhood, the gift we receive.
- *Communion*: Brotherhood, the gift we share.
- *Mission*: Brotherhood, the gift we give away.[10]

Each spiritual family of the Church has the responsibility to nurture each of these elements of Christian life among its members. The way that it does this will not only be a pointer of its authenticity as a charismic tradition, but will also be a measure of its integrity and a predictor of its ongoing vitality. Each family is called to be a school of holiness, a school of community, and a school of mission for its members. The same imperative can be extended to the hermeneutics of ministries of the spiritual family, nowhere more so than in those concerned with education. This was captured well in the decade after the Council by the US Catholic Bishops in their defining document on Catholic education, *To Teach as Jesus Did*:

> *The educational mission of the Church is an integrated ministry embracing three interlocking dimensions: the message revealed by God (didache) which the Church proclaims; fellowship in the life of the Holy Spirit (koinonia); service to the Christian community and the entire human community (diakonia). While these three essential elements can be separated for the sake of analysis, they are joined in the one educational ministry. Each educational program or institution under Church sponsorship is obliged to contribute in its own way to the realisation of the threefold purpose within*

---

9   These three chapters of *Vita Consecrata* describe the essential contribution of the consecrated life to the wider life of the Church.

10   This is the basic structure of the document *Identity and Mission of the Religious Brother*. See also the document released by the US Catholic Bishops Conference to mark the thirtieth anniversary of the Decree on the Laity. It adopts the same structure, with the addition of a fourth element concerning personal maturity. USCCB (1995), *Called and Gifted for the Third Millennium*, USCCB, Washington.

the total educational ministry. Other conceptual frameworks can also be employed to present and analyse the Church's educational mission, but this one has several advantages: it corresponds to a long tradition and also meets exceptionally well the educational needs and aspirations of men and women of our time.[11]

The first element is concerned with an individual's growth towards maturity, both humanly and spiritually, as a fulfilment of his or her baptismal vocation. The dimension of human growth and maturity is critically important, and also telling. Membership of a spiritual family should foster in people their integral human growth and all that this implies. This can be a danger for a spiritual family, a problem potentially sourced in two factors that may be at play. The first risk is cultism, either around a founder or a founding vision; the second risk is institutionalism. Both can inhibit human growth, resulting in such malaise as emotional dependency, arrested psycho–emotional development, unhealthy denial of freedom and dampening of initiative or, at its worst, the infantilisation of people. Both older monastic orders and religious institutes as well as newer ecclesial movements have attracted criticism on these scores in the past. While such groups may continue to grow and to sustain themselves, their authenticity as Christian spiritualities is compromised. It becomes a cultural issue for them: their culture cannot be considered to be an adequately charismic one.[12] It will, as a result, not be one that is conducive to bringing people into encounter with Jesus as, in Johannine terms, his 'friends'. It is a cultural issue that concerns not only the inner life of the spiritual family, but one that is likely to find expression also in ministries of the spiritual family, most obviously its educational institutions. The primary task of the Catholic school to foster the 'integral education of the human person,'[13] will also risk being compromised as a result.

The perspective of a Catholic anthropology proposes that human and spiritual development are inextricably linked, two sides of the same coin. The former does not, however, automatically lead to the latter; rather, it creates conditions favourable for it to happen. Discipleship is the key concept here, something that involves both choice and learning. Each Christian

---

11   United States Conference of Catholic Bishops (1973) *To Teach as Jesus Did, A Pastoral Message on Catholic Education*. Washington: USCCB. #14.

12   As mentioned earlier in this book, from the time of the Conclave which elected him, Pope Francis has been particularly critical of such communities of the Church, describing this malaise as 'self-referentiality'.

13   This phrase is a constant in official Catholic teaching as well as in innumerable commentaries on Catholic Education. See, for example, *The Catholic School on the Threshold of the Third Millennium*, #4. It is the underlying premise on which the Congregation for Catholic Education built its 2017 document *Educating to Fraternal Humanism*. See Chapter II: 'Humanising Education'.

spirituality is Christ-centred, and sourced in personal encounter. It came into the life and mission of the Church as a consequence of an intense spiritual experience of a founder or founding group, and the spirituality which grew from the founder's charism will have integrity only to the extent that such mystical intuitions are developed in the spiritual family. Each Christian spirituality's accumulated spiritual wisdom and expertise, its approaches of prayer and liturgy, its ways of living and acting, all facilitate and foster this to occur. Membership of a spiritual family of the Church is not limited to nurturing human or even evangelical values in people, but goes further to lead them to friendship with Jesus Christ. It will draw each person both into an inner life where such encounter is fed in stillness, contemplation and prayer, and also it will be expressed in the outward signs of a life in the Spirit that Saint Paul describes in such traits as joy, kindness, patience, compassion, forgiveness, generosity and, most especially, faith, hope and love. In the context of the Catholic school, it is the witness of the educator's personal Christian faith and discipleship which is the most fecund factor in the mission of evangelisation.

The second dimension stated in *To Teach as Jesus Did* states that every Christian spirituality will be inherently communal and ecclesial. It is lived in, through and from a relational base, as an expression of the triune God who is relational.

> *... communion and mission are profoundly connected with each other; they interpenetrate and mutually imply each other, to the point that communion represents both the source and the fruit of mission: communion gives rise to mission and mission is accomplished in communion.*[14]

For a person to be a member of a spiritual family, he or she will have that spiritual family – or, more usually, a local expression of it – as one of those networks of relationships in his or her life. In turn, that spiritual family will be embedded within the wider community of the Church, and interrelated with other communities. One body, many parts. A person may be a member of more than one ecclesial community, and usually will be. For example, someone may be a member of a recognised community such as the Franciscans as a lay person, a religious or a priest; additionally, he or she could be a member of a local parish; and further could be active in social action in a private association recognised by the Church, such as St Vincent de Paul. Before each of those communities, the person is also likely to be part of a 'domestic Church' in his or her family.[15] All of these

---

14   *Christifideles Laici*, #32.
15   Cf. *Lumen Gentium*, #11.

will be the source, the means and the fruit of spirituality.

Our concern here is with the nature of community in the Church's spiritual families. A spirituality will not survive if it becomes disconnected from its community; it simply makes no sense to speak of a Christian spirituality apart from its lived expression in an ecclesial community. To be such a community, in the first place, the human relationships need to be real. That is, people need to know one other, and well. They need to have a sense of care and responsibility for one another. They need to have a shared sense of stewardship of the charismic tradition which not only gives them a gospel path to follow, but the authenticity and integrity which is theirs to ensure and to develop. The vitality of a spiritual tradition and the vitality of a community are completely correlational.

One of the deepest hopes of John Paul II for the new ecclesial movements was that they would be 'schools of communion' and offer a 'spirituality of communion'.[16] It has also been a hope often expressed for Catholic schools.[17] At one level, this means respectful dialogue, welcome and hospitality, a sense of bonding and belonging, and shared responsibility. But it is more than that: it is the conscious forming of *Christian* community. It is one thing for a group to share values, to have a certain *esprit de corps*, and to have a commitment to sound human processes that build co-responsibility, inclusion, respect and right relationships, as genuine as all of this may be as signs of the Kingdom. But it needs to go further, to be attentive together to the movement of God's Spirit and to be open to be transformed by it. It is to gather consciously for the sake of *missio Dei* and to share in this mission together. It is to have a sense of responsibility beyond one's own ecclesial community for the Church more broadly, all part of the Body of Christ. Finally, it is to be a Eucharistic community – the 'source and summit' of the Christian life.[18]

A spiritual family that is the steward of one of the Church's spiritualities will be self-consciously building, strengthening and reviewing itself as a Christian community. It will have inspired means and collected wisdom for so doing, and it will give priority to this. It will, in consequence, be effective as a leaven of communion in its ministries, such as schools:

> *What makes this testimony really effective is the promotion, especially within the educational community of the Catholic school, of that spirituality of communion that has been indicated as the great prospect awaiting the Church of the Third Millennium. Spirituality of communion means 'an*

---

16   Cf. *Novo Millennio Inuente*, #22; *Christifideles Laici*, #14.
17   See, for example, *Educating Together in Catholic Schools*, #12-14.
18   *Lumen Gentium*, #11. See also *Catechism of the Catholic Church*, #1322ff.

ability to think of our brothers and sisters in the faith within the profound unity of the Mystical Body, and therefore as those who are a part of me', and 'the Christian community's ability to make room for all the gifts of the Spirit' in a relationship of reciprocity between the various ecclesial vocations … In that special expression of the Church that is the Catholic school, spirituality of communion must become the living breath of the educational community, the criterion for the full ecclesial development of its members and the fundamental point of reference for the implementation of a truly shared mission … This spirituality of communion, therefore, must be transformed into an attitude of clear evangelical fraternity among those persons who profess charisms in Institutes of consecrated life, in movements or new communities, and in other faithful who operate in the Catholic school.[19]

The above naming of the Catholic school as an 'expression of Church' claims for it a deep responsibility to aspire to be ecclesial, an ecclesiality which is professed in the Creed as 'one, holy, catholic and apostolic'. Without such an orientation in its community, a spiritual family will become self-absorbed, and its development of its spirituality will not be fed by what needs to feed it: the Holy Spirit alive in the evangelical needs of people, seeking to strengthen and to unify.

The third constitutive and interrelated element of any Christian spiritual family is its sharing in *missio Dei* outside itself. It is the bringing about of the reign of God in time and place, in persons and human society. It is the way that an ecclesial community has pondered the call of Jesus to the attitudes of discipleship described in Matthew 5:1–7:29 and goes about fulfilling them in the kind of prophetic action figuratively captured in Matthew 25:31–46 with the hungry fed, the thirsty quenched, the strangers welcomed, the naked clothed, and the sick and imprisoned visited. Prophecy can be understood as bringing the mind and heart of God, the very life of God, to engage practically with the world in love. It may be in word or in deed, but it will be concrete and it will be self-giving, and it will be in redress of need and evangelical dystopia. The principles and themes of the Church's social teaching – such as human dignity, solidarity, the common good, equity, right of participation, a preferential option for the poor, care of creation, peace among nations[20] – are a way of expressing this. It is in this sphere that spiritual families will not only demonstrate their authenticity and integrity,

---

19   *Educating Together in Catholic Schools*, #16–17.
20   There is a rich literature on the social teaching of the Church. Its core themes and principles are expressed variously. For useful introductions and links, see the sites maintained by the US Conference of Catholic Bishops (http://www.usccb.org/beliefs-and-teachings/what-we-believe/catholic-social-teaching/index.cfm) and the Australian Catholic Social Justice Council (http://www.socialjustice.catholic.org.au/social-teaching).

but they will also nurture their vitality. To the extent that they become self-referential – to employ the term with which Pope Francis has challenged the Church from the time of the Conclave which was to elect him – and insulated from need, they will have their evangelising impulses dulled.

The Catholic school is a privileged locus of ministry for a spiritual family to share in *missio Dei*. Placed among teachers, students, their families, and the wider community of the school, the spiritual family comes into direct contact with the world of today. It has a mandate to educate. It is expected to educate. From this mandate and this expectation, the potential for the school to be an agent of evangelisation is considerable. It has enormous opportunity to draw on the inspired tradition and resources of the spiritual family to invite and to nurture people as disciples, and to bring forth the Kingdom in them and from them. But simply to conduct a school with the brand 'Catholic' does not of itself ensure anything. To be described authentically as a Catholic school it will be a place where the gospel of Jesus is heralded and the way made smooth for its being taken up. It will be a place of evangelisation – in word and deed, in sign and symbol, in values and practices – in ways that are appropriate and effective for the community which is being served. The gospel will be lived credibly, and practices that are antithetical to evangelical value will not have sway.

THE WHO AND WHY OF A SCHOOL'S GOVERNORS AND EDUCATORS

This raises an interesting and important hermeneutic for the Catholic school, and indeed for all the ministries of the Church. What makes them Catholic? Is it that simply they are acting in ways consistent with Matthew 25:31-46 or Luke 4:16-21 or John 13:1-15? Is it enough that human need is being served equitably, that people are being empowered with dignity and possibility, and that causes of poverty and injustice are being reduced? Is it enough that young people are educated in integrated and effective ways to become humanly mature, critically aware, and productively engaged? Is it enough that they are helped to grow into just, honest and compassionate adults? Is it enough that they become sensitive to goodness, beauty and truth? All of those things help to bring about the Kingdom; indeed, they are expressions of it. They are not inconsiderable achievements if they can be realised. Any Christian would welcome them. A Catholic school, like any ministry of the Church, will be pursuing them, and consciously so. But there needs to be a deeper hermeneutic at work in a Catholic school: the WHY of these activities and the self-understanding of the WHO.

It is a matter of purpose and identity. Why are we doing what we are doing, and how do we collectively identify ourselves as we do it? These are questions that can be validly posed to any entity that has governance of a Catholic school or to those who lead and educate in one. The purpose and identity of the Catholic school are sourced in the gospel of Jesus Christ and the community of Christian disciples who today take up this gospel. But a Catholic school – like a spirituality – is not an abstract concept. It comprises real human beings. To state that a Catholic school derives its purpose and identity from the gospel and the Church means, *ipso facto*, that the people who conduct such a school do this. Their reason for doing what they do is to bring about the reign of God. They are motivated from their own Christian discipleship and their own evangelical vision for young people and for society. They have a sense of themselves as part of Church, and feel co-responsible for the whole of Church.

This is an ideal, of course. It is more realistic to acknowledge a range of orientation and motivation among those who govern, lead and teach in Catholic schools, especially those schools where Christianity is a minority faith community, or in social contexts that are experiencing significant pluralising and detraditionalising. This does not, however, diminish the validity of the questions. Or the importance of asking them. They are questions for the pastoral leadership of the Church at large, and also for ecclesial communities such as religious institutes and newer PJPs who act in the name of the Church. There will be a critical point at which it is no longer valid to describe a school as a work of the Catholic Church. It will be determined by the moment when there is no longer a critical number of people in the governance and work of the school who are active in their Christian discipleship and their ecclesial membership, and who have the moral authority to shape the identity and purpose of the school accordingly.

In his very first homily as pope, presiding at the Mass *Pro Ecclesia* the day after his election, Francis reflected on the gospel passage that formed part of the liturgy: Matthew 16:13-20. He focused on the question Jesus put to Peter and the other disciples: 'And who do you say that I am?' The Holy Father challenged himself as Peter's successor, along with the Cardinal electors, and the whole Church:

> ... *if we do not profess Jesus Christ, things go wrong. We may become a charitable NGO, but not the Church ... When we journey without the Cross, when we build without the Cross, when we profess Christ without the Cross, we are not disciples of the Lord, we are worldly: we may be bishops, priests, cardinals, popes, but not disciples of the Lord. My wish is that all of us, after these days of grace, will have the courage, yes, the courage, to walk*

in the presence of the Lord, with the Lord's Cross; to build the Church on the Lord's blood which was poured out on the Cross; and to profess the one glory: Christ crucified. And in this way, the Church will go forward.[21]

His insight was that it would be as 'disciples of the Lord', consciously so, that the Church needed to undertake its works. The challenge for every community of the Church – and most especially its spiritual families that have grown up primarily to give credible and effective voice to the gospel – is to attend to forming Christian disciples among those who act in its name: in their personal faith, in their belonging to one another, and in their impulse to evangelise.

TEN POINTERS TO CHARISMIC AUTHENTICITY, INTEGRITY AND VITALITY

Spirituality is an inherently organic concept. Living it out in a Christian community is not easily, or perhaps not even validly, able to be quantified and measured. Like other organic concepts relating to people, such as a person's health or well-being, there are, however, telling indicators and predictors that can be diagnostically assessed. And, like the test results from a medical examination, they are important but not always self-explanatory or definitive. They need interpretation and contextualisation. The following ten markers are proposed from this perspective. They may offer a school community, one that seeks to draw on a spiritual tradition of the Church, a set of lenses through which to examine the authenticity, integrity and vitality of the spirituality of the Church with which it seeks to give shape and impetus to its life and work.

The list is not exhaustive. Further, it does not suggest phenomena that will be acting independently of one another. Not does it propose that some kind of pre-packaged multivariate analysis can be made of spirituality in schools. The pointers are offered more as different faces of the same diamond.

1. Coherence in culture and community

For a school's culture to be functional, its rhetoric needs to align with the reality of what happens among its members in their day-to-day lives, and how this impacts on their relationships; how judgements are made and how value is determined; what is honoured and what disregarded; who is included and who ostracised; which behaviours and attitudes carry most

---

21   http://w2.vatican.va/content/francesco/en/homilies/2013/documents/papa-francesco_
      20130314_omelia-cardinali.html

weight and which are not much tolerated; what is proclaimed and what is muted, and so on. The community of the school is built around such things, or it falls apart because of them. Catholic schools are intensely relational in their character, and purposively so, because it is in and through the collegial relationships and the educative relationships in the school that its spiritual, academic and wholistic growth goals are pursued. It is done relationally and communally. The 'spirituality of communion' to which the Church calls each Catholic school is reflected most tellingly in the quality of the inter-personal relationships in the school. Every genuine Christian spirituality will bring people into relationship and will foster community. Their various charismic cultures, when they are creatively faithful to their founding intuitions, will offer facility for nurturing this. The language which different spiritual families use may differ, the symbols and rituals will have their own tradition and impact, the mix and feel will have its own distinctiveness, but a school community infused with Christian values will always be the result.

A school may claim to be animated by a specific spirituality, but it needs to ask itself to what extent this is only window-dressing. It is easy to put a name on the entrance gate, or a logo on a letterhead, but how are the evangelical intuitions that gave rise to this spiritual tradition reflected in the way the school community – most especially its staff – prays and worships, articulates its purposes, infuses its teaching and learning, celebrates and mourns? What can be found in its documents, policies, symbols, and rituals? Is there an explicit and common language that most people use, or shared ways of acting and reacting, of judging and intuiting, of prioritising and evaluating, and of relating and organising, that would be readily identifiable as emanating from that spiritual and apostolic tradition? To what extent do staff and students have a self-understanding that they are part of the tradition and belong to its wider story, and indeed that they are the ones who are writing its next chapter? The extent to which such questions can be answered in the affirmative will give an indication of how deeply the spirituality runs among the members of the school. Such coherence of rhetoric and reality makes it more likely that the symbolism and ritual of the school will have meaning.

Some dysfunctionality or even toxicity can emerge in a school's culture when significant gaps open between its rhetoric and its reality.[22] An extreme example, but one that has been tragically true in some school cultures in past decades, was the scandal of sexual abuse and the inadequate institutional responses to it. How did it come to pass that a Catholic school's culture, or

---

22 See Arbuckle (2016), *op. cit.* for a discussion on 'myth drift' in the context of Catholic schools. In Gerry Arbuckle's conceptualising of culture, myths play a central role as the way that a community makes meaning or, in his terms, brings 'cosmos' from 'chaos'.

that of a sponsoring spiritual family, became in any way facilitative of such criminality or a host to such pathology? How did it become negligently blind to it? Another example was the use of harsh corporal punishment on children. Despite the possibility of its being culturally normative at one time, it was simply and objectively antithetical to an evangelical approach to education. Another example, one which pertains more to the present day, may be the degree to which a school's emphases on competitiveness and individual attainment, or its enrolment policies, hinder a cultural receptivity to the principles of the social teaching of the Church.

A core question for a school, then, is to look at the character of the community it constructs. On what is it built? What is the mortar that binds its bricks? To what extent do these accord, for example, with the qualities that Paul proposed to the Church of Colossae as the foundation of community: compassion, gentleness, kindness, humility, patience, forbearance, charity, forgiveness, gratitude, peace and love?[23] Each spirituality, and the culture which grows from it, is a way of incarnating the God of love.

2. Connectivity

The spiritual traditions of the Church typically have had their origins in the graced ways that people took up discipleship of Christ in ways that spoke compellingly in a moment of history, and attracted others to take up gospel similarly. A personal charism of a founder grew into a spirituality because it connected with people. That spirituality – or, least a specific community's living of it – will continue to be useful for the Church for as long as it connects with the reality of people's lives. The spirit of *Gaudium et Spes* enjoins the Church, and each expression of Church, in an ongoing project of engagement with the core of people's daily living. 'Jesus would never speak to the crowds except in parables,' the Evangelist tells us.[24] For the Catholic school's sharing in Jesus' ongoing mission of evangelisation, the same approach is always required: to put the gospel in frames of meaning that people already have, and in those terms to invite people to discipleship.

The trends in Australian Catholic school communities that have been revealed by the empirical data of the Enhancing Catholic Schools Identity Project suggest that such a figuratively 'parable approach' to evangelisation is not working. Increasingly, the 'kerygmatic dialogue' school, which the researchers acknowledge has served the Australian Church well, is losing plausibility with all sections of school communities – leaders, teachers, students and parents. The trend is to a preference for the 'recontextualising

---

23   Col 3:12-15.
24   Matt 13:34.

dialogue' school.[25] The data suggest a diminishing of connectivity, a growing ineffectiveness of approach for people whose world is detraditionalising and pluralising. Frames of meaning are changing, and Catholic schools need to adapt accordingly to find new parables. When Catholic schools – or the Church more generally – speak in a language that is not understood by those being addressed, when it is primarily absorbed by issues of its internal functioning and doctrinal disputations, when its proclaimed and subliminal messages do not accord with how most people are experiencing and evaluating things, when its priorities and patterns of acting appear to be culturally anachronistic, then they are not teaching as Jesus taught.

What does not change in a changing world is, of course, the human condition. People of all eras seek the same things: they want to find security and happiness, to have reason to live, to belong and to be connected, to build relationships, to love and to be loved, and to live a fulfilling life. In the Christian understanding, they also need to have meaning that transcends the mortal and the temporal. Nor has God changed God's place of residence: God dwells in each person and in people together. The task for those who take up the challenge of evangelisation is always to join the two. They are essentially the same, for all human yearning is God's yearning in us.

A school needs to look for the signs. How is the religious education curriculum being taken up by both staff and students? How are liturgical events engaging people? How broadly are social justice programs being embraced? How readily does Christian discourse flow from the lips of staff and students in ways that relate to their day-to-day living? What place do contemplation and stillness have in the culture of the school? How do people pray at school? Is 'Church' spoken of in the first person? For a school that attempts to shape its evangelising around a distinctive spirituality, each of these questions can be sharpened in terms peculiar to that spirituality and to the story of the spiritual family.

Jesus connected with people dialogically and respectfully. Yes, he proclaimed and taught; yes, he forgave and healed; yes, he used signs and wonders. But Jesus used dialogue – with the Twelve, with the Pharisees and doctors of the Law, with his friends, and with those outside and on the margins. He asked and listened and helped people come to understand what it was they really wanted. He also touched, sat with, and ate with. He connected. A school will also proclaim and teach, it will bring wholeness, and it will use its skills and resources. But it needs to connect, to engage people respectfully where they are – staff and parents, as well as students – and from there move together to new places. Rather than presenting and

---

25   Pollefeyt and Bouwens (2014), *op. cit.*, pp. 279ff.

insisting upon some precast, take-it-or-leave-it vision of Christian living, the Christian community will treasure the opportunity that the Catholic school gives it for encounter with the actual lives of people. It will be an encounter that listens first, that knows how to approach the other with respect and humility and a sense of privilege.

3. Credibility

For connectivity to be effective, those initiating the connecting must be credible in the eyes of those with whom the encounter is taking place, their message needs to be plausible, and there needs to be a climate favourable for affirming and supporting the message. These are the three factors that are likely to impact most strongly on establishing and maintaining credibility for the gospel message among students and staff in the environment of the Catholic school. These factors relate to the personal authority of those who teach the gospel and witness to it, the prevailing discourse abroad in society, and what peers signal to be important and acceptable. Each is important.

First, without the witness of personal integrity, a school leader or teacher is likely to bring little moral authority to the work of evangelisation. No one has antennae more attuned to pick up inconsistency and hypocrisy than does a school student. While they may sometimes be hoodwinked or misled by messages in mass media and social media, it is unlikely they will put much store in words that seem to them to be hollow, or gestures that come across as empty. And, even if they are fooled for a time, if they do unfold hypocrisy in their teachers, the judgement of students can be brutal and not readily revised. Similarly, there are few groups with a more robust scepticism and disarming pragmatism than change-weary teachers. They spend their lives buffeted by both proposals and people, and are typically quite astute judges of each. Their allegiance will not be won automatically, nor simply as a function of their employment.

Again, it is to Jesus that we turn for modelling on how to evangelise: unlike the scribes, Jesus was heard attentively 'because he spoke with authority'.[26] It was an authority sourced in what he did and in who he was. He healed, he forgave, he liberated, he welcomed, he nourished, and he brought *shalom*. In doing so, he found that he needed to reinterpret and recontextualise the Law, and to reposition people in relation to it. What was the Sabbath? What was it that made someone clean or unclean? How should a sinner or outcast be treated? Of what did true worship consist? Who was to be regarded as a neighbour?[27] Jesus went about such reframing

---

26   Cf. Matt 7:29; Lk 4:32.
27   Cf. Mark 2:23-28; 3:1-6; Matt 12:1-14; Luke 10:29-37.

of the Torah not to win popularity or to attract easy recruits, but because the Torah sat deeply in him. He personified it. He could listen and speak with authority. It will be the same for today's evangelisers.

Such credibility allows leaders and teachers, and schools institutionally, to offer an alternative source of authority than those which may prevail in the broader social narrative. Matters such as social inclusion/exclusion, so-called border sovereignty, capitalist hegemony, criminalisation of behaviour in preference to treatment of illness, start-of-life and end-of-life questions, or gender identity, are all examples of moral issues on which public commentary is not lacking. Not always, indeed too rarely, is such commentary and opinion nuanced evangelically. Catholic schools have a responsibility to do this, not only for their students, but also among staff, parents and alumni. It is often to the school – directly through means such as principals' editorials in newsletters and indirectly through all manner of ways – that people turn for authoritative and critical engagement with the issues of the day. When such credibility is diminished – such as has tragically happened to the Catholic Church institutionally through the revelation of its members abusing children and its acting inadequately in response – then the efficaciousness is commensurately diminished. Every spiritual tradition has its language and its symbolic ways of bringing an evangelical lens to life. Its capacity for doing so will depend on the way that that tradition – and the essence of the tradition rather than its trappings – are in the bone and marrow of those who lead and teach in its name.

The third factor at play in establishing credibility is in peer approbation. It is all about what is signalled to be acceptable or, more colloquially, what is regarded as 'cool'. From the first day that a child goes to preschool or kindergarten, peers play an important role in determining peer endorsement. Four-year-olds connect intuitively, as do young people of any age. By the time of adolescence – as no teacher would need to have pointed out – peer approbation is critical, perhaps the most critical factor in the shaping of behaviours. Behaviours become habits become attitudes become means of self-identity. Often in short-order. Acceptable behaviour is driven by the need to be accepted; what is cool is what the cool kids do. All of this is normal, necessary and good – or has the potential to be – because it is normal and necessary growth in a cultural context. People find meaning and identity within cultural contexts. Cultures provide a framework for this to happen. The challenge in a school context is to build a culture where there is alignment between what is evangelical and what is cool. It is part of the culture and the network of inter-related sub-cultures that every school tries to build: what a person needs to be and to do to win kudos in the cultural context(s) of the school. There will be student cultures, staff cultures, and any number of sub-cultures among and within them. In dysfunctional and toxic cultures, it will be the bullies, the class clowns, the 'jocks', the fashionistas, the cynics, the non-participants who carry weight. The cultures or sub-cultures they create will be divisive, demeaning, debilitating, fearful, and passive. In healthy and enabling cultures peer authority will be nurtured differently. The direction of much of this comes down to the need for skilful cultural leadership. At their best, the charismic traditions in Catholic education are in positions of strength and comfort here; it is what they do best. It is why and how they started in the first place.

4. Critical mass

When it comes to building cultures in schools, it is axiomatic that there is a need for people who are culturally in sync with one another. A living culture is people. It is not a top layer or a small cell of people who dictate to everyone else how to act; nor is it a word-smithed vision-and-mission statement that sits in the reception office, nor a comprehensive and contemporary document or website based on a particular educational philosophy. It is people. It is how the people who constitute a school community make meaning and determine relative value, how they ritualise and reinforce that meaning and those values among themselves, and how they understand their purposes and choose to express their identities. In any school community, the reality is that the staff will act out of a range of religious faiths and practice. So, also, will this be the case when a school is part of a charismic tradition. At one end of the spectrum will be those who identify strongly with the tradition: it is their preferred personal spirituality; it defines their pedagogical and pastoral style; they feel in communion with others in the same spiritual family; they even take responsibility for articulating it, for nurturing it, and for inducting new people into it; they may even have actual membership of a third order, oblate branch, or some other kind of formalised association of people from that tradition. There will be others who are broadly supportive but with less personal commitment, some will have no more than a passive awareness of the values and intuitions of the charism, and possibly there will be others who tolerate the religious emphases of the school because that is where it seems that fate has landed them.

If a school is to be compelling and convincing in its evangelising and educating within one of the spiritual traditions of the Church, there needs to be a critical mass of people at the strongly-identifying end of the spectrum.[28]

---

28 Jill Gowdie provides helpful references and commentary on 'critical mass theory' as it applies to Christian communities. See: Gowdie, J (2017), *Stirring the Soul of Catholic Education. Formation for Mission*, Vaughan Publishing, Mulgrave VIC, pp. 114–117.

Among these people needs to be the principal, along with, ideally, the rest of the leadership group. So, also, it is helpful that the people on staff who carry the most influence among their colleagues identify with similar clarity. These may be longer-serving staff who carry the corporate memory of the school, or it may be others who have moral authority on staff, but they need not be in any predetermined role. Every school has them. They may be the receptionist or the deputy principal or the sports coordinator or the school nurse. They may be younger or older, and preferably both. Whoever they are, these are the people who need to know the story of the spirituality, to own it, to be able to share it with others, to carry it within their hearts, and to inspire others in their appropriation of it. In the Australian Church context of today, they will be people who see themselves living out this spirituality fully as lay people; they will not understand themselves as riding on the coat-tails of religious, or doing their best in the absence of religious. Indeed, although they may have a deep appreciation and even affection for the religious institute which introduced the spirituality to the school, they will themselves now be taking responsibility for it.

To put even more focus on this understanding, in a Lasallian school there will be a critical mass of people who would be comfortable to describe themselves as Lasallians, in a Dominican school a critical mass of Dominicans, in an Augustinian school sufficient people committed personally to the Augustinian way, and so on. It is more likely than not that there would be only one or two, or more usually none among them, who are ordained or religiously professed. If there is not a critical mass of such people on staff, then a spirituality is unlikely to have much significance in the day-to-day life of the school. It will be diluted and diffused. It will not be fore-of-mind among either staff or students. It will not have a defining influence on their living identity. Worse still, there could be a dysfunctionality among centres of influence in the school. A genuinely Carmelite school culture will be created by Carmelites, a Franciscan one by Franciscans, an Ignatian one by people for whom Ignatian spirituality and pedagogy shape their way of the gospel. Who and how many such people will be within a school community will vary, but there needs to be a certain number of them and they need to be the culture shapers.

5. Christian discipleship

Every Christian spiritual tradition and ecclesial community is a means of nurturing people's discipleship of Jesus, and of bringing them into communion with others in and for *missio Dei*. This nurturing is a spiritual thing, primarily and essentially, and it is Christocentric. It invites people, with urgency and inspiration, into a lived and loving encounter with Jesus Christ, and sustains them in it. In proposing what he described as the 'six criteria of ecclesiality' for discerning the value of any new lay group within the Church, John Paul II's first measure was the extent to which the group could be considered as a 'school of holiness' that promoted a 'unity of faith and life'.[29] That is, by belonging to a particular group or movement, lay people would grow spiritually. Similarly, the eight criteria proposed by *Iuvenscit Ecclesia* begin with a movement's needing to be a way for Christians to respond to the universal call to grow in holiness, to take their baptismal priesthood.[30] The other seven criteria are framed from this primary assumption.

One of the inherent dangers for any movement, including an ostensibly spiritual one, is a disproportionate focus on the founder or the founding events. This is not surprising because founders are often such inspiring and large personalities. They can be immensely attractive, and the story of their lives can continue to touch and inspire people for generations. It has made them saints. Story and myth are central to any culture, a charism–inspired one as much as a completely secular one. There is a risk, however, that the founding story can come to focus on the personal traits or achievements of the founder rather than on what drove and sustained these, the latter always being an intense relationship with Jesus. Other factors can amplify this focus on the founder, for example a set of principles or guidelines for ministry written by the founder or the community, or the inclusion of the founder's own name in the name of the spirituality or the ecclesial community. What can occur, and it does, is that the founding story can come to replace the Jesus story, or the story of God's people in scripture. The founding documents, or even more recently written ones, can come to replace the Scriptures and the dogmas of the Church. Rituals framed around the community's values and legends, which at their best should be small 's' sacramental, can come to replace the big 'S' sacraments.

The charismic traditions of Catholic education are not merely sets of characteristic patterns of pedagogy, or care, or shared human values. While we may validly describe a Mercy way of educating, or an Ignatian pedagogy,

---

29   *Christifideles Laici*, #30.
30   *Iuvenescit Ecclesia*, #18, 22. Cf. *Lumen Gentium*, #10.

these are expressions of a deeper experience. At its best, all Christian spirituality leads to and from relationship with Jesus. For a spirituality to be Catholic, this encounter will be significantly found in the sacramental life of the Church, and within its shared pastoral mission. A school could well ask itself, for example, the extent to which it is normal for its staff to pray and worship together, to be nurtured spiritually, or to be linked into the life of the Church. It may want to look at the meaning it puts around the stories it tells students and that it ritualises for them at signature school events: do they compellingly lead to the gospel of Jesus and are they aimed at nurturing Christian discipleship? It may pause to consider who are the shapers of the school's culture in the eyes of students, those whom the students see as carrying the soul of the school. The deputy principal? The long-serving 'Mr Chips' teacher? The twenty-something young gun? The coach of a top-level sports team? The student leaders? And then the school might examine the way that such people exemplify an unambiguously Christian discipleship.

These are questions that probe the degree to which a school – most pointedly its teaching faculty – identifies a community of Christian disciples. It will be a sounding of the depth and breadth of 'spiritual capital' in the school, to use the term proposed by Gerald Grace,[31] but extending it broadly across staff. It is perhaps useful to consider 'spiritual density' in a school as well as spiritual capital. This is different from ensuring that there is an adequate level of theological education, something that is important especially in school leadership teams who need to articulate the purposes and identity of the school, and in those who teach religious education. Spiritual density is more organic and cultural than that, closer to the

---

31 Gerald Grace has written extensively on this concept, developing Pierre Bourdieu's concepts of economic, social and cultural capital (See Bourdieu, P [1986] 'The forms of capital', in Richardson, JG [ed.] *Handbook of Theory and Research for the Sociology of Education*. New York: Greenwood Press). It is something that he has identified as the sustaining and inspirational factor in Catholic schools – most especially among heads of schools – and critical for securing their future as Catholic schools. Professor Grace's ideas were triggered especially by his own research of leaders of inner-city English schools, and also by the earlier longitudinal research of Bryk et al in the United States. He has also in more recent years commented on the potential contribution of the charismic traditions of the Church in Catholic education, but has written mainly from the perspective of religious institutes sharing their spirituality with lay Catholic educators, rather than from the perspective of possible new and more inclusive and dialectic paradigms for the Church's spiritual families. His entry into this discourse is found in: Grace, G (2002a) *Catholic Schools: Mission, Market and Morality*. London; RoutledgeFalmer. See also: (1998) 'Realising the Mission: Catholic approaches to school effectiveness', in Lee, R, Weiner, G, Tomlinson, S (Eds) *School Effectiveness for Whom?* London: Falmer Press; (2002b) *op. cit.*; (2010) 'Renewing spiritual capital, an urgent priority for the future of Catholic education internationally', *International Studies Catholic Education*, Vol. 2, No. 2, pp.117-128; Weeks, N and (2007) *Theological Literacy and Catholic Schools*. London: Centre for Research and Development in Catholic Education, University of London. The issues are more broadly explored in Grace, G & O'Keefe, J (2007) (eds.) *International Handbook of Catholic Education* (2 Vols.). Dordrecht: Kluwer Academic Publishers. See also: Bryk, A, Lee, V, & P Holland (1993) *Catholic Schools and the Common Good*. Cambridge MA: Harvard University Press.

concept of the 'Christian village' proposed by Tom Groome.[32] Drawing on the dictum that a village is needed to raise a child, or the self-evident truth that an Irish community is needed to create an Irish person, so the nurturing of a Christian requires a Christian community. To take that a step further, the grace and wisdom of a spirituality of the Church, needs a living community of people who have embraced that path of spirituality.

6. Continuing formation

Religious institutes have long recognised the importance of what the Church often calls 'formation'. This is not a term that has much currency in the English language, but one that has been appropriated from Latin languages where it has the more general sense of education and training. In the Church, it is usually associated with guided personal and spiritual development. Although it usually carries this specialist meaning in English, it is useful not to attribute to it some esoteric mystique that is the preserve or secret business of the initiated. It is normal, as spirituality is normal.

Just as Jesus took the Twelve apart to teach them, in order to invite them deeper into their appropriation of the gospel, so is it necessary for his disciples in any age to be schooled in holiness. Again, this should be an area of strength of the spiritual traditions of the Church, their accumulated wisdom and practised expertise being able to offer ways and means for this to happen. A spiritual family should be most at home when it is helping its members to be attentive and responsive to the movement of the Spirit seeking to irrupt in them. Fortunately, some of the richest programs and resources for spiritual development and formation are those produced by the spiritual families of the Church. At their best, this is their greatest contribution to her spiritual vitality. Among the most attractive benefits for lay people to become part of one of these traditions for their own spirituality and mission are the opportunities for ongoing formation that they offer.

Members of religious institutes have typically benefited from a mindset of life-long formation, and most religious institutes have invested significantly in it. While a good deal of formation can and does happen through critical and guided reflection on normal life experience, the value of formal programs, courses, reading, and spiritual direction or accompaniment cannot be overlooked.[33] If the members of a spiritual family who are lay people are to develop in their embrace of that tradition, and allow it to develop in their discipleship, they need structured formation opportunities, and ongoing

---

32 Groome (2011), *op. cit.*
33 See Nicholson, *op. cit.*, for a discussion of the importance of formation for lay people in this sense.

spiritual accompaniment. This is for their own benefit, and also for that of the wider spiritual family, because a spirituality will only ever be as vital and convincing as its community. For schools, and for the spiritual families which conduct them, the allocation of resources to the spiritual formation of staff can be a litmus test for how important the spirituality is seen in defining what the school is about. A vital spiritual family will not leave such matters to chance, or simply trust that some kind of spiritual osmosis is occurring any more than it will neglect its teachers' continuing professional learning.

As they have considered the growth and place of new ecclesial communities, the pastors of the Church have understandably zeroed in on the quality and integrity of spiritual formation.[34] This will be taken up further in Chapter 7.

7. Constancy of orientation

It takes both time and intention to embed a particular spirituality into a school's culture, and strategic care to keep it there. When such a spirituality does become a defining feature of that school community – where there is indeed a congruence between what the school claims and what its members actually are and do, where there is an active critical mass of people who have a self-identity defined by that spirituality, and where a distinctive form of Christian discipleship is at the heart of it all – then a school is likely to have something powerfully evangelical at work from which to shape its identity and its educational approaches. But this will not happen overnight. It requires sustained leadership, and a certain 'constancy of orientation' to use a way of understanding charism that was proposed by Pope Paul VI.[35] For a spiritual family, and one of its ministries such as a Catholic school, to develop into a real 'school of holiness', in the sense that John Paul II used the term, it will need people who are steeped in the spirituality, and a continuity of leadership.

This constancy of orientation, while careful to be a way of presenting Jesus and the gospel and not an alternative for them, should be enhanced and reinforced at all the levels of the school – in its myths and rituals, in its documents and symbols, and in its day-to-day modus operandi and intuitive ways of acting, judging and prioritising. Then the school will be alive.

In the context of the Catholic school, the principal is the single key person to lead this. In situations where there is co-principalship, or where

---

34 For example, the documents *Christifideles Laici*, *Educating Together in Catholic Schools* and *Iuvenescit Ecclesia* both have this as a major focus.

35 Paul VI (1971), *Evangelica Testificatio, On the Renewal of the Religious Life according to the Teaching of the Second Vatican Council*, #12.

a principal works collegially under a rector or president or something equivalent, this may vary in its expression and be more complex. The key point to make is that whoever is leading the community culturally must be someone who is imbued with the spirituality that is named for the school. It is the leader of the school community – typically its principal – who will be the one to witness convincingly and teach wisely about the way that the particular spiritual tradition can provide an 'integration of faith, culture and life'.[36] If this person is not able, willing, or naturally disposed to do this, or to do it with sufficient credibility, then it is unlikely that the spirituality will grace the mission of the school in the way it could otherwise do. This has significant implications for criteria of principal selection and support. It is when a school changes its principal that its culture is most vulnerable. This is especially the case when that culture has been built — perhaps unwittingly — around the personal charisma of the principal, something that is not unusual especially in founding or long-serving principals. When a school taps into a gospel-sourced cultural and pedagogical narrative that is bigger than the school itself, the arrival of a new principal is less likely to trigger the cultural identity crisis it otherwise might. The issue of leadership will be explored further in Chapter 6.

In some countries movement of teaching staff and senior leaders is both common and encouraged. Australia is one such place. Many principals see this as a healthy and rejuvenating thing when it remains around the ten per cent mark each year. When it exceeds twenty or thirty per cent, however, problems can occur not only in confusion over '*how* we do things around here' but at the more important level of *why*. It is even more likely when there is a high turnover of members of the school's leadership team. School mission statements and multi-year strategic plans go some way in maintaining constancy during such changes. Documents, however, can only do so much, especially when they are documents that have been written by others. It is important to recognise that what will matter most in a school is what is in people's hearts — their instinctive ways of acting and judging, their key intuitions, their loyalties and sense of belonging, their shared and often unstated values and working assumptions.

Past generations of Catholic educators took constancy of orientation for granted. People spoke, for example, of the distinctive approach of 'Jesuit education', perhaps without being able to explicate it very clearly but having a sense that whatever the personalities and knowledge of the individual Jesuits who may be administering or teaching in a school, there would be a commonality of style and substance that could be expected to

---

36   *Educating Together in Catholic Schools*, #21.

be present and recognisable. When religious institutes trained their own members, using not only the same texts and methods, but sharing the same folklore, such a situation was not surprising. The spiritual families of today's Church, however, often comprise only a minority of members who are religiously professed and who have been formed in this way. Most people come to the spiritual family as adults, often with experience in a range of faith communities and spiritualities. The building of community and the role of formation is more important than ever, and taken up in more detail in Chapter 7.

8. Critical dialogue

In some ways providing a counter-theme to the previous marker is the imperative for spiritual families and for their schools to be evolving continually. In one of the more challenging sections towards the end of *Evangelii Gaudium*, and one likely to have created some nervousness in the corridors of more than one Vatican dicastery, is Pope Francis' insight that 'realities are greater than ideas':

> There also exists a constant tension between ideas and realities. Realities simply are, whereas ideas are worked out. There has to be continuous dialogue between the two, lest ideas become detached from realities. It is dangerous to dwell in the realm of words alone, of images and rhetoric. So, a third principle comes into play: realities are greater than ideas. This calls for rejecting the various means of masking reality: angelic forms of purity, dictatorships of relativism, empty rhetoric, objectives more ideal than real, brands of ahistorical fundamentalism, ethical systems bereft of kindness, intellectual discourse bereft of wisdom.[37]

Strong cultures can be insular in their lived expression. Schools often have such cultures, as do ecclesial movements of more recent origin, which have not been nuanced and opened by time. Strong cultures sometimes do not go easily to dialogical, humble and vulnerable spaces. But this is how Jesus engaged with people,[38] and this is the intuitive way a spiritual family needs to live. For the Spirit can only be perceived through attentiveness and vulnerability.

An ecclesial community and a school are called to develop a disposition for both internal and external critique, with a concomitant openness to

---

37   *Evangelii Gaudium*, #231.
38   Groome (2011), *op. cit.*, p. 33, proposes a useful 5-point paradigm for Jesus' dialogical method: he begins with people's lives; he encourages their own reflection on this; he teaches them God's ways with authority; he invites them to see for themselves and take his teaching to heart; he encourages them in their decisions for living faithfully as a disciple.

change. It is a call to be alert and interpretative, and a caution against the ossifying risk of resistance to being different as circumstances change.

> *Realities are greater than ideas. This principle has to do with incarnation of the Word and its being put into practice: 'By this you know the Spirit of God: every spirit that confesses that Jesus Christ is come in the flesh is from God' (1 John 4:2). The principle of reality, of a Word already made flesh and constantly striving to take flesh anew, is essential to evangelisation. It helps us to see that the Church's history is a history of salvation, to be mindful of those saints who enculturated the Gospel in the life of our peoples and to reap the fruits of the Church's rich bimillennial tradition, without pretending to come up with a system of thought detached from this treasury, as if we wanted to reinvent the Gospel. At the same time, this principle impels us to put the Word into practice, to perform works of justice and charity which make that Word fruitful. Not to put the Word into practice, not to make it reality, is to build on sand, to remain in the realm of pure ideas and to end up in a lifeless and unfruitful self-centredness and gnosticism.*[39]

More than being simply infertile, a self-absorbed culture can be toxic. To adapt Eric Fromm's phrase 'pathology of normalcy',[40] there is a danger that a spiritual tradition can become, at least in part, antithetical to the gospel. To take an obvious example, the use of corporal punishment on children in the past may have been normal in a school and normal at the time in the stratum of society that the school served, but such normalcy was pathological. Strong norms can engender collective blindness and numbness. Equally, and perhaps less obviously, a school and/or its parent community may have normalised characteristics such as exclusive enrolment practices, the valuing of students' worth based only on achievement and dominance, punitively based pastoral care strategies, neglect of social justice education, or lack of resourcing for catechetical programs. All of these can reinforce the status quo, often to the detriment of evangelisation.

The Catholic school culture in Australia was partly shaped for over a century by reactionary, protective, circle-the-wagons narrative. At least from the time that public funding was withdrawn in the late nineteenth century, but probably also before that, Catholic schools served as something

---

39   *Evangelii Gaudium*, #233.
40   The phrase was coined by Fromm in relation to mental health, and how this can be socially (and artificially) determined. A person's rightful individuality can be compromised by pressure to conform to what is regarded as normal. It was first posited by him in a four-lecture presentation in 1953. See: Fromm, E (2010), *The Pathology of Normalcy. Edited and with an Introduction by Rainer Funk*, American Mental Health Association, New York.

of a bastion and vanguard in the face of a Protestant hegemony.[41] That is a generalisation that like all generalisations needs nuancing, of course, but it can be argued that such a collective attitude did not always make for a culture of critique. Perhaps it still does not in some quarters, particularly on some questions of secularisation, ethics, and social inclusion. The time has long since passed from when Catholic schools were places where Catholics went to school, and Catholics from a homogenous sub-cultural group. Data suggest that today's Catholic schools draw students from across the socio-economic, ethnic, and faith spectra. This is the reality which is greater than the ideas.

The disruptive questions that can emerge from such social change can create confusion, and generate what some social anthropologists call 'chaos'.[42] An important anthropological axiom, however, is that cultural chaos can be the precursor to growth.[43] It may not, of course. It may alternatively prompt the wagons to be circled more tightly. To show 'creative and active fidelity' to its charismic tradition,[44] a spiritual family is called upon to bring the lens of its founding charism to new contexts, and to allow for an interrogative dialectic to play out between the spirituality and contemporary culture.[45]

9. Contemplative practice

The transformative social action that is often mythologised in a founder or founding event, especially in spiritualities associated with apostolic religious institutes, can sometimes overshadow the intense experience of God that is always found in the origins of a new Christian spirituality. Founders of spiritual movements are intensely spiritual people. They are contemplatives. They pray. They pray deeply. They typically insist on the absolute centrality of prayer and contemplation for any who would follow them. And genuine prophets are always genuine mystics, for the two go together.

It can be a challenge to thread such a contemplative intuition into the culture of an institution, most especially one shaped by frenetically pragmatic teachers. This is where a charismic culture can come adrift from its moorings. Activism can take over. Historically, spiritual movements have needed to be proactive in maintaining the *ora et labora* balance on which

---

41 Gerald Grace discusses this from the experiences of the United Kingdom, the United States, and Australia.

42 'Chaos theory' proposes that apparently random and disordered phenomena can come to be seen in a new and previously unperceived order and beauty. New patterns of meaning are developed. The theory has been applied to a range of fields of knowing from physics, chemistry, biology, sociology, psychology and anthropology, to philosophy and theology.

43 Gerald Arbuckle is a strong proponent of this conceptualising, and it underpins much of his writing around refounding. See, (2016), *op. cit.*, pp.68ff.

44 The phrase is used specifically with regard to the role of religious in Catholic schools, in Congregation for Catholic Education (2002), *op. cit*, #13.

45 *Ibid.* #14

Benedict insisted. Eremitical and monastic groups have daily times set aside – typically long and several. Apostolic groups have developed various approaches, but have not always been successful in establishing patterns and rhythms that are conducive to nurturing the inner lives of their members. Many find that without the safeguarding of appropriate time and space in daily life, then it can be neglected.

It is the best of times and the worst of times for developing contemplative attitudes and practices of stillness. While spiritual wisdom concerning contemplation has never been more accessible and more adaptable,[46] lay spirituality never more promoted and valued, and non-work time never more potentially available, the modern complaint is that people feel that they are time-poor. We have, in addition, never lived in environments where sensory stimulation had been more intense and less easily escaped. We are connected; we find it hard to put our devices aside. The naturally contemplative capacity with which we are born seems to be often squashed by our contemporary lifestyles. Such cultural behaviours are well attested. Yet we know from the revelation of Scripture that God's Spirit speaks gently in stillness, in silence.[47] To create moments of stillness, to learn techniques of prayer and contemplation, to build this into habits of life – these become special imperatives of the present time, and arguably one of the richest contributions that spiritual families have to bring to the Church's work in Catholic education. At their best Catholic schools are schools of holiness. As such, they need to draw on their wisdom, but also generate methods that suit the people of this age.

10. Church communion, a reciprocating relationship

No single spirituality is the complete expression of Christian discipleship, and no spiritual family the fullness of the Church. They are integral parts of a single Body, in the Pauline sense. Each needs the Body for its identity and purpose, and the Body needs all of them to pursue its purposes and to be whole. It is a reciprocal or, more accurately, a reciprocating relationship, an active mutuality.

How to deal with diversity is an abiding issue for the Church, as it is for any institution. There are normal human factors at play – issues of politics and power, of autonomy and accountability, of 'us' and 'them'. Even among

---

46   Apart from the established wisdom of various spiritual traditions and masters of the spiritual life, there have emerged in the last half-century a number of modern schools of Christian meditation and *lectio Divina* (such as the World Community for Christian Meditation, which has influenced such initiatives as the diocese-wide teaching of Christian meditation in schools in Townsville, Australia) and of contemplation (such as Centering Prayer, associated particularly with Thomas Keating OCSO, and the Center for Action and Contemplation, led by Richard Rohr OFM).

47   Cf. 1 Kgs 19:12; Ps 46:10

people of good will, the ideals that are described in Church documents are not always realised and it is well for us to be honest about realities on the ground. They play out at all levels of the Church, from the parish, to the diocese, to the province or national scene, to the Vatican. It was the same for the churches to which Saint Paul wrote; it was the same for the first Council of the Church in Jerusalem. The Church has a necessarily institutional aspect to its life and mission, but can be damaged when this falls into institutionalism. 'Institution' itself is not an inherently negative concept; the hierarchical dimension of the Church inevitably operates this way to some degree, and needs to do so, as indeed does its charismatic dimension. But to operate institutionally, and to have an institutionalised mindset, are two different concepts. The former is necessary, the latter to be avoided. An institutionalised Church would be one where authority diminishes to control, and collaboration fades to passive compliance. Saint Paul might have had something to say about the workings of law and grace in such a church.[48] The Church at all levels, local and universal, and within its various communities and spiritual families, needs always to have cultures and structures that can remain responsive and agile to the promptings of the Spirit. One way that this can be assisted is through their being animated by Church spiritualities. The spiritual families of the Church themselves should look to how they can contribute their distinctiveness within the unity of the Church at all levels, particular and universal.

No single imaging of the Church provides a perfect understanding of it because each is analogous and figurative, even that of Saint Paul. Indeed, he does not restrict himself to the analogy of the Body of Christ in giving an image of church.[49] It is important for members of the Church – including those who are members of spiritual families as much as those whose principal identification may be as a curial officer – to maintain a multifaceted perspective of the whole, because the activity of the Spirit itself is manifestly multiform. Pope Francis has put it this way:

---

48   See especially Romans 1-8 and Galatians.

49   Conceptual imaging of the Church has been a major focus of post-conciliar ecclesiology. Avery Dulles' 1974 book *Models of the Church* quickly became a classic of this scholarship. Dulles described five historical paradigms of the Church: as 'institution', as 'mystical communion', as 'sacrament', as 'herald', and as 'servant'. He later added a sixth: 'community of disciples'. See: Dulles, A (2001) *Models of the Church* (expanded edition), Doubleday, New York. Each is a way of understanding the Church; each has validity; but none is complete of itself. John Fuellenbach is one who has critiqued and developed Dulles' modelling, and has added two additional conceptualisations: church as basic ecclesial communities and church as a contrast society. See: Fuellenbach (2002) *op. cit*, especially Chapters 3,6 and 7: 'The Meaning of "Church" in the Teaching of Vatican II'; 'The Use of Models in Ecclesiology'; and 'Two Models for the Future Church'. Other writers have taken up the emphasis that Yves Congar preferred – that of *communio* – as discussed earlier in this book.

Differences between persons and communities can sometimes prove uncomfortable, but the Holy Spirit, who is the source of that diversity, can bring forth something good from all things and turn it into an attractive means of evangelisation. Diversity must always be reconciled by the help of the Holy Spirit; he alone can raise up diversity, plurality and multiplicity while at the same time bringing about unity. When we, for our part, aspire to diversity, we become self-enclosed, exclusive and divisive; similarly, whenever we attempt to create unity on the basis of our human calculations, we end up imposing a monolithic uniformity. This is not helpful for the Church's mission.[50]

Pope Francis' language is strong and it carries weighty responsibilities especially for those in leadership roles, both in charismic families and in the hierarchy of the Church. When a charismic family or one of its ministries seeks to operate independently or exclusively from the rest of the Church, it will also hinder the mission. When bishop or priest in a pastoral office – directly himself or indirectly through a parochial or diocesan agency – attempts to impose a 'monolithic uniformity' on the Church community, this will impede its mission. These co-responsibilities of leadership and whole-of-Church perspective will be taken up again in Chapter 6.

From the standpoint of a Catholic school that is conducted by a spiritual family, these matters can play out attitudinally and culturally. They can do so at the levels of the school's canonical authority, its civil governing body, its principal and leadership group (including a key person such as a director of mission or a director of Catholic identity), and among the school community more generally – staff, students, parents, and alumni. Questions for each group would include, for example: What does it mean to you that your charismic heritage belongs not privately to you but to the Church for the work of the Church? To what extent do you feel co-responsible for the work of the Church, specifically for the vitality and the development of the Catholic education sector generally? How do you exercise this co-responsibility collegially with other Catholic school authorities? How deeply do you feel part of the Church, and that this school is a ministry of the Catholic Church? In which ways do you bring the spirituality which shapes this school to the life of the diocese or the parish? Of course, the degree to which such questions can be answered favourably will be influenced by how favourably the pastoral structures of the Church welcome the diversity that the various traditions bring, and the strategies they have that are conducive to their expression.

---

50   *Evangelii Gaudium*, #131.

Spiritual movements typically begin as renewal movements. Those that are most helpful for renewing or reforming the Church are those that find a place in its life, rather than apart from it. An example is the Franciscan movement from the time of its founding. In an address to members of the Franciscan family, Pope Benedict XVI reflected on Francis of Assisi's intuition, even in his spirit of quite radical reform, to place his mission within the Church, and not outside or alongside it.[51] Francis need not have done so, observed the Pope: he could have tried to reform the Church from the outside as some other well-intentioned reformers have done. The Franciscan way has made such a perennially fruitful contribution to 'rebuilding the Church' because Francis took the option that he did, something Benedict XVI urged present-day Franciscans to continue to do. He pointed out to them that 'charism and institution are always complementary' for the Church; it needs both. One of the unhealthy directions which any community needs to be alert of is that of insularity. When a group becomes too clubby, or defines its identity or its mission differently from the Church, it runs the risk of losing the ecclesial identity that gives it authenticity.[52]

BEING A COMMUNITY OF MISSION, IN *COMMUNIO*

In the end, it all comes back to mission, *missio Dei*. All charismic traditions, and the spiritual families which have been entrusted with those heritages and which continue to recontextualise and renew them, are about enabling the Church for that mission. In every Catholic school which draws its identity from one of these traditions, lies the hope that it will invite people into the discipleship of Jesus and associate them together as a Christian community so that they can become a 'community of mission'.[53] Thus the school becomes a community among communities, springing from the charismatic dimension of the Church, helping, through its own authenticity, integrity and vitality, to bring the same qualities to the mission of the Church more broadly so that the Reign of God may be embraced by today's generation. This is the final criterion and the ultimate goal for any Christian spirituality. If it effects that, then we can all shout 'Amen!' So much depends on community, and how a community understands its identity and its purpose.

It is important for a Catholic school community to have means for

---

51 Pope Benedict XVI (2009), *Attract to Christ Men and Women of All Times*, Castel Gandolfo, April 20.
52 'Ecclesial identity' is a recurring theme in the magisterium of successive post-conciliar popes. See, for example: *Evangelii Gaudium*, #131.
53 See: *Educating Together in Catholic Schools*. This is a major theme of the document.

critiquing its authenticity, its integrity, and its vitality. All three. This will involve an examination both of its essence as a Christian community, as well as of the charismic distinctiveness from which it has sprung at the promoting of the Spirit and in which it has been mandated by the Church. Any such critiquing would therefore need to involve people and instruments using both sets of lenses.[54] The first focus is the trifold role that any spiritual family needs to assume for its members as a school of holiness, a school of community, and a school of mission. The pastors of the Church have a right and a responsibility to expect this; and, in their role of pastoral oversight, the right and the responsibility to be involved in evaluating it. The second focus is the community itself, which needs to have ways of critiquing its creative fidelity to its own charismic intuitions. This has an inevitable chicken-and-egg aspect to it, since the capacity to undertake such self-reflection with validity will be a function of the degree to which such creative fidelity does live on in the community. Without a community which is actively living out a spirituality, and doing so at the heart of the school, then the spirituality will fade or will morph into something much dimmer than the compelling way of the gospel of Jesus that it once was.

---

54 An interesting research project that, at least in its conceptualisation, meets this criterion, is the ECSIP research being conducted by KUL, Belgium, on behalf of Catholic education authorities in various countries. The latest aspect of this project, still in trial phase as this book is in print, is a fourth research which has the working title of the 'charism scale'. If such an instrument can be developed validly, it would be able to drill down into two hermeneutics: first, the degree to which a school community has an authentic charismic tradition, and second, how this correlates with other measures of Catholic identity. It would thus shape the lenses of both the Church as a whole and that of the particular ecclesial community, and have a way of relating the data generated from each source.

5

GRACE AND WISDOM
FOR WHAT WE DO

The Word takes flesh, and abides

Jn.1:14

A CONTEXT OF ACCOUNTABILITY FOR
EFFECTIVENESS AND IMPROVEMENT

Catholic schools, and schools generally, have never operated in an environment of greater scrutiny. For the most part, this is a good thing. Huge resources are invested in them, enormous trust placed in them, and so it is not surprising that there are expectations for hard evidence of acceptable returns on such investment. 'Transparency', 'outcomes', 'value-add', 'equity' and 'school improvement' have become buzzwords. Since at least the 1980s, efforts to measure and report the effectiveness of schools have grown significantly. Later focus became more centred on integrated school improvement. People want to see the data. They want these data to inform teaching and learning, funding and planning, progress and social gain. In the context of Catholic schools, they want to see how evangelisation permeates all of this.

Again, these are welcome developments in the main. Closed and opaque systems are rarely healthy. In too many ways, classrooms were just that in the past. Another term that has also come more frequently to be used is 'stakeholder'. While some educationalists do not like it because of its origins in commerce and gambling, it does attempt to capture important truths: education is a matter that concerns the whole community; a range of interests are affected by what happens in schools; chance should be minimised. With such volume of expectation, various sources of it, and so many pressures generated by it, there can arise, however, degrees of debilitation, confusion, and disproportion in schools as they go about delivering what they feel to be demanded of them. Such debilitation, confusion and disproportion are most harmful when they affect purpose and identity. Clarity on these two aspects of the Catholic school is needed for it to discern what effectiveness and continual improvement really mean for it.[55]

Clear sight of the big trees of purpose and identity can easily become blurred by the density of the multi-variegated leaves, the leaves that have been developed to ensure that schools operate in appropriately-governed, legally compliant, and risk-minimised ways. A labyrinth of legal and regulatory requirements deals with matters such as: minimum standards of competence and credentialing for governing authorities, administrators, teachers, and other professionals; curriculum standards and delivery; financial administration and acquittal of income; child protection; workplace safety; industrial matters and human resource management; privacy.[56] Each area requires procedures for ensuring both due attention and attestation of attention. While all of them may be necessary, and serve worthwhile purposes, their number and complexity can enervate those in governance and leadership. Obviously, these people need to develop systems for distributing, devolving, and possibly out-sourcing authority and management in appropriate ways, so that those with overall responsibility can keep their eyes and energies on the big picture. But what is that big picture?

Expectation also comes from other stakeholders potentially adding to the blur as well as the pressure. These may be parents, alumni (who may also be benefactors), church leaders and agencies, and religious institutes and spiritual families associated with the school. Additionally, students and teachers will have their own expectations of the kind of school they want to be. All these need to be engaged respectfully and dialogically because they are constitutive members of the school community. A school's governors

---

55 Extensive commentary and research exists on school effectiveness generally, and effectiveness in Catholic schools more specifically. With regard to Catholic schools, one sociological study that was influential in shaping later discourse was that of Bryk, A, Lee, VE, & PE Holland (1993), *Catholic Schools and the Common Good,* Harvard University Press, Cambridge MA. Anthony Bryk, as founding Director of the Center for Urban School Improvement at the University of Chicago (his later roles being at Stanford University and as President of the Carnegie Foundation for the Advancement of Teaching) is an example of a researcher who has led the discourse from a focus on accountability and effectiveness to one more centred in holistic school improvement, underpinned by moral imperatives such as relational trust. See, for example, Bryk, AS & Schneider, B (2003) 'Trust in Schools: A Core Resource for School Reform', *Educational Leadership,* Vol. 60, No. 6, pp. 40-45; Bryk, AS, et al (2010), *Organizing Schools for Improvement, Lessons from Chicago,* Chicago University Press; Bryk, AS, et al (2015), *Learning to Improve: How America's Schools Can Get Better at Getting Better,* Harvard Education Publishing, Cambridge MA. In the UK, Gerald Grace (who was himself influenced by Bryk *et al.*) has been a leader in research and commentary. For a selection of his main works, see: Grace, G (2016), *Faith, Mission and Challenge in Catholic Education. The Selected works of Gerald Grace,* Routledge, New York. Grace is concerned always for Catholic schools to centre on mission.

56 In Australia, for example, it has been estimated that more than sixty separate pieces of State and Federal legislation and regulation affect schools, with many of these often being changed and developed. Source: www.complispace.com.au. This is an example of the kind of specialised consultancy firm that school authorities are increasingly needing to engage.

and leaders can only do this, however, when they themselves are clear on what they want the school to be.

More subtly, but no less powerfully, the social and cultural currents of the day can also make their demands on a school. Again, this cannot or should not be ignored. Especially in those schools, such as Australia or Belgium or Ireland' where most funding comes from the public purse, society at large has a legitimate interest in what a school is doing. But even where a school may be more independently supported, its existence is not helpfully regarded as somehow private or cocooned from the society in which it sits, and which it must inevitably serve. Its graduates will become co-responsible for making that society. As Church documents have recurringly stated, the Catholic school has a duty to society to help to educate engaged, capable and critically contributing citizens who can do this.

In a myriad of ways, unless they are attempting to exist in their own parallel society like the Amish in parts of the United States, the members of every school community will also be inescapably and significantly influenced by broader social discourse. This will happen through media they access every day, and the issues and values that have hegemony there. The school's active engagement with such discourse is, therefore, also essential. As with its own extended community, however, any such dialogue will be unable meaningfully to take place if the school itself – and most especially those in leadership of it – enters the process with weakness in clarity concerning their own purposes and identity. This is the same principle which guided the 'Courtyard of the Gentiles' initiative and which underpins the ECSIP research.[57]

This cocktail of expectation can often be distilled in simplistic and reductionist ways. Tabloid reporting of school league tables based on the outcomes of public examinations or standardised testing instruments is an example, one that often brings frustration and lament from teachers who know that test results often provide only one measure of learning, and not always the richest one. The fostering of rigour in scholarship and excellence in achievement – worthy pursuits for a school – are not always validly assessed in atomised testing. Similar examples of myopia in both purpose and measurement can be fuelled by political and economic agenda. The typically broadly-based and nobly-phrased aspirations that are described in formal documents such as Australia's 'National Goals for Schooling in the Twenty-First Century',[58] are not always matched by the thrust and parry

---

57   See Benedict XVI (2011), *op. cit.* This is also the underlying conceptualisation of the 'dialogue school' model proposed by ECSIP. See Pollefeyt and Bouwens (2014), *op. cit.*

58   Education Council (2014), *The Adelaide Declaration on National Goals for Schooling in the Twenty-First Century,* Council of Australian Governments (COAG), Canberra. These goals are prefaced by this hope: 'Australia's future depends upon each citizen having the necessary knowledge, understanding, skills and values for a productive and rewarding life in an educated, just and open society. High

of politicians who might zero in on national scores on the OECD's PISA tests or decry the skills shortage in this or that industry. Such utilitarian narrowness is at odds with the tradition of Catholic education which has emphasised a wholistic education for the individual, and a service to the building of a just and critical society.[59]

Without for a moment seeking to shy from any of these responsibilities and accountabilities, or to undervalue the hopes and expectations of its various stakeholders, a Catholic school does need to engage them from the standpoint of its own *raison d'être*. Judgements need to be made, priorities and emphases discerned, without of course neglecting the realities of viability and sustainability. Dialogue needs to take place both within the school community, and with other parties outside of it. For this to happen so that the school does not become the pawn or puppet of an agenda that is not its own, it needs to be clear on what it wants to be and to do.

Why does it exist? By which measures does it evaluate its effectiveness and strategise its ongoing improvement? A Catholic school can be a completely legally-compliant institution without its needing to make legal compliance its purpose. It can be a financially sustainable organisation with efficient administrative practices, without its naming business efficiency and viability as its core goals. It can meet enrolment targets and undertake ambitious capital projects without its turning growth and expansion into its principal KPIs. These objectives are all important things for a school to pursue. But still, that does not mean they are central to its purpose and identity. There are also responsibilities of a higher order to consider. These include such things as the school using fair and just employment practices, managing personal information with care and privacy, handling complaints with promptness and compassion, ensuring a physically and emotionally safe working environment,

---

quality schooling is central to achieving this vision.' They carry a vision for education which is broad and wholistic: 'Schooling provides a foundation for young Australians' intellectual, physical, social, moral, spiritual and aesthetic development. By providing a supportive and nurturing environment, schooling contributes to the development of students' sense of self-worth, enthusiasm for learning and optimism for the future. Governments set the public policies that foster the pursuit of excellence, enable a diverse range of educational choices and aspirations, safeguard the entitlement of all young people to high quality schooling, promote the economic use of public resources, and uphold the contribution of schooling to a socially cohesive and culturally rich society.' The Adelaide Declaration was preceded six years earlier by a similarly-pitched and arguably richer document: Ministerial Council on Education, Training and Youth Affairs (2008), *The Melbourne Declaration on Goals for Young Australians,* Council of Australian Governments (COAG), Canberra. It carried just two goals: 1. Australian schooling promotes equity and excellence; 2: All young Australians become: successful learners, confident and creative individuals, and active and informed citizens.

59   Both imperatives are developed at length by the Congregation for Catholic Education in *The Catholic School* (1977) and in each of its documents through to *Educating to Fraternal Humanism* (2017). The narrowness of an economic rationalist agenda in education is powerfully contested by Dom Mark Patrick Hederman OSB in his critique of Irish education in: (2013), *The Boy in the Bubble,* Veritas Publications, Dublin.

and implementing effective communication methods. All are important; all are justifiably up for scrutiny; all bear on a school's effectiveness. But none of these activities define the school's *raison d'être*.

So, to deal with effectiveness and school improvement, we are drawn back to the question of the purpose and identity of the Catholic school. This is a well-hoed field, of course. No one involved with Catholic schools is likely to be a stranger to vision and mission statements, school strategic planning or annual reporting. Since the publication of *The Catholic School* four decades ago, Catholic school leaders have led their communities in exploring together questions of what has variously being called climate, ethos, mission, core values, and vision. This has coincided, not insignificantly, with the time when the proportion of religious in Catholic schools was already in sharp decline, and also with the emergence of the excellence movement in the corporate world and the role played by organisational culture in achieving excellence. The educational field was to embrace this thinking, and from the 1980s to recast it to some degree. What had perhaps been taken for granted in the past came to be named more overtly and pursued more intentionally. Universities began to offer specialist courses in Catholic education and Catholic educational leadership, conferences began to be held, statements and documents produced, and books written. With such programs for skilling educational leaders and administrators, and ample theological and academic discourse to inform them, schools came to have available to them both expertise and experience for distilling their purpose and identity.

British educationalist Gerald Grace is among those who have been challenging Catholic schools to analyse their effectiveness and improvement through the lens of their deep mission as Catholic schools. Two decades ago, he identified particular elements as the common themes in the mission statements of UK Catholic schools which he studied, and suggested that such values needed to inform strategies for considering effectiveness. These elements for effectiveness were:

- Developing a love for and commitment to Jesus Christ, the Catholic Church, and the gospel message of love, peace, truth and justice.
- Establishing a community based on love and care of the individual, where faith gives meaning to all of the community's activities.
- Developing the spiritual awareness of pupils.
- Promoting the spiritual growth of all in a community through prayer, the sacraments, and chaplaincy. [60]

---

60   Grace, G (1998) *op. cit.*

More recently, the Center for Catholic School Effectiveness based in Loyola University's School of Education (in Chicago) developed what has come to be adopted and promoted by the National Catholic Education Association as the 'National Standards and Benchmarks for Effective Catholic Elementary and Secondary Schools' (NSBEC's). It identified seven standards or benchmarks, that Catholic education must be:

- Centred on the person of Jesus Christ.
- Contributing to the evangelising mission of the Church.
- Distinguished by excellence.
- Committed to wholistic education.
- Steeped in a Catholic world view.
- Sustained by gospel witness.
- Shaped by communion and community.[61]

These NSBECS aim to

> provide Catholic school sponsors and stakeholders with a sound set of criteria which they can confidently use to develop tools and resources for authentic accreditation, self-assessment, reflection, strategic action, and collaboration. Surveys, rubrics, checklists, exemplars, published articles, research, and links to professional development based on the Standards support implementation of best practice and growth in excellence at the school and diocesan/network levels.[62]

This kind of approach, one also reflected in Australian Catholic education,[63] is quite religiously explicit and catechetically specific. Many Catholic theologians, philosophers and educationalists, as well as the authors of official documents of the Holy See and most Bishops' Conferences, have tended, however, to be noticeably wider than this in their cast regarding the identity and purpose of Catholic schools. Tom Groome, for example, named eight defining characteristics that would make a Catholic school Catholic. It would operate out of:

- a Catholic *anthropology*, which understood the human condition to be an image of God, and which therefore called for respect for persons, with a belief in their goodness and possibility
- a Catholic *cosmology*, which understood creation and culture as essentially good, and so called for an education that positively

---

61   The Standards were developed in 2012. See: https://catholicschoolstandards.org
62   *Ibid.*
63   See, for example, *Catholic Schools at a Crossroads* (NSW/ACT Bishops, *op. cit.*)

engaged and cared for this, and which, through seeing God in all things and all things in God, was engaged sacramentally
- a Catholic *sociology*, which recognised that people grow in their humanity in and through community and their interpersonal relationships
- a Catholic *epistemology*, which promoted knowledge of the whole person, education for fullness of life, and life–long learning
- a Catholic *historicity*, which valued the wisdom of the sciences, the humanities and the arts, and drew on that wisdom
- a Catholic *politic*, which worked from a social conscience and for justice
- a Catholic *spirituality*, which recognised the 'God–shaped hollow in every human heart' that only God could fill, and in this the various spiritual traditions of the Church had much to offer
- a Catholic *universality*, which was inclusive, open–minded, and embraced all of life, including its paradoxes.[64]

Groome later refined this octangular understanding of the distinctiveness of Catholic education as five 'theological' and three 'cardinal' characteristics,[65] and has continued to develop his understandings.

In a summary of documents produced by the Congregation for Catholic Education, of which he was Secretary for a time, Michael Miller has summarised his five 'essential marks' of Catholic schools as being:

- inspired by a supernatural vision
- founded on a Christian anthropology
- animated by communion and community
- imbued with a Catholic world–view in its curriculum
- sustained by gospel witness.[66]

Other writers and Church authorities will have different lists and will describe what is characteristically Catholic in other ways. The point here is not to quibble over which list has better claim than the other, but to recognise that, in this liminal time, it is likely that a broader framing of mission is going to

---

64 Groome (2001) *op. cit.*

65 See Groome (2004) *op. cit.* The theological characteristics were: a positive anthropology; the sacramentality of life; an emphasis on the communal in human and Christian living; a commitment to tradition; an appreciation of rationality in learning and the value of education, as faith seeking understanding. The cardinal characteristics that linked and bound these were: commitment to personhood (an ontological concern); to justice (a sociological concern); and to catholicity (a concern for universality).

66 Miller, M (2006) *The Holy See's Teaching on Catholic Schools*. Sydney: St Paul's. Cardinal Miller's third point has been amplified subsequently by the Congregation's 2007 document, *Educating Together in Catholic Schools* (which emphasised a 'spirituality of communion') and its 2017 publication *Educating to Fraternal Humanism, Building a Community for Love.*

be more helpful. As is evident from Miller's summary, this has long been the perspective of the universal Church. Individual bishops, religious institutes, or other Catholic education authorities may sometimes have had a narrower confessional understanding of the character and purpose of their schools, but this may in turn have been a function of the more homogeneous clientele that those schools served. For the Church across the world, there has been, however, the broader recognition that Catholic schools exist and have a place across a large range of religious and cultural contexts.

This is a liminal time, most especially in Western countries and for the Church in these countries, including its spiritual families. Perhaps especially for its spiritual families. It is a time when religious and cultural contexts are in flux, but that is the very kind of context that gave birth to most spiritual families. Liminality leads to a reframing of identity and purpose. As observed by Michael Putney, identity and purpose are not shaped only by one's own tradition but by engagement with the other.[67] It will be the same for the Church, for its spiritual families, and for their schools in this era of change. What is critical to bring to any discussion on effectiveness and improvement of Catholic schools at the present time is a breadth of understanding and perspective. It is a time to listen to the ideas of thinkers, to heed prophets, to read the signs of the times, and to dialogue and discern.

There will be a range of thought and vision, both within and outside the Church. Richard McBrien was an example of a theologian who explored the changing context in which the Church – and the Church's ministries such as its schools – was needing to rethink its identity and purpose. He regarded it to be something of pressing importance. He proposed five trends that would occur as the Church did this. He saw that it would:

- become less Roman and more catholic
- become less inwardly focused, recognise the communion that already exists among churches, and be more collegial
- as a result of its sacramentality, become more inclusive
- become more concerned with social justice, human rights, and peace
- remain a eucharistic faith–community, 'gathered proclaiming and hearing the Word around the Lord's table, reaching out beyond itself to those in need, witnessing in all that it says and does to the coming of the final reign of God'.[68]

---

67 Putney (2008) *op. cit.* p. 18ff. Bishop Putney names seven aspects of ecclesial life which the Catholic school, as a function of its ecclesial identity, needs to bring into dialogue with the world of the twenty-first century: communion in Christ; missionary orientation; ecumenism; inter–religious dialogue; working for justice; bearing the tradition; and contemplation.

68 Among McBrien's many works, for an accessible introduction to this thinking, see: (2004), 'Catholic Identity in a Time of Change', *The Furrow*, Vol. 55, No. 9, pp. 455-464.

In another example of a reading of the signs of the times, social anthropologist Gerald Arbuckle concurs with Peter Berger's interpretation that religious culture disintegrated in the 1960s and 1970s. For Catholics, he sees that this has resulted in a cultural chaos from which identity reformulation is still under way.[69] Like McBrien, he suggests there are trends that are taking place with which the Church needs to engage. Arbuckle proposes that in these trends there are indications of a tentative cultural transition away from the more negative aspects of post-modernity to something he calls 'paramodernity' which will be marked by greater emphases on interdependence, collaboration, gender equity, imagination, education of the heart, dialogue and non-violence.[70]

Again, the purpose here is not to undertake a discussion on the merits of interpretations such as those provided by McBrien or Arbuckle, or by any other particular theologians, anthropologists or commentators on church and society. It is, rather, to emphasise that it is incumbent upon those in pastoral, charismic, and educational leadership in the Church to have the perspective and agility to engage with such commentary and interpretation, and to bring their communities into engagement with them. To do so is no different from the dialogue of faith, culture and life that the Church has consistently proposed, since the Vatican Council, as the goal of the Catholic school.[71]

The ECSIP (Enhancing Catholic Schools Identity Project) concepts of 'post-critical belief' and the 'dialogue school' are pertinent here. They are founded on the imperative of such a critical engagement, a befriending of the cultural and religious realities of the school community. Data from ECSIP suggest that, in the Australian context, the impact of liminality is being experienced in ways that are moving the typical Australian Catholic school from being a 'Kerygmatic Dialogue School', which has been the prevalent model in Australia, to a 'Recontextualising Dialogue School'. For the theorists behind ECSIP, this is seen as a healthy and necessary shift of paradigm. To maintain the 'Kerygmatic' model may be to insist

69   Arbuckle (2016), *op. cit.* p. 114. See: Berger, P (1977), *Facing Up to Modernity*, Penguin Books, Harmondsworth. See also: Arbuckle, GA (2013), *op. cit.* Arbuckle describes twelve models of Catholic identity, and argues for an interactive approach that accommodates this in the formation of people in Catholic institutional ministries.

70   He names twelve themes of the emerging mythology of paramodernity: spirituality; inclusion; interdependency; the importance of storytelling; the return of mythology; the role of intuition; deconstructionism; critique rather than rejection of meta-narratives; supportive smaller groupings of people; the reality of death; an acknowledgement of evil; and non-violence. The intentional engagement of a range of Catholic identities is something that has a wider discourse. See, for example: de Sousa, M (2014), 'Religious Identity and Plurality amongst Australia Catholics', *Journal for the Study of Religion*, Vol. 27, No. 1, pp. 210-233.

71   For a discussion on the approach of the Catholic school to eschew an anchoring in confessionalism in favour of dialogue, diversity, truth-seeking, learning and wholistic education, see the discussion paper prepared by the Congregation for Catholic Education in the lead-up to its 2015 International Congress: *Educating Today and Tomorrow, A Renewing Passion.*

on something that has lost its plausibility for the school community. The problems of continuing with it are seen to be threefold:

- ethical, because the old approach would not be invitational and respectful
- theological, because it would foreclose the narrative of the community, seeking to preserve rather than to evolve
- pragmatic, simply because it risked becoming counter-productive to evangelisation.[72]

The community of the school, the culture more generally, is no longer marked by a sufficient level of faith homogeneity, something that contributed in the past to the effectiveness of the 'Kerygmatic' model.

It must be recognised, however, that there is a variety of school communities and, for some, a more confessional approach to build a school's culture may continue to be appropriate and effective. This is not to imply an imposed re-confessionalist or a closed-minded restorationist attitude, but simply an attitude that makes plausible connection to the meaning-making dynamics that are already sufficiently at work in the community. It is likely to do so by drawing on Catholic liturgy and ritual; on tradition and Scripture; on the spiritual, doctrinal and cultural richness of the Church; by including catechesis in religious education programs; and by explicitly embedding gospel values across the curriculum.[73] A Recontextualising Dialogue school, to continue with the ECSIP terminology, is not one where people of faith need to run up some figurative white flag, and surrender their intentionality around evangelising or ecclesial identity. It is, rather, to recognise what the school community is in reality, not to pretend that it is something that it is not, and then to work from there. Whether a Catholic school authority does or does not agree with the conceptualisations of ECSIP, its means for developing purpose and identity needs to start here. There is deep wisdom in the Thomist maxim that 'grace builds on nature'.[74] The starting point for today's Catholic school leaders is the same as it was for Jesus: to engage with people wherever it is they are, particularly those who are far from the gospel, to help them discover for what it is that they yearn, and to offer them the opportunity to fulfil that yearning. It cannot

---

72 Pollefeyt and Bouwens (2014), *op. cit.* pp. 277–79.
73 *Ibid.*, pp. 297ff. First among the authors' recommendations include the continuing of confessional elements in schools, and the inclusion of prayer and liturgy. Empirically, they have been shown to be effective in Australian schools.
74 This famous sentence from St Thomas Aquinas is sometimes misinterpreted in a Pelagian sense. It is better understood to mean the truth that God's Spirit dwells in human reality, and is active at the core of human existence seeking to come to life – in the way that this is presented particularly in the Johannine and Pauline Scriptures.

sacrifice its role to have a transformative impact on the lives of students and teachers.[75]

The focus on the actual life situations of people – which needs always to be the starting point – can sometimes lead back to the confusion of the descriptive with the prescriptive that has previously been discussed. It can leave little room for change and *metanoia*. It can underestimate the power and grace of inspirational leadership, and of life-changing experiences. What *is* should never be the determinant of what *has to be*. It is simply where things start. If a move away from 'kerygmatic' as a descriptor implies a discrediting of *kerygma* itself, then it would be misplaced. Schools can be better than that, and good schools are.

The nature and means for transformation will vary as the character of school communities vary. It is likely, perhaps inevitable, that in a country such as Australia there will indeed be some variety of approach in Catholic schools. A one-size-fits-all approach is unlikely to be appropriate. But the Church has long been comfortable with this, as the documents of the Congregation for Catholic Education attest. Around the world, Catholic schools serve a range of communities, from those that are predominantly Catholic to others where the Catholic percentage is minimal. The mission of every Catholic school, nonetheless, will always be an expression of *missio Dei*; it will need always to be rooted in the cultural and religious realities of its community, and to aspire always to facilitate rather than to impede God's Spirit coming to life in that space. That is where the Spirit will be and that is what the Spirit will be seeking to do. One lens for considering how the school shapes that identity and pursues that purpose is provided by looking at the organisational culture that it seeks to build.

BUILDING A CHARISMIC CULTURE

Let us not over-egg the pudding. What is proposed here is a simple proposition. The charismic traditions of the Church can be greatly advantageous in gracing Catholic schools to be mission-effective. How does that happen? Good schools have strong and functional cultures. Such cultures are built around shared meanings expressed in deep purpose, and bonded by compelling communal identities. The Catholic school is a school; its deep purpose is *missio Dei*. It will be mission-effective when it has that purpose embedded in the heart of such a culture. Christ-life is sacramentally

---

75   See D'Orsa, J & T (2013), *op. cit.* pp. 21–23. Therese and Jim D'Orsa describe the four common responses in times of liminality: denial; traditionalist; critical or iconoclastic (that is, dismissal of tradition); and transformative (providing creative continuity through new perspectives). They argue that the mission-thinking of schools should aim to be transformative in these liminal times.

mediated through such cultural expression; it seeks incarnation in time and place, in people and their lived reality. Second, the primary identity of the Catholic school is ecclesial; it is a work of the Church, undertaken by a faith community of the Church. Among such faith communities of this Church are those which live out of its spiritualities, which have proven to be both enduring and agile. They have provided the Church with some of its most accessible paths of Christian discipleship, community and ministry. Most of them have emerged from contexts of dire evangelical need and, at their most authentic, they continue to thrive when faced with commensurate challenge. Such spiritualities, when they are lived communally, and when the ecclesial communities which are entrusted with their heritage and development are creatively faithful to the integrity of the spirituality, can offer Catholic schools compelling cultural narratives. They provide schools with inspirational ways of giving the gospel contextual plausibility and impulse, and of being good schools. They allow schools to draw on their myth and story, and their accumulated spiritual wisdom and resources, to build gospel-oriented cultures – charismic cultures – where God's Spirit gifts the school to life.

However let us overstate the argument. This is also a proposition with qualifications. First, to opt to draw on one or another of the Church's charismic traditions is not the only or necessarily the best way for a Catholic school to build a culture which gives its faith a community, a shared purpose and clear identity. It is but one way. It may or may not suit the context of a particular Church, or the needs of a specific educational situation. It may or may not adapt comfortably within an individual culture, society, parish, or diocese. It may or may not be possible for the spirituality to be supported by a viable or sustainable community that lives out of that tradition. There are many sources of holiness in the Church. Each believer, each pastor, is charismically gifted, in order to fulfil his or her baptismal right and responsibility to be holy, and to share in God's mission in and from the Church. Each parish and diocese is a community of faith. It will always be a local matter to discern the relative merits for a school or group of schools to build identity and purpose around one of the Church's spiritualities.

Second, the Catholic school is not the only faith community to which a person can belong, or the only locus for living out his or her Christian discipleship. *Social Identity Theory* is also applicable to faith communities.[76]

---

76 Social Identity Theory postulates that a person's self-understanding and social behaviour can come from more than one identity through that person's membership of different social groups. A person – including a young person – can have, for example, a self-concept in family, another at school, another at work, another with a separate peer group, etc. See: Turner, JC & Reynolds, KJ (2010), 'The story of social identity', in Postmes, T & Branscombe, N, *Rediscovering Social Identity, Core Sources,* Psychology Press, New York. pp. 13–32.

People will be members of their own family; they may also be members of a parish, of a group such as St Vincent de Paul; they may be regular participants in a study or special-interest group; or use the print or electronic prayer resources produced by another community. These memberships and associations are also likely to change during the course of their lives. In each of them, and at different phases of a person's life's journey, they can be nurtured in their personal faith, have some experience of Christian community, and be impelled into mission. Even though a student or teacher may attend or minister in an educational institution of a particular tradition, such as Ursuline or Vincentian, and may indeed use the nomenclature of that tradition to describe themselves in that school's context, it is unlikely that it will represent their entire ecclesial identity or capture their whole personal spirituality. It will play its part for them to a greater or lesser degree, giving God's Reign a favourable cultural context for that part of their lives. It will be one part of the whole of their lives, and usually for only a period of their lives. Those caveats acknowledged, the charismic traditions of the Church do have much to offer Catholic schools, especially in times of need and change.

But intentionality is required. Whether a school's opportunity to draw on a spirituality of the Church is the result of a discerned decision, or whether it is because of its historical association, ownership or governance, the constructing of a culture infused with this spirituality will not just happen as a matter of course. The window-dressing delusion has been discussed above. Culture is not something a school community *has* or acquires; it is better understood as what it *is* and seeks to be. It has a hermeneutical dimension that is key: how people make meaning in their lives, specifically how they interpret the movement of God's Spirit in their lives. So, the foundation blocks for building a charismic culture are not names and logos, customs and rituals, legends and heroes, protocols and policies. Elements such as these need to be expressive of something that is happening at a deeper level, a spiritual level, both individually and communally in the school. The expressive elements of a culture can serve to generate corporate identity, even a quite strong identity, but without connection to deep purpose they could just be empty gongs clanging. Lots of noise, little Christocentric substance.

John's account of Jesus' encounter with the Samaritan woman at the well is instructive for how to go about this.[77] Typical of the fourth Gospel, it is rich in its figurative language and works on different levels: thirst and hunger, life and death, reaping and sowing, and the finding of transformative

---

77   John 4:1-42.

meaning in the here and now. The woman's experience of Jesus, as also the experiences of the disciples and the Samaritans, brings awakening in them and impels them to belief. Without embarking on an exhaustive exegesis of all the meaning and allusion that is packed into this wonderful passage of Scripture, let us focus just on a few points.

First, Jesus comes to Samaria and there he speaks to a woman of Samaria. Both scenarios would have disturbed the religious sensibilities of a first century Jewish reader. In the Jewish mindset, God dwelt in the Temple in Jerusalem above Mount Sion and was encountered there, not on Mount Gerazim, and certainly not among the apostates of Samaria. But Jesus comes to a well — a symbolic place of Divine encounter — in that non-Jewish country to draw water, a symbol of life. He speaks with a woman there — a taboo — and probably a woman who had been ostracised even in her own town for some reason — most likely because of her sinfulness or disease — since she was forced to come to the well in the middle of the day when the other women were not around. She is going about normal things, working to satisfy everyday human needs, trying to do what she can manage in the circumstances of her own life. It is in that situation that the encounter takes place.

Second, Jesus engages in dialogue with her and, through that dialogue, prompts her first to puzzlement, and then to reassessment. This is not a disconcerting or alienating confusion for her, but one that opens her. From that, Jesus leads her to new vision, and to fullness of life.[78] He does that principally not by talking about himself or the Law — even though he remains clear on his own Jewish identity as he speaks — but by revealing to her the truth about herself. 'He told me everything I have ever done.' He taps into her deeper longings, and reveals himself as the one for whom she is waiting. 'I am he.' He offers her a breadth of vision — to be the kind of person who comes to God 'in spirit and truth'. The woman's response is to be so enthralled by this, albeit with only partial understanding, that she is moved to become the unlikely herald and advocate of the gospel amongst her townspeople. 'Come and see ... I wonder if he is the Christ.' And many did come to believe. The whole town was affected. Community is implied. Meanwhile, in their search for food, the disciples do not yet understand; they cannot yet see beyond the immediate. Their epiphany will come in similar circumstances to that of the Samaritan woman, in the great eucharistic Chapter 6 – 'I am the Bread of Life' – and culminate in Peter's

---

78 The fourth Gospel pivots on its centrepiece verse in 10:10: 'I have come that you may have life, life in its fullness.' The encounters in the first half of the Gospel, such as the one with the Samaritan woman, and the 'I am' statements of Jesus build up to this. Jesus is this life. And the way, and the truth.

profession of faith: 'Lord, where else could we go? You have the message of everlasting life.'[79] Meanwhile as Chapter 4 closes, the reader is left in no doubt as to the significance of what has happened in Samaria as Jesus returns to Cana and gives the second sign of the Gospel: the desperately worried official's son is cured – 'Your son will live.'

The great spiritualities of the Church at their most authentic have cultures rooted in John 4 intuitions. Their founders were graced to understand and to live the gospel in their own time and place, however unlikely or apparently Godless that situation may have appeared to be. In was in that very 'Samaria context', as jaded or fractured as it might have been in its ecclesial connections, where they led people to encounter Jesus and to find fullness of life. They used language and developed patterns of discipleship that were accessible, invitational and ultimately transformative. It was language and metaphor drawn from life experience, plausible in that life experience, but which dialogically led people to see themselves and their ordinariness in new ways. It changed them. It inspired them. It impelled them. But ultimately it led to Jesus. That is their deep purpose, forged in liminal times. As time went on, identity also built. It grew around story usually, because story is so inherently attractive, especially family story.

Family story is something to which people are naturally drawn. It holds intrinsic interest. They feel they belong to it and in it – it's their story. So, also, for a spiritual family. Their community is their deep story and a primary shaper of their collective identity.[80] The same attraction can happen more locally in a single school community. Indeed, it is one of the common and most effective unifiers that schools use to build culture. Drawing on the story of the school is done in a myriad of ways: honour boards, building names, house names, trophies and awards, heroes and legends, alumni bodies, rituals, mounted photos and story boards, and so on. Schools also tell the story of their wider spiritual family and draw on it in various ways – its founder, the founding events and challenges, maxims and teachings, the sites that have become sacred and are now places of pilgrimage, the story of the family as it spread around the world. All the stuff of culture-building. It can be one of the most concrete advantages of being able to tap into a spirituality of the Church. Both teachers and students relate to these expressions of story. They tell it to one another. It helps them shape who

---

79   John 6:67.
80   Reference was made in Chapter 2 to this preferred term of Bernard Lee (2004), *op. cit.* Lee's conceptualising of 'deep story' was in relation to apostolic consecrated life in specific religious institutes, but the concept can be extended more broadly to a spiritual tradition. Anthropologists such as Gerard Arbuckle might prefer to speak about this as 'myth'.

they are collectively. It gives them something of a corporate personality, and a means for describing the kind of community they are.

The critical thing is to keep this story in touch with the purpose that germinated it. Any group or organisation can have a corporate story – a computer company, a football club, a political movement. Even groups which have come to be defined by considerable malevolence – such as the Khmer Rouge, Nazism, or ISIS – exploit story in ways that give them identity. While it is highly improbable that a Catholic school community would sink into any collective pathology like that, it does need to be attentive not to allow its identity-shaping story to become decoupled from the founding intuitions of that story. To do so is to risk creating a distance from its gospel essence. If it is not careful it can be antithetical to the gospel, even insidiously so. How the story is customarily presented in the school setting is quite telling from this perspective, and even more telling is how the hearers are positioned to receive the story. This will reveal the mythology which really underpins the culture of the school or community. Which elements of the story are emphasised? And why? Which elements are less emphasised or omitted altogether? And why? What is honoured and celebrated? Where is there quietness or even silence?

When its essence stays tightly aligned with the intuitions of its founder's charism, then the story can provide not only identity, but draw the members of the school community into its deeper charismic purposes. The language may evolve, the content may be adapted for the place and the audience, the means for telling it will be various, but it will remain primarily concerned with the gospel of Jesus Christ. It will show people what this gospel can look like in their context: what forgiveness and mercy can look like, what patience and kindness can look like, what compassion and service, peace and justice, resilience and commitment all can look like, and what faith, hope and love can look like. What being Christian can look like. What a good school can look like. What Church can look like. And it will invite and nurture people into Christian discipleship in those ordinary life situations.

Many schools do this wonderfully well.[81] They seize the opportunities that their charismic traditions offer them to bring spirit and truth to the

---

81   One case-study of how this can play out is that done by Margaret Lee. See: Lee, MJ (2015), *The Institutionalisation of Charism in a Faith-Based School. A case study of a school in the Dominican tradition*, PhD thesis submitted in the Australian Catholic University. In a comprehensive study, Lee shows how the Dominican charismic tradition has been built into a school's culture in a way that allows members of the school community, who are otherwise quite disconnected from Church and who have rejected its authority, and whose lives are influenced by individualism, secularism, and pluralism, to develop a practical gospel-authentic spirituality. She found that Dominican spirituality – through its core values, language, formation opportunities, infusion into the curriculum, and in other ways – gave students and teachers a 'credible and palatable' way to process meaning, form identity, and develop spiritually. It allowed for a gospel-based culture to be fostered across four areas: mission and identity; governance and leadership; academic excellence; and operational viability. She concluded that it gave the school a way to be a Catholic school.

actual life situations of people in their school communities, as Jesus did in John 4. As that happens, then the spiritual and ministerial wisdom of the tradition, its resources, practices, expertise, and accumulated insights, are at hand to facilitate and drive it. Teachers and leaders draw on the pedagogical principles and learning of the tradition, and they access professional learning and formation opportunities that they find meaningful. They have links into the Church nationally and internationally, to youth ministry options, a sense of connection with others who share a resonant mindset and heartset in the tradition across the world – the whole range of attractions that are frequently reported as benefits of being part of a spiritual family of the Church. Approaches to learning and teaching, values and priorities, behaviours and language, allocation of time and resources, accepted ways and means for relating, justifications for initiatives and responses – all these develop normative patterns at many levels of the school.[82] It is a mutually reinforcing and multi-dimensional relationship between purpose and identity. Successful school leaders will be attentive to all of this and proactive in ensuring it, something to be developed further in the next chapter.

The set of markers of authenticity, integrity and vitality of a Christian spirituality's presence in a school, discussed in Chapter 4, are directly applicable also to its culture. This authentic, integral and vital spirituality will be at the very heart of a genuinely charismic culture. Mission-oriented schools need always to be attentive to what is at their corporate heart, and the degree to which, in the cultures out of which they are living and ministering, identity aligns with purpose, and both align with the gospel of Jesus. In an incarnated religion, as Christianity essentially is, there is no dichotomy between means and ends. Both are expressions of love, of God revealed in Jesus. Both lead to love and from love. From another perspective, however, the distinction between means and ends, between identity and purpose, is an important one to maintain. Not to do so risks replacing the latter with the former. This can happen – and frequently enough does to some degree – when there is a disproportionate emphasis on the movement's founder, and/or on the spiritual family.[83] It is one of the attendant dangers of having an especially inspirational founder or a particularly well-bonded

---

82 For examples of the myriad of concrete ways that schools can be advantaged in this way, specifically in their cultures, see Cook, TJ (2015) *op. cit.* Tim Cook canvasses the subject broadly, and cites the ways that various individual school communities have used the charismic opportunities they have. Others have researched the subject in a more focused way, for example Jennifer Elvery's study of teachers who occupied middle leadership positions in a secondary school of a particular tradition: Elvery, JM (2013), *Understanding and Implementing the Marist Charism from the Middle: The Experience of Middle Leaders in a Marist School*, PhD thesis submitted in the Australian Catholic University.

83 An example of this was found to be the case in the Elvery's study, *op. cit.* and also in the schools studied in the author's own research: Green, MC (1997) *The Charismatic Culture of Marist Secondary Schools in the Province of Sydney*, PhD thesis submitted in the University of Sydney.

and fine-spirited spiritual family. Its strength can become its greatest flaw: the very characteristics that attract and keep people are those that may keep them from coming to know and love Jesus and to feel at home in the Church. At its worst, it can become cultish, self-referential, or develop into a kind of parallel church.

Another risk for schools is to slip into what might be called 'heritage thinking'. Heritage is important because it is that part of the community's story that has gone before them, has helped to shape and define them, and out of which they have emerged. But it is a word that refers to the past. Culture, on the other hand, is about the present. Spirituality is about the present. When a school speaks, for example, of its 'Mercy' or 'Ursuline' heritage, it needs to be careful that it has not given its founding spirituality a virtual 'heritage listing' – something to be preserved as it was, a relic of what was, a treasure of a time gone. When a spirituality is primarily linked to a religious institute rather than a more inclusive group of people, this can happen. When the name of the spiritual family is something that relates mainly to ownership or governance, or to past links, but is not embedded in the living culture of the school in explicit and broadly-owned ways, then it can happen.

Again, the critical role of community presents itself. A Christian spirituality dies out without a living and sustainable Christian community which exercises co-responsibility for developing and continually recontextualising the tradition which it has inherited. So, also, it is fanciful to imagine that a spirituality will be able to provide the heart of a school's culture if it is not animated by a local Christian community of sufficient size and influence, also at the heart of the school, for whom that spirituality is a significant element of the way they are answering their baptismal call. They will be people immersed deeply in that spirituality: they will have been intuitively attracted to it; they will know it; they will be able to talk about it and induct others into it; they will be confident in expressing it culturally and pedagogically; they will feel co-responsible for it. It will speak to their now as much as their past. Anything else is a house of cards.

DIVERSITY OF TRADITIONS

One situation about which schools need often to make a determination is what to do when a school finds itself with more than one tradition or spirituality on which to draw. This may be the result of an amalgamation when two or more schools from different traditions have combined to form a new institution. It may be that the school bears the name of a saint but that saint comes from a different spirituality than the spiritual family which is conducting the school or with which the school is affiliated. It may be that a school of one tradition is in a parish of another. Or there may be competing spiritualities for another reason, such as the withdrawal of a religious institute from governance despite an ongoing presence of the spirituality among members of the school community, or when conduct of an institution is handed over from one religious institute or other PJP to another of a different tradition.

In matters such as these there are several paths that schools can take and a range of factors that are likely to bear on their decision-making. One option is for a school to attempt to name and retain the richness and integrity of both traditions, drawing on each in various ways, and staying connected with the spiritual family and/or religious institute associated with each. Many schools opt to attempt to go that way. Another is to settle on one of the traditions, and respectfully let the other(s) go. Another is to try to combine or to blend them in some way. A fourth is to choose another spirituality of the Church and to build the school's identity and community around that. Or, a school could opt to focus on its own story, developing its own identity as part of its local church, without recourse in a unifying kind of way to any one spiritual tradition. All of these paths have been chosen, and each has its adherents. Each school's context will be different, and the relative merits of the different options are likely to play out differently. There can also be some keenly felt sensitivities and deeply held allegiances to take into account. And more than a little politics. It can be a delicate matter.

What needs to be at the heart of any discernment process is a clear intention to seek whatever is going to be most conducive for facilitating and giving expression to the life of the Spirit for the present school community. An outcome is needed that brings the gospel compellingly into dialogue with the actual lives of students and staff and which helps to build Christian community. That may mean a change or a new direction, something that always requires sensitive and skilled cultural and spiritual leadership. To propose change is not to dismiss or demean what could be a strongly held attachment to one or other of the spiritual traditions that have been important in the past. What is being recognised here is that new contexts call for fresh contextualising of the gospel. It is also to recognise that if a school wants to build its identity and shape its mission around a spirituality of the Church, then that spirituality has to be something deeply culturally embedded in the community and able to be supported by a community of that spirituality, which remains at the heart of the life of the school.

Otherwise an affiliation with a particular spiritual tradition will simply be window-dressing, and its capacity to bring effect to evangelisation in real and engaging ways will be minimal.

Let us consider the potential attractions and hurdles that each of the above options may offer. Such a consideration is necessarily hypothetical and cannot take into account the subtleties of meaning and feeling that may exist in a real-life situation. Some principles can, nevertheless, be identified.

First is the option to proceed with more than one spirituality. Arguments in favour of this can include the view that a school will be doubly graced by having two or more spiritualities of the Church, and having the resources and wisdom of two or several spiritual families to support it with respect for the school's own history. It may also be argued that, given the range of people in a school community, some may connect more readily with one spirituality ahead of another. From one perspective, such arguments have obvious merit. Indeed, a welcoming of the 'multiformity' of the activity of the Spirit is central to respecting the charismatic dimension of the Church:[84] the Spirit, blowing where it will, will be continually renewing, refreshing and re-presenting the gospel of Jesus. The Spirit will be inherently diverse in its expression, from one point of view its expression will be as diverse as the individuality and charismic giftedness of each person. Why, then, would a school not seek to foster such intentional heterogeneity? The argument against this strategy – against proceeding with more than one spirituality – is one based on pragmatic and cultural reasoning, rather than theological. It is, simply, harder to do, and more likely to come to little. The kind of charismic culture that has been described earlier in this chapter – one that is woven densely through a school's life – is a more straight-forward proposition if it is built around a unified and unifying mythology. This is true of any organisational culture, and no less so for a charismically-based one. In the microcosm of a single school, in its day-to-day life and ways of proceeding, it is just simpler culturally to tap into the story, symbolism and ritual, the pedagogical principles and evangelising emphases, the values and language, of a single tradition. The written policies and protocols of the school, its ritualising and honouring, its agreed ways of judging and prioritising, its youth ministry and student leadership strategies, its branding and campus iconography – all examples of how to embed a Christian spirituality deeply into a school's culture and self-identity – are more effectively developed when there is clarity of voice.

---

84   Cf. *Iuvenescit Ecclesia*, #1, 2, 4, 8, 9.

Diversity can too easily dissipate into symbolic busyness and cultural confusion. It can lead to weakness and unhelpful complexity in the naming of the collective values and identity of the community. There can be continual questioning around perceptions of equitable attention to the different traditions of the school, something that can result in a paling of both. Principals can feel that they are treading on egg-shells every time they draw on one spirituality but not another in writing an editorial, designing a learning initiative, welcoming back an alumnus at an assembly, or offering a staff retreat. At their least effective, the traditions can diminish to little more than tokenism, for example, symbols on badges or names on buildings or one or two 'spirituality days' in the course of the year when a founder or tradition may be acknowledged, but with little day-to-day connection or cognisance among students or staff in ways that influence their Christian discipleship or define the community. It would be a different matter, of course, for a larger church community such as a parish or a diocese, or indeed a larger institution such as Catholic university. The letting of many spiritual flowers bloom in those situations is what broader ecclesial life should be. A primary or secondary school is, however, more typically a smaller and more cohesive entity. The role of organisational culture in helping it to be an effective educating and evangelising community is a more focused phenomenon.

The reality is that, for various reasons, one of the spiritual traditions often offers more to the school than the other(s). The ongoing presence of a community attracted to that spirituality – at the heart of the school and in influential leadership of it – is foundational.

It may also be that one spirituality:

- is more readily taken up by students and staff
- is more effectively supported by personnel and resources outside the school
- is sourced in a larger spiritual family of the Church
- is better adapted for lay inclusion
- is growing new forms of ecclesial expression rather than shrinking in older ones
- seems to be engaging more critically and dialogically with contemporary issues
- seems to be more missionary than insular, and/or
- provides more opportunities for students and staff outside the school in areas such as spiritual formation, youth ministry, social justice projects, professional learning, or career development.

Not to be able to take up those opportunities because of a concern to attend to each tradition equitably is an obvious impediment for a school.

Another factor to consider is that the traditions may not be culturally comfortable partners. While each is, of course, a graced expression of the one and the same gospel of Jesus, their cultural histories do not always make for them to be easily compatible. For example, a tradition that began in pre-emancipated Ireland, addressing need in a people denied education, full citizenship and unencumbered religious expression, may be likely to have developed cultural emphases and intuitions different from one that emerged from a long monastic experience in a Catholic country in continental Europe. A spirituality developed by semi-enclosed religious women may have evolved different cultural expression from one associated with apostolic male religious. A clerical religious institute may be different in its cultural approach from a wholly lay one, either female or male. All Christian spiritualities have the same tridimensional essence that has been discussed above. It is in their cultural expression that their distinctiveness is felt, but it is in this cultural expression that they can be most efficacious.

Most spiritualities have had their progenitors, and have been at least in part a blend of pre-existing spiritual bloodlines. Ignatius Loyola, for example, was affected by his reading of Ludolph of Saxony (a Carthusian), by the Benedictines of Montserrat, and by the example of Francis of Assisi. Dominic initially followed the Augustinian Rule. John of the Cross, a Carmelite, was educated by the Jesuits. Most of the founders of apostolic institutes in France in the eighteenth and nineteenth centuries were formed in the seminary by either the Sulpicians or the Vincentians (Lazarists), and influenced by the currents running through the 'French school' of spirituality, notably that of Francis de Sales among others. And all of them would have been shaped by the experiences of their life – first in their families, and later in the people in need with whom they came into contact. The novelty and timeliness of every spiritual tradition has, in this sense, some blending of the Christian story that has gone before it. Cannot a school, therefore, also rightfully blend the spiritualities from which it has emerged? Theoretically, of course. In practice, however, to attempt to do so would be an ambitious endeavour indeed! The great spiritualities of the Church have had the benefit of saints and masters of the spiritual life; they have a rich spiritual patrimony to pass on. They often have the wisdom and experience of many contexts both of time and place, right across the Church. From that has come the 'constancy of orientation' of which Paul VI spoke and to which reference was made in the previous chapter. New ways of the gospel, and indeed inspired new Christian pedagogical approaches, do continue to emerge. There are founders and saints in the Church of this generation. There remains, nonetheless, considerable practical benefit for a single school to draw more deliberately from an existing spirituality to which people are attracted, and to help its wider spiritual family to recontextualise it.

One of the helpful decisions for a school community to be able to make is to distinguish disinterestedly between its past and its future. Recognising that, for the reasons considered above, that it is likely to be easier to build a strong charismic culture from a single spiritual tradition, and to tap into this for its evangelising and educating, a school may need to let go gently and respectfully of one or more aspects of its history. These aspects will continue always to be honoured as heritage, and unambiguously so. But it will be as heritage, as completed chapters that have shaped the history of the school. Now, in the interests of evangelisation rather than nostalgia, new chapters are to be written. The future will look different. For example, a school that has amalgamated from two or more schools or traditions may continue to have ways in annual traditions, and in building-names and iconography, of honouring its past. Its present culture, however, will be built around a chosen single spirituality, either one of those which is already in its story, or a new one. It will be likely, if the decision comes as the fruit of discernment rather than the outcome of politics, that the spirituality chosen will be one with which the school community is familiar rather than something with which it does not. This would allow it to build on the existing spiritual depth already in the school, both personally and communally.

Therefore, in most situations, the surest way forward for a school wishing to draw on the Church's spiritualities could be for it to choose one of them. It should be a discerned choice, not a political or emotional one. It will be one that draws on the criteria explored in the last two chapters. The discernment will be rooted in the evangelical, educational and personal needs of the current school community, in the vitality and credibility of the wider spiritual family that could be associated with the school into its future, and in the possibilities that exist for nurturing faith, community and mission in the actual people who constitute the school community. It will be driven by mission-thinking.

THERE ARE MANY DWELLINGS: A PROMISE AND A CHALLENGE

Five times in Chapter 14 of the fourth Gospel the word 'abide'/'dwell' appears, once as a noun and four times as a verb (μένω, *menó*). It is a key Johannine theme, and one that flows through the entire Last Supper discourse. It speaks of the God who abides, who remains, who dwells in people, in time and place.[85] We are assured that there are many indwellings of God – Father, Jesus, Spirit – as many as there are those who believe. It is the great promise of Jesus in John's Gospel that the Spirit will continue to reveal this truth. It is also the great challenge of the fourth Gospel: abide in God, for to be cut off from God brings powerlessness and lifelessness. You can do nothing.[86]

Among those dwellings are enduring communities of disciples who run Catholic schools. These communities are the custodians of some rich ways that have been efficacious for keeping the branches and the vine as one. They are entrusted with the Church's great spiritual traditions, not for their safe-keeping but for the life and mission of the Church. God abides with them, if they abide with God. God is in their midst – in the lived realities of their schools. God seeks to take flesh in the culture of those schools, for Divine incarnation can only occur in a human cultural context. They have developed ways for educating young people to wholeness of life, for building schools as communities, for serving society, and for leading people to know that now is the favourable time. If those spiritual families are to endure and to continue to be able to participate with effect in *missio Dei* through the work of Catholic education, they need to remain being schools of holiness, schools of community and schools of mission. And for that to occur, there needs to be leadership.

---

85   Cf. John 14:2,10,14,23,25. Johannine scholar Mary Coloe PBVM has written extensively on this topic. See: Coloe, M (2001), *God Dwells with Us: Temple Symbolism in the Fourth Gospel,* Liturgical Press, Collegeville, MN (2007) *Dwelling in the Household of God: Johannine Ecclesiology and Spirituality,* Liturgical Press, Collegeville. An accessible introduction is found in: (2013), *A Friendly Guide to John's Gospel,* Garratt Publishing, Mulgrave. See also video clips on: www.marycoloe.org.au/homepage.

86   John 15.

6

CHARISMIC LEADERSHIP

The people were astonished at his teaching, for he taught them as one having authority, not like the scribes.

Mt.7:28-29

LEADERSHIP MATTERS. A LOT.

In whichever ways it may be conceived or exercised, effective leadership of any cultural group or organisation is both essential and defining for that entity. For a Catholic school or spiritual family of the Church, given its intensely relational and intentionally communitarian character, the goodness of leadership is a *conditio sine qua non* for it to coalesce as a genuine Christian community of disciples, of learners, and of apostles. The jury is in on the question of the pervasive impact of leadership – or, alternatively, the absence or inadequacy of leadership – and it has been in for some time. Research abounds.[1]

---

1   The topic of leadership is an immense subject of theory and practice, in both the fields of organisational culture and of school education. While any adequate representational survey of the literature associated with it is well beyond the scope of this book, it would be important, nonetheless, that the reader have a reasonably informed understanding of the research and commentary of the last forty years. Such an understanding is assumed in the discussion of this chapter, particularly regarding the emphases that have emerged for leaders of Catholic schools. Some pointers may be helpful. 'Leadership' – in contradistinction to 'management' or 'administration' – began to emerge strongly in research associated with the excellence movement and organisational culture in the 1980s, first in the corporate world and then more specifically in schools where the school effectiveness movement developed its own emphases. Prominent and somewhat concept-setting in this research and commentary were Peters and Waterman (1982), *op. cit.* and Deal and Kennedy (1992), *op. cit.*, already cited in Chapter 2. They were strong in their correlation of an organisation's or school's success with the quality of leadership in it. Also highly influential in the research associated with school leadership between the 1980s and 2000s was Tom Sergiovanni (1984; 1990; 1994; 1996; 2004), *op. cit.* in his emphases on the importance of the symbolic and cultural leadership of the principal and, later, community leadership. On this subject, for some examples of other contemporaneous research and theory, see: Purkey, SC & Smith, MS (1982), Synthesis of Research on Effective Schools, *Educational Leadership,* Vol. 40, No. 3, pp. 64-69; Wilson, BL & Corcoran, TB (1988), *Successful Secondary Schools: Visions of Excellence in American Public Education,* The Falmer Press, London; Millikan, R (1987), School Culture: a conceptual framework, *Educational Administration Review,* Vol. 5, No. 2, pp. 38-56; Duignan, PA (1987), 'The Culture of School Effectiveness', in Simpkins WS, Thomas AR & Thomas EB (eds) *Principal and Change: The Australian Experience,* University of New England Press, Armidale; McGaw, B et al (1992), *Making Schools More Effective: Report of the Australian Effective Schools Project,* Australian Council for Educational Research, Melbourne; Newton, C & Tarrant, T (1992), *Managing Change in Schools,* Routledge, London; Starratt, RJ (1993), *The Drama of Leadership,* The Falmer Press, London; Grace, G (1996), 'Leadership in Catholic Schools', in McLaughlin, T O'Keefe,

But what is it that makes leadership good? More specifically for our concerns here, what would make a good leader of a community that draws on a particular Christian spirituality to support its members' sense of faith, community and mission? On that question, the jury of theoretical and empirical enquiry may not be quite as unanimous in its verdict, but it is not far from being so. At least when it comes to Catholic schools and other ecclesial communities, there is considerable consensus around what matters and what works.

In the context of this discussion, 'good' presents itself as a better reference point than 'effective'. Critique of good leadership has long absorbed both scholars and practitioners. From Thucydides and Plutarch in the ancient Graeco-Roman world,[2] to Niccolò Machiavelli and William Shakespeare in early modern times,[3] to contemporary academics such as James McGregor Burns and Warren Bennis,[4] the exercise of leadership has proved a compelling subject of study. In our own time, a long list of descriptors has accreted around the noun *leadership*, as theorists have opted to place the weight of emphasis and perspective on one aspect or another. Some have emphasised cultural leadership, moral leadership, visionary leadership, inspirational leadership, purposeful leadership, or strategic leadership; others have preferred authentic leadership, servant

---

J & O'Keeffe, B (eds) (1996), *The Contemporary Catholic School: Context, Identity and* Diversity, The Falmer Press, London; Beare, H (1987), 'Metaphors About Schools: The principal as a Cultural Leader', in Simpkins WS *et al., op. cit.* The role of vision and purpose in leadership emerged as quite significant. In addition to the above, see also, for example: Ramsay, W & Clarke, EE (1990), *New Ideas for Effective School Improvement: Vision, Social Capital, Evaluation,* The Falmer Press, London; Lightfoot, SH (1983), *The Good High School: Portraits of Character and Culture,* Basic Books, New York; Coleman, JS & Hoffer, T (1987), *Public and Private High Schools: The Impact of Communities,* Basic Books, New York. Two of the themes that gained most strength from the 1990s, both in research and theory, were the moral bases for school leadership and authenticity in leadership. Sergiovanni, Starrett, Beare and Duignan have all been champions of this emphasis.

2   The Athenian historian Thucydides' *The History of the Peloponnesian War* has long been studied as a masterpiece of counterpoint, contrasting the approaches of culture and leadership in ancient Athens and Sparta. Plutarch, writing four centuries later, composed biographies of noted Roman and Greek leaders, including some of the more famous and infamous of the emperors. In *Parallel Lives* he also provides moral counterpoints of moral virtue and want of it.

3   Machiavelli is best known for his influential work, *The Prince,* for which his times provided ample sources of study of the exercise of power and governance in contexts of moral ambiguity, contest and conflict. A number of Shakespeare's plays are themed around characters in leadership, for example *Macbeth, Hamlet, Richard III,* and *King Lear.* It is, though, *Henry V* (and to a lesser degree *Henry IV, Part 1* and 2) which is often studied in the context of leadership, and used for leadership seminars and workshops in a great number of contexts. For an enlightening exploration of the way Shakespeare deals with leadership, using *Henry V* as a source, see: Olivier, R (2013), *Inspirational Leadership. Timeless lessons for leaders from* Shakespeare's Henry V, Nicholas Brealey Publishing, London.

4   American academics Jim Burns and Warren Bennis were pioneering giants in the field of leadership studies in the latter part of the twentieth century. While neither was associated primarily with education or church leadership, each was influential in shaping thought and debate around moral or ethical leadership. Burns, in particular, was an advocate from the 1970s of what he called 'transforming leadership.' See, for example, Burns, JMcG (1978), *Leadership,* Harper and Row, New York; Bennis, W (1989) *On Becoming a Leader,* Basic Books, New York; (1993), *An Invented Life: Reflections on Leadership and Change,* Basic Books, New York.

leadership, community leadership, or value-based leadership; yet others have sought to stress distributed leadership, change leadership, leadership for learning, empowering leadership, horizontal leadership, peer leadership, or transformational leadership; others again have been more utilitarian and clinical in their attention to evidence-based measures of a school leader's ability to induce staff and students to value-add to learning processes and outcomes, to build enrolments and community satisfaction, to align with public policy priorities, or simply to meet or exceed the leader's designated KPIs. All these approaches have their validity, of course, for each is based on an understanding of goodness, of purpose, and of utility.

And now, to this long list of adjectives, we presume to add yet another: 'charismic'. In doing so, there is no implied dismissal or diminishment of most of the above descriptors, emanating as they have from both valid and reliable empirical analysis and from informed conceptualising and considered hermeneutical reasoning. They offer ways of understanding and evaluating good leadership in schools. It is well established in the literature that such leadership, in the context of a values-driven and coherent culture, is strongly correlated with school effectiveness and school improvement. There should be no suggestion — other than the caveats concerning gospel-compromising effectiveness that were named in the preceding chapter — that a Catholic school be anything less than a successful school. This has been an explicit working premise since at least the promulgation of *The Catholic School* over four decades ago. Indeed, a number of the leadership descriptors listed above — especially those derived from higher moral purpose and with the creation of intentional community — will dovetail readily into the discussion which follows concerning charismic leadership.

The discrediting of 'great man' and 'command-and-control' leadership over recent decades has not been uniform or without turnback. Especially in contexts of uncertainty, struggle, or threat — whether these be genuine or whether they be dishonestly confected in the popular imagination — people's focus, hope, and expectation can tend to remain invested in the single leader. And those single leaders can be adept at exploiting this human tendency, even to the branding of their leadership or policies by use of their own name. It happens in public life, in church, in corporate entities, and in schools, often fuelled by media or social hype of one kind or another. It can be simplistic and disingenuous, and even demeaning and disenfranchising for followers, but it can also work for a time. Political, social, and religious movements, even those with informed and critically engaged membership, do it. Tabloid reporting of it abets them.

There remains, nonetheless, and there needs to remain, a valued place for the inspirational leader, the person of vision and character whose capacity to imagine, articulate, excite, coalesce, and call people to transcend the mundane, to build community and effect enduring change and growth. In the school context, the research is unequivocal that this will necessarily include in first place the principal. A school without an influential and effective principal will likely have a dysfunctional culture, and be a fractured and fraught place to learn and to teach. But it is equally clear that leadership cannot reside in the principal alone. What underpins the arguments of those who advocate more inclusive, shared and broadly infused styles of leadership in a school, is the clear evidence that schools with multiple founts of influence and channels of confluence are places of achievement, contentment, momentum, and mutually reinforcing values.[5] This calls for leadership at all levels: from those on the senior leadership group; from those in middle leadership positions in academics, pastoral care and the co-curriculum; from teachers in classrooms and coaches of sports teams; and no less from those who sit behind the reception desk, run the library, offer counselling, or service the IT desk. Then there are some of the most influential players in a school environment: the students themselves, both those with designated leadership positions as much as others who hold sway in classroom and playground. Peer influence has enormous impact and a school neglects it at its peril. Almost no-one in a school will be without a sphere of some influence. In this sense, it is neither trite nor cute to describe everyone as a leader. It is, rather, a recognition of how influence works in a school. And, with this comes both opportunity and challenge.

Of course, not everyone gets leadership readily, because not everyone immediately sees the big picture, has a sense of shared responsibility for the whole, or even is alert to look for it. The oft-told anecdote of the medieval stone-masons is instructive. A traveller comes upon a building site where a group of masons is busy with chisel and mallet, mortar and trowel. Curious to know what is happening, he approaches one of the masons to enquire as to what he is doing. 'I am shaping this stone. It's a finely quarried stone, sir, and it needs to be accurately measured and cut, and then carefully placed.

---

5 'Distributed leadership' is a widely used term. Others, such as Patrick Duignan, prefer 'sustainable collective leadership', or other terms such as shared leadership or co-responsibility in leadership. See: Duignan, PA (2012), *Educational Leadership. Together creating ethical learning environments,* Cambridge University Press, Melbourne. For research on the effectiveness of distributed leadership in schools, see: Harris, A (2010), 'Distributed Leadership: Evidence and Implications', in Bush, T, Bell, L & Middlewood, D (eds), *The Principles of Educational Leadership and Management,* Second Edition, Sage Publications, London; Leithwood, K, Mascall, B & Strauss, T (eds) (2009), *Distributed Leadership According to the Evidence,* Routledge, New York; Fullan, M (2006), *Turnaround Leadership,* Jossey-Bass, San Francisco. For some further background see: Harris, A (2009) *Distributed Leadership: Different Perspectives,* Springer Press, Dordrecht; Spillane, J (2006), *Distributed Leadership,* Jossey-Bass, San Francisco; and the complete issue of the *Journal of Educational Administration* Vol. 46, No. 2 (2008).

The master-mason has given me clear directions for how this is to be done.' The traveller is impressed by the skill and application of the mason. He approaches another, and asks him what he was doing. 'My brother masons and I are getting these stones ready for the east wall,' he says. 'We know that we need to have them laid before the winter so that the mortar will set well.' Again the traveller admires the diligence and workmanship of the craftsmen, and he moves onto a third mason who is chiselling away on a small stone, to ask him the same question as to what he is doing. This time, however, the response is different: 'I am helping to build a cathedral.' Leaders are always about cathedrals. They are prompted by grandness of vision, nobility of purpose, and a compelling sense of endeavour. And they can inspire those about them to the same. Some in a school will be proactive in seeking such vision and purpose. It will sit easily with them, and they with their place in it. Others will need more assistance to have their eyes opened and their hearts inflamed, but they will be grateful and graced when this happens. Indeed, they need for it to happen if they are to take some share in leading and influencing.

LEADING WITH AUTHORITY

The research on authentic, ethical and moral leadership reveals that, in the final analysis, goodness in leadership is centred in the personhood of the one who is leading. To be good, leadership requires someone who credibly personifies that to which the organisational entity aspires. For the Catholic school, that means *missio Dei*. A leader in a Catholic school will be someone who thinks, judges, feels and acts in ways that are resonant with what God wants, and who draws forth such resonance to be amplified in others. Thus it was for Jesus: he was heeded because it was recognised that he taught 'with authority',[6] in contrast to what is portrayed, in the Synoptic Gospels at least, as the hypocrisy of the scribes and pharisees. Whatever knowledge and diligence the scribes and pharisees might have demonstrated, it was not what mattered to people. Jesus, however, lived out in his own life the kind of discipleship that he espoused in Chapters 5 to 7 of Matthew. He was therefore able to perform miracles of healing. In the Gospel of John, Jesus was 'one with the Father'.[7] His whole identity derived from this, as did his hope for his disciples into the future. It is from such union of love that the Spirit will come. It will be no less so for a school leader. It is in this that authentic Catholic school leadership rests and authority is sourced.

Authority is different from power. Authority, in the sense that Jesus

---

6   Cf. Matt 7:29; Luke 4:32; Mark 1:22.
7   Cf. John 10:30; 17:20–26.

exercised it, is concerned with the action of grace. It is not 'great man' leadership; it is not instrumentalist or controlling. It is not vertical or top-down. Rather, it is dialogical, life-giving, unifying, and facilitative of the faith, hope and love in which it is itself sourced. Its signs and fruits are as St Paul describes – joy, kindness, patience, resilience, forgiveness, selflessness, compassion, gratitude, and so on. But, who among us can presume to be one with God? Who is an ordinary Catholic school principal to claim such profound authenticity in his or her leadership? Or a battling Head of Year Ten, or a data-smothered Head of Mathematics, or a no-minute-to-spare Year Three classroom teacher, or a hormonally-charged class captain of 'Room 9-3'? Jesus' disciples had a similar question, fearing that none of them would be able to pass through the eye of the needle.[8] Jesus answered simply: humility before God is the key. Humility is always the path of a person's spiritual journey – making space for God to act, and trusting that action. On that basis, Jesus reassures them that they will share the throne with him.

A school with a deeply driven and shared sense of identity and purpose – a school where 'we' and 'us' are used a lot more than 'they' and 'them' – is one where such distributed leadership for *missio Dei* can potentially be exercised in a multi-faceted and mutually-enriching way. When a sports coach knows that the deep purposes of the school are served when a player learns about self-discipline and collaboration, when an instrumental tutor knows that to help a student to master the violin with elegance and skill is a way of teaching about the beauty of all life, when a counsellor knows that to guide a suicidal teenager towards hope and a sense of self-worth is to share with God in the creation of life, when a Year One teacher knows that to teach a child to read is a gift that will bring with it dignity and engagement with the world, when a Year Twelve Coordinator knows that a disciplinary sanction for a student is better when it is educative rather than punitive, when a student is greeted by name on entering the school campus in the morning – these and a myriad of other encounters and judgements, day in and day out, are all ways of bringing Christ-life to birth, of realising the reign of God. They are expressions of *missio Dei*, and all members of a school can be influential in bringing it about. That 'the glory of God is humanity fully alive' is true now as it was when first written by Saint Irenaeus in the second century.[9] To teach and to learn, to read and to write,

---

8   Cf. Matt 19:23-26.

9   *Gloria Dei vivens homo* is the original Latin (*Adversus Hæreses* IV, 20, 7.) Saint Irenaeus's great work *Adversus Hæreses* (Against the Heresies) was written especially against the heresy of Gnosticism, prevalent in the second century, which denied the full humanity of Christ, and also promoted a kind of dualism that distinguished the spiritual from the carnal in human beings, extolling the former and denigrating the latter. It was not only a denial of the Incarnation, but also a denial of the possibility of experience of the Divine in the here and now of everyday life – thus, a rejection of the incarnational theology which underpins the argument of this book.

to coach and to play, to counsel and to be mentored, to guide and to grow, to inspire and to serve others, to form relationships that are nourishing and liberating – all of this is mission-centred activity. It incarnates God who is mission. All who share in it and influence others through it are sharing in mission-oriented leadership in a school.

But Irenaeus is often undersold in that famous line. The full quotation reads: 'The glory of God is humanity fully alive, and the life of humanity is the vision of God. If the revelation of God through creation already brings life to all living beings on the earth, how much more will the manifestation of the Father by the Word bring life to those who see God.' The profundity of the first sentence is what creates the *opportunity* in a Catholic school for a broad and deep embrace of *missio Dei*, but the second sentence is just as important. It is in this that a Catholic school can face more of a challenge for those who are its leaders, for this requires God to be made explicit. They are two sides of the one coin: to nurture the full expression of human life is to resonate absolutely with the vision of God, but it is by bringing people to knowledge of Jesus – the Word of God – that life comes to fullness. It is to 'see God'. Here is the rub for authentic leadership in a Catholic school.

To the extent that the work of a school or the nature of leadership are concerned with human development – even without any reference to the spiritual sense of this development – then they may be consistent with serving God's mission, but they will not be wholly expressive of it, or fully congruent with it. Those who share leadership of the Catholic schools – and especially for our concerns here, the principal and others who are most significant in naming identity and shaping culture – will have a diminished expression of authentic Catholic school leadership if they themselves are not people of committed Christian faith, people who have been affected by the gospel of Jesus, who have taken up discipleship with him, and who share this journey in communion with fellow disciples. There will be, inevitably, a range of faith experience, maturity and perspective among the staff and students of a Catholic school. Not all will be ready, willing or able to exercise such fullness or authenticity of leadership. Of relevance are the number and influence of such people in a school.

The transition from religious to lay leadership of Catholic schools over recent decades, and this in the secularising and detraditionalising societal contexts in which Catholic schools in western societies have increasingly found themselves during the same period, has brought this concern into sharper focus. In the 1990s and early 2000s it attracted heightened attention from researchers and Church leaders.[10] Concern was raised as to the readiness of the next generation of school leaders to lead spiritually. Both their theological literacy and their capacity for confident, informed and credible spiritual leadership of their communities were under question.[11] To some extent, it was a matter of ensuring that people had the appropriate skills and adequate theological, scriptural and doctrinal knowledge to enable and enhance credible spiritual leadership, but more deeply it was a matter of the spiritual intentionality and maturity of the leader.[12] It was about their hearts more than their minds and hands. To what degree was their growth in faith and discipleship being nurtured in ways that matched the development of other dimensions of their human growth? What kind of spiritual accompaniment or direction were they receiving? What were they reading and how were they sharing their faith? With whom? How did they pray and worship? What was the nature of their critical engagement with the major discourses of the Church?[13] What was their own involvement in

---

10　One influential leader of research and international discourse on this question has been Gerald Grace. See especially Grace (2002; 2010) *op. cit.* Grace's concept of 'spiritual capital', already mentioned in Chapter 4, applies in a heightened sense to leaders. His earlier research indicated that competence of principals in leading learning and teaching, business management, HR, strategic planning and PR, was not always matched by understanding or readiness concerning the more explicitly spiritual dimensions and purposes of the Catholic school. The sources of spiritual capital in the past, according to Grace, were in family faith and practice, and ways that members of religious congregations were schooled, benefited from initial and ongoing formation, and lived their lives of prayer and faith practice. With these bases dissipating, there was the challenge as to what would nurture the spiritual capital in Catholic schools of the future. The matter of new approaches to formation will be taken up in Chapter 7.

11　The National Catholic Education Association in the USA, for example, has been alert to this concern and responsive to it. Two parallel broadly-cast studies conducted by Merylann Schuttloffel in 2003 and 2013 addressed a wide range of issues associated with the recruitment, induction, support, responsibilities, formation of school principals. See: Schuttloffel, M (2003), *Report on the Future of Catholic School Leadership*, National Catholic Education Association, Arlington VA; (2014), *Report on Catholic School Leadership, Ten Years Later*, Arlington VA: National Catholic Education Association. On the subject of capacity-building in principals around spiritual leadership and theological education, she found that the 'glaring inadequacies' of 2003 had been significantly redressed in the ensuing decade.

12　Ron Rolheiser (2014) *op. cit.*, for example, writes of 'stages of discipleship', a growing spiritual maturity. In doing so, he attempts to put into contemporary language the insights of mystics such as John of the Cross who wrote of the inner or upward journey of the spiritual life. Rolheiser distinguishes three stages: first, the 'essential discipleship' of adolescence and early adulthood that parallels John of Cross's 'dark night of the senses'; second, the 'mature discipleship' of full adulthood that parallels the 'proficiency' stage of John of the Cross; and third, the phase of 'radical discipleship' that parallels the 'dark night of the soul'. Another contemporary master of the spiritual life, Henri Nouwen, also draws from the Catholic mystical tradition, to which he brings his knowledge both as a pastoral theologian and as a clinical psychologist. He emphasised the movements of the Spirit through a person's life, which consisted of the early adulthood, mid-life and mature stages. See, for example, Nouwen, H (1975)' *Reaching Out: The Three Movements of the Spiritual Life*, Doubleday, New York. His life's work has been more recently visited and edited by Michael Christensen and Rebecca Laird in Nouwen, H (2010), *Spiritual Formation: Following the Movements of the Spirit*, Harper Collins, New York.

13　In the theoretical framework of the ECSIP research, the question may be framed in terms of the 'post-critical belief' of the leader: the degree to which a person had moved from naïve belief through critical engagement of faith and life, and was continuing perennially to reappropriate it into life.

the broader community of the Church, and their lived sense of belonging? What was their level of comfort in self-consciously taking the lead missiologically in their schools?[14]

Authority, in the way that it is used by Jesus in the Gospels, emanates from an interiorly sourced integrity. It is not a credibility that comes simply from 'walking the talk', as important as that also may be. It is, more, a personal alignment with God and the will of God, something that is nurtured over time, and only through an intentional and sustained discipleship of Jesus. In terms of Catholic school leadership, authenticity is found here. That is not to suggest that competent authentic leadership would then happen as if by magic. There is, of course, a set of specific capacities to which to be attentive, to learn, to practice, to critique, and to improve – personal ones as well as professional.[15] But if it is not fundamentally spiritual, then it will be something less than authentic. It will also be something less than effective if it is the building of a charismic culture that is being attempted.

It comes back to mission. Always. The vision and purpose of the Catholic school stem from the intention to realise in time and place, in people and action, the reign of God who is mission – the bringing to birth and the nurturing of Christ-life in people, of bringing people into oneness with Christ, with one another, and with God's plan for creation. Although it will ideally be shared by many in the school, through resonant and intersecting fields of influence, the most authentic leadership in this mission will primarily reside in people for whom such spiritual communion is a lived experience.

---

14 The D'Orsas' emphasis on the challenge of ensuring adequate quality of 'mission thinking' is pertinent here, as it will apply most especially in the context of Catholic school leadership. See: D'Orsa, J & D'Orsa, T (2013) *op. cit*, pp. 244ff on what they describe as the six key elements of mission thinking. It is unlikely that a school leader would be creating figurative 'God-spaces' in the life of a school, if such spaces have not been created in his or her personal experience.

15 Three noted writers on leadership who have identified a range of specific and practical competencies through which a principal can exercise moral or ethical leadership, based in solid theory and empirical learning, are Michael Fullan, Patrick Duignan and Jerry Starratt. While each presents these competencies and strategies from a non-specifically religious perspective, the application of their frameworks fits readily into how authentic Catholic school leadership can be imagined and developed. Each explores and proposes what might be described as the *craft* of authentic leadership. See, in particular, the trilogy on change leadership that Fullan did for Jossey-Bass: Fullan, M (2001), *Leading in a Culture of Change,* Jossey-Bass, San Francisco; (2008), *The Six Secrets of Change,* Jossey-Bass, San Francisco; (2011), *Change Leader: learning to do what matters most,* Jossey-Bass, San Francisco. In the third book, Fullan describes a 7-faceted approach that builds on action ('the crucible of change' for him), resolve, motivation, collaboration, confidence, use of data, and 'simplexity'. Duignan (2012), *op. cit.* develops a set of 30 personal, relational, professional and organisational capabilities that authentic leadership requires. Starratt, RJ (2004), *Ethical Leadership.* Jossey-Bass, San Francisco; (2012), *Cultivating an Ethical School,* Jossey-Bass, San Francisco.

AUTHORITY WITHIN A SPIRITUAL FAMILY

When a school community aligns itself with one of the Church's spiritual families, and seeks to draw on the spiritual, communal and educational wisdom of that tradition to help it to shape its identity and enliven the way it shares in God's mission, and further, as it aspires to become or to remain a living community of that tradition, then there emerge important additional considerations for those who would have authority within it. The essential conceptualising of such authority is the same as suggested above for any authentic leadership in a Catholic school: modelled on Jesus' oneness with the Father, a unity from which the Spirit proceeds. But if it is within a charismic tradition, then further imperatives emerge. Authority in a spiritual family is sourced in the community's identity, as long as that community itself is a genuinely spiritual family, a community of the Spirit and self-consciously placing itself within God's people, the Church. For authority to be authentic in such a community it will be rooted in the charismic giftedness of that family, its spirituality – in its distinctive way of Christian discipleship, in its communal life, and in its intuitive and cumulative wisdom in education. It is a tri-faceted authority. Put simply, for someone to lead, for example, a Benedictine community, that person needs to be Benedictine. The leader will have a self-awareness that aligns with that, and he or she will be accepted by fellow-Benedictines as such. For that to be so, the leader's full Christian identity does not, arguably should not, need to be solely Benedictine. But Benedictine spirituality will be, first, one of the principal ways through which that person embraces of the gospel; he or she will be intuitively attracted to it and it will work for them. Second, the person will feel at home with others who follow the Benedictine way and will have a felt sense of belonging to them. Third, the leader will be able to articulate cogently and to exemplify personally an educational approach and an overall ministerial manner that is an expression of Benedictine style, priorities and emphases.

To be a Benedictine school leader, or one of any other spiritual tradition, is not simply to put on a name badge or lapel pin in the morning as part of a person's professional dress. But symbols will be part of it, as will conscious professional practices. It is not to read some books and to swat up on all things Benedictine. But learning and study of the story and wisdom of the tradition will also be an essential part of it. It is not to show up to gatherings of Benedictines in the same way that duty calls a leader to be present at other school-related events. But involvement and presence will be an indispensable element of it. To be a Benedictine school leader will be, however, something more intuitive, heartfelt and owned than any position description, policy manual or history book can name. It will be personal. It will be of the heart. Head and hands will follow.

The three sources and expressions of any living spirituality apply with added significance to those in leadership roles in an educational ministry of that spiritual family: it will be for the leader a distinctive path of personal discipleship; it will be communal, both in a sense of belonging to a community and in feeling part of its story; and it will be a characteristic way of evangelising through education. Just as the three elements are interrelated in the spirituality, they need to be in anyone who is going to exercise authority in that spiritual family. In a school, this is inescapably the principal, but it needs also to be true for others who play influential roles, irrespective of whether these people are or are not in formally designated leadership roles. More than this, those in formal and informal positions of influence also need to have a sense of their shared responsibility for the ongoing nurturance and perennial recontextualising of the spirituality. They more than anyone, will be responsible for inducting the next generation into the spiritual family, and for forming them with integrity. Leaders are also co-responsible, continually, for developing fresh language and symbolism that speak to emerging contexts, for applying founding intuitions to contemporary needs and experiences, and for imagining new paradigms for belonging and ministering. Ideally, their leadership will be quite widely distributed and variously exercised through a school, but it always falls to those with more influence to be people for whom all three elements of the spiritual tradition are personally appropriated, and to be people who feel co-responsible for both the present and the future vitality of the tradition.

As the school leaders help to create, sustain, and develop a charismic culture in the school, all the expectations around cultural leadership come into consideration for those in influential roles.[16]

These expectations will require them to interweave their spiritual, communal, educational, strategic and administrative leadership as five threads of the same fabric:

- in the ways they articulate, ritualise, reward, honour, and symbolise the core hermeneutical narrative of the school
- in their manner of relating and nurturing community
- through the ways they plan, prioritise and allocate resources, and the aspects of the life of the school to which they give most attention and energy

---

16 The earlier discussion on leadership and school culture is relevant here, that of the 1980s and 1990s (a discourse that has been led by writers such as Deal, Sergiovanni, Beare, Caldwell, Duignan and others already cited) as well as more recent understandings of culture in the school setting, and its links with collective identity (for example, D'Orsa & D'Orsa, Arbuckle, and others as already cited.)

- in the kind of professional learning that is offered and expected
- in deciding who is appointed to which roles, and why, and
- in generating the bases for policy-setting, making judgements, and establishing pastoral care styles.

All this will be woven through their entire leadership style and emphases. The power and grace of the charismic traditions are incarnated in all these lived realities of the school and its culture. Important among them will be the leaders' responsibility to be the keepers of the story – to know the story not only of the school (which is a given) but of the spiritual family also, to feel part of that story and to own it, and to ensure that it is broadly known and appropriated. It is from such radical knowledge of the deep story of the group – its mythology – that leaders can exercise their equally important responsibility for being imaginative.[17] Too frequently, imagination can be undervalued as a quality of leadership. There must always be a vision offered for the future, but where are its sources? They are found in the deep story of the group, in its defining intuitions of grace. The leaders must be people who have learnt to intuit the same way.

Authentic leaders of a charismically identifying school – people who need to be able and ready to speak and act with authority in the community – are therefore called to be people deeply immersed in its identity. In addition to the other skills and experience that will equip them for school leadership, they will need to belong to that ecclesial community. They will be invested with it spiritually; they will have learnt personally from that spirituality and they will live it. Such profound personal approbation does not happen easily or quickly, of course, and in that lies a real-life challenge. The reality for many Catholic education professionals is that they are likely to move among several spiritual families in the course of their careers. When they first come into positions of greater influence in schools, such as middle and senior leadership roles, they will come to them as adults. Their own identities will be already formed. They will have their own families and significant others. They will belong to one or more faith communities, not least their parish. They will have a personal spiritual history, and often enough have a developed spiritual maturity augmented by a sound theological education. They may not have had previous experience of the spirituality in which

---

17   David Ranson makes interesting comments on this interplay between story and imagination. See, for example, Ranson, D (2001) 'Memory and Imagination: New Sources of Catholic Identity', *The Furrow*, Vol. 52, No. 11, pp. 605-11. On the subject of story, Ranson recalls the practice of the Vikings in their raids of Saxon villages. The first people they sought out to extract were the village story-tellers because they knew – as people who honoured story themselves – that severed from corporate memory, a group loses its orientation and can fall into hopelessness. Arbuckle (2016) *op. cit.* approaches the same idea using his preferred terminology around 'myths'.

they now find themselves immersed. Where does that leave them, and where does it leave their community?

In a precarious position, is the short answer. In the balance. The would-be leaders will need to act sensitively, strategically, and intentionally. What they bring, presumably, are their sense of baptismal commitment, a personal history of following Jesus, and their experience of being the ecclesial and spiritual companions of others. They bring an understanding of the purposes of Catholic education and their own vocational commitment to it. Most will bring a proven ability to lead successfully in a Catholic school context; that is probably why they won their appointment. And they bring themselves. All of that can position them very well. From one perspective, all the foundation rocks are in place for them to be authentic spiritual leaders. But, from another point of view, there are lurking risks. People suited well to charismic leadership will be alert to these. If they are not then they risk leading the school into an identity crisis, and inadvertently creating some cultural dysfunctionality. They also risk drying up one of richest founts of evangelising that the school community has: its charismic giftedness.

Wise leaders will know that they are in positions of leadership of a spiritual family, and so they will recognise, first, the critical importance of their being or their becoming invested in that family spiritually. That family comprises people – people who define their collective identity in graced ways and have distinctive approaches for sharing in God's mission. Those people will seek both to be part of that family, and to develop a sense of responsibility for its future. Second, they will know that they need to learn. There is a humility in that. The thing about a spirituality, however, as discussed in Chapter 2, is that it can indeed be taught and learnt. It will have developed a language, an accumulated wisdom, an expertise, a history, ways that it ritualises and symbolises, and a whole set of cultural mores through which Christ-life comes to life in the community. All those things can be learned. Third, there is the heart. Here is the greatest risk. Leaders will need to ask themselves if this spirituality and this spiritual family sit well with them. Do they connect intuitively? Does it inspire and sustain? Is it them? If the answers to those last questions tend to the negative, then there is an inherent problem. It is unlikely to work.

That is not to propose that the people who are likely to be suited to lead a school of a particular spiritual tradition of the Church are best sourced from within that tradition itself. Often they will be, and it is strategic for a spiritual family to be identifying and developing potential new leaders. But there are also dangers of narrowness when no fresh bloodlines are introduced into a spiritual family. A closed-shop mentality can breed insularity, dullness, cultism and, at its worst, a xenophobic mistrust of the outsider. That would not be healthy for it, culturally, educationally or evangelically. Nor would it be healthy ecclesially. It is well to remember that the spiritual traditions of the Church do not belong to the individual ecclesial communities which live and nurture them; they belong to the whole Church, for the life and work of the Church. They are called to *communio*.

A community has responsibility, when choosing its leaders, to appoint people who are likely to be able to develop genuine spiritual authority within that community. Some will already be well along the way to having such authority; others will need to attend to building it. Just as important as their professional competencies will be their readiness to embrace and to nurture this path of the gospel in themselves, not as an outsider or as some kind of associate or critical friend, but as a member of the spiritual family. The broader spiritual family that has conduct of the school has a duty to set in place appropriate strategies and adequate resources for a leader's induction, formation, sustenance, and sense of belonging. If those are missing, then it will make it difficult for a person to assume the kind of authoritative leadership that the school community will require if that spiritual tradition is to continue to be at its heart.

MARIAN LEADERSHIP

Charismic leadership is essentially Marian. Just as the spiritual families of the Church are helpfully understood in essence as manifestations of the charismatic dimension of the Church, as expressions of its Marian principle,[18] so also is leadership within them helpfully conceptualised in Marian terms. Indeed, this must be its defining character. For it to be otherwise is to risk compromise of both its charismic integrity and charismic vitality.[19] To share leadership in a spiritual family of the Church – and specifically in a ministry of such a family, such as a school – is to have a fundamentally Marian disposition to one's leadership. Whatever other competencies may be required professionally, or whatever the particular responsibilities or

---

18 See the discussion in Chapter 3 concerning the nature of the Church's spiritual families in the context of the co-essential hierarchical and charismatic dimensions of the Church, and the Balthasarian conceptualising of this in terms of the Petrine/Marian principles of the Church. For a consideration of this strong theme in the theology of Von Balthasar, which in turn, influenced the thinking of Saint John Paul II on how he interpreted the growth of the new ecclesial movements, see: Leahy, B (2000) *op. cit.* pp.124-39.

19 For an interesting study which surfaced examples of how leadership in a charismic tradition can become usurped by other imperatives, see: Finn, CJ (2013), *An Exploration of how Identity Leaders Perceive and Institutionalise the Edmund Rice Charism*, a Doctoral Dissertation submitted in the Australian Catholic University. Finn looks at how criteria such as self-preservation and uncritical pursuit of success can distort a leader's priorities and attention away from the founding intuitions of the tradition.

tasks that a position description may name, it is first to be Marian. Mary is the archetype of the one who is alert to the movement of God's Spirit within her, who is vulnerably open to it and in dialogical communion with it, whose unequivocal and complete 'yes' allows Christ-life to become incarnate, and so it is she in whom and through whom God's life-giving and love-inducing mercy finds life in time and place, in people and events. Mary is holy. It is because of this that she is prophetic.[20] It is she who can proclaim with all authority and all humility: *Holy is God's name*.[21] Deeper than a leader's sense of belonging to one spiritual family or another, or to its works, and more profound than a leader's immersion in the distinctive spirituality of that community, however rich and fecund it may be, is this: to be Marian. Indeed, the degree to which Marian leadership is expected and valued in a community is likely to be a measure of how true it is to the graced intuitions of its founding.

What does it mean to be a Marian leader? There are various ways that Marian theology and tradition would allow us to frame responses to that question. We could go to the Lucan imagery of Mary in the Gospel and Acts, especially the Annunciation, the Visitation, and Pentecost; we could draw on the symbolism of the Johannine image of Mary as 'mother of Jesus' at Cana and Calvary; we could approach it from one or more of the perspectives offered by the array of titles and imagery that dogma, tradition, culture, art, and popular piety each give us. We could draw on the Marian theology of the early theologians or that of contemporary ones. It is an immense storehouse of insight and wisdom, built over centuries of experience of Christian discipleship, scholarship, and religious imagination. Each would have its own validity, offering us a perspective on what it is to be Marian. Indeed, individual spiritual families do draw on particular Marian imagery in ways that bring power and grace to their own traditions. But, to explore the Marian principle in leadership more generically, let us return first to the traditional iconography of the Ascension that was introduced in Chapter 3. It is a visual theology that allows us to ponder Mary as leader. She plays a leadership role in realising *missio Dei*, something that is sourced in her being found at the heart of the gathered disciples, arguably an even better phrase than 'First Disciple' which may imply some kind of precedence of position. It is to that which a school leader is called. It will draw that leader

---

20 For a conceptual exploration and empirical study of the interplay between the mystical and prophetic dimensions of Catholic school leadership, and its implications for leading in a contemporary ecclesial context, see the doctoral thesis-project of Professor David Hall FMS: Hall, DA (May, 2010), *Forming Australian Marist School Leaders in Uncertain Times: Friends of a Compelling God*, a doctoral dissertation submitted in the Catholic Theological Union, Chicago. Hall develops a method for contemporary Catholic school leadership, drawing specifically on the founding intuitions of Marist education.

21 From the *Magnificat*: Luke 1:49.

to the same personal holiness and alignment with Jesus Christ. Second, it will bring the person into communion – with God, with others, and with the cosmos – and position him or her as an agent of communion. Third, the leader will be a source of life and love, of the very mercy of God. And all this will be played out in a context of eschatological vision and hope, lived out in the here and now, in *ekklesia*. Let us step through all of that.

Before looking at Mary's place and role in this icon, let us focus on the cosmology of what we are contemplating. It is clearly concerned with heaven and earth, but there is something curious in the ways they are depicted. Mary and the Apostles are very much on earth – the solidity of the brown rock and the living green of the foliage ground them there. And, certainly, the ascended Christ is obviously in heaven above – regal, magisterial, celestial and Divine. But there is an incongruity with the angels in each place. Those attending Mary are, like her, haloed in heavenly gold. They are robed in celestial, pure white, with gilded wings. By contrast, the angels attending Christ are clothed – along with some red of humanity and royal purple – in the colours of the earth, in browns, greens and duller reds. Yet there are, simultaneously, threads of eternal blue among all four of them, both those on earth and those in heaven. What is going on? Put simply, it is that heaven has come to earth and earth has gone to heaven. This is an image of a redeemed cosmos, and a redeemed people. The reign of God is

---

22 This icon of the Ascension was written by Australian iconographer Michael Galovic in 2014. It is used as something of an ecclesial and spiritual *leitmotif* by the Marist Association of St Marcellin Champagnat, an Association of Christ's Faithful, in its aspiration to promote the Marian principle of the Church.

realised in earth and in heaven. This reality gives a perspective to all that follow: no longer does the mortality or finiteness of the earth prevail. The reign of God and the eternal vision it promises are possible, now, in time and place. It is an image, literally, of *enthusiasm*. It offers hope.

Turning to Mary, there are several important things to highlight, and implications to draw for what this could mean for spiritual leadership in a school context. First, and before all else, is her absolute alignment with the ascended Christ. The vertical axis of the icon, its balance and symmetry, pivot on this. Mary's significance and authority pivot on this. Her horizontal positioning among the Apostles – at their centre or, perhaps better, at their heart – is not derived in any way from her own importance. Her place and authority among them are defined primarily by her holiness – by her being one with Christ. This is signified not only by the vertical alignment, but also by the blueness of her inner garment and the radiating gold of her halo. Her hands are in the *orans* or praying gesture. It is her holiness that matters. She is the one who has said yes, an all-embracing and eternal yes to God. Her primacy in the icon is therefore one that has a spiritual source. Like the Apostles, she is on earth. She is one among them – not higher in any hierarchical sense. She attracts the attention or adulation of none of them; everything is in relation to Christ. Marian leadership in a school setting will witness to a similarly transparent yes, to prayer, and to contemplation. It will lead people to discover Jesus, because that it is what anchors the leadership of the school. The leader will first be contemplative, and Christocentrically contemplative – aspiring to be able to pray with St Paul that 'I live now, no not I, but Christ lives in me'.[23] It is only as a contemplative that he or she will be able to foster contemplative attitudes and practices in the culture of the school, or that part of the school for which he or she has responsibility. The leader will have credibility as a Christian disciple: centred on Jesus Christ and his gospel, on daily living of the pascal mystery of Christ, sustained by the interior joy and hope that this brings. It will radiate. It is only as a disciple that the leader can nurture discipleship. This is what every saint and founder has known; it is what was at the birth of every new spiritual tradition of the Church. Those who continue to lead communities of these traditions will be similarly characterised.

Second, the Church in all its giftedness and diversity is alive around Mary. The icon is an icon of the Church, of what it means to be an ecclesial community. Peter, clad richly to signify his role of pastoral leadership, is on her right, Paul the missionary on her left. John the beloved, clothed in the intimacy and passion of red, fully and humanly alive in Christ, is on her

---

23   Gal 2:20.

far left. James holds the Scriptures. All are constitutive of church. All have a place and find *communio* around Mary, yet each remains focused on Christ: the Petrine institutional/pastoral dimension of the Church; the Pauline apostolic/evangelising dimension; the Johannine mystical/sacramental dimension; and the Jacobean Scriptural/traditional dimension. A Marian leader will want to nurture all four of these elements of ecclesial life in the school community: to want them nourished by the Word of God; to have in the school's culture a valued and normal place for prayer and worship, and to be encouraging of contemplative practices. A Marian leader will also want these elements of ecclesial life to be integrated into the wider Church and its pastoral program; and for the school itself to be self-consciously motivated as an evangelising community. But for this to happen in the school, and to become embedded in the culture of the school, it will first need to be real in the leader.

Spiritual leadership in a Marian way will include the leader's creating of time and space for personal contemplation on his or her own life, and for lectio divina, prayer, celebration of the Sacraments, engagement in the pastoral life of the Church, and active participation in the work of evangelisation. While specialists in the school may bring their own expertise to how the school pursues each of these with staff and students, it is not so much a matter of delegation as it is of distributed leadership. Delegation and distribution are not the same, certainly when it comes to authentic spiritual leadership in a school. For example, a principal may justifiably and responsibly delegate entirely to the science department the teaching of physics, or to the finance office the management of the school's accounts, and may beg off on both because of lack of expertise. But when it comes to spiritual leadership, the principal does not pass responsibility over to others, but rather shares it with them collectively, dialogically and collaboratively. It becomes distributed across the school and expressed in its culture at all levels, and in myriad ways. It becomes a charismic culture.

A pointer to the third element is Mary's shoes. They are red, a colour with a range of meaning in iconography. It can carry a sense of full human life, of passion and compassion, of witness and martyrdom, of love and of indwelling divine life. Mary's simple shoes signify each of these to some extent. And they touch the brown earth. In these shoes, Mary brings God's mission to time and place. Christ at the top of the icon, the red shoes at its foot. Mary – in and through her personal alignment with Christ – brings the life-giving love of God to this community and this lived context. She personifies the mercy of God.[24] To understand Mary's role here, it is

---

24 Walter Kasper provides a comprehensive theological consideration of centrality of mercy in the

helpful to depart a little from the visual imagery of the icon and to delve into the Scriptural significance of mercy. The English word 'mercy' is a pale rendition of the Scriptural sense of mercy. There are two words in the Hebrew Scriptures that we translate by the word 'mercy'. The more common is *hesed* (דסח) – the faithful, covenanted, loving kindness of God. It is a rich concept. But it is the other word, less frequently used, that perhaps has more relevance in a consideration of Marian leadership: *rahamim* (סימחר). Its root is the same as *rehem* – the womb of the mother.[25] *Rahamim* (a plural noun) alludes to the maternity of God, the God who gives birth, who brings the lifeless to life, flesh to dry bones, the God who gathers, nurtures, forgives, animates, renews, who loves life into life.[26] This is what it is to be Marian. Like all of us, Mary is an image of the Divine. It is the Mary who sets out in haste, brimming with inner joy, to her cousin Elizabeth and, in their embrace, new life stirs. Her very being and her all her life magnify God. It is the Mary who gives birth in Bethlehem, to the wonder of outcast shepherds. It is the Mary who is with the dis-Spirited disciples in the Upper Room on the day of Pentecost as they become fired and enthused. This is the Mary who gives life in real-time to the God who is mission.

What would a leader imbued by *rahamim* look like in a school? It would be someone whose presence and action are life-giving and love-inducing. In this sense, it will be a missional leadership that transforms, a sharing in the action of God-who-is-mission. A culture is created where staff and students flourish – psycho-emotionally, academically, professionally, socially and spiritually. The signs of Christ-life abound because there is a focused effort to nurture, honour and reinforce it, signs such as those which Saint

---

life and work of the Church in: Kasper, W (2013), *Mercy, the Essence of the Gospel and the Key to Christian Life*, Paulist Press, New York. The final chapter of the book (Chapter 9) deals specifically with Mary as the personification of this mercy, especially her title of 'Mother of Mercy'. This book figured in a famous interchange between Cardinal Kasper and then-Cardinal Jorge Bergoglio at the Conclave that went on to elect the latter as Pope Francis. When Kasper showed his new book to Bergoglio, the future Pope was taken by its title: 'Mercy', he is reported to have said, 'that's the name of our God.'

25 For a critical introduction to the metaphor for God as mother, see Sister Elizabeth Johnson CSJ: Johnson, EA (2002), *She Who Is, The Mystery of God in Feminist Theological Discourse*, Herder and Herder, New York. For a consideration of the images of God as mercy in the Hebrew Scriptures, including that of 'mercy as womb-compassion', read Sister Veronica Lawson RSM: Lawson, VM (2015), *The Blessing of Mercy. Biblical Perspectives and Ecological Challenges*, Morning Star Publishing, Northcote VIC, pp. 19–42.

26 Some contemporary Marian theology, particularly from the fresher perspectives of feminist theology, has pushed back against images of Mary as an expression of the maternity of God or the feminine dimension of the Divine, and against the idealising or philosophising Mary in ways that compromise the cogency of who Miriam of Nazareth was, humanly and historically. Elizabeth Johnson argues this way. See: Johnson, EA (2003), *Truly Our Sister, A Theology of Mary in the Communion of Saints*, Continuum, New York. Johnson is critical of the masculine/feminine dualism she sees in the theology of Balthasar, and the kind of way Mary is typed in it in an almost depersonalised way in her ecclesiology. Although she still argues for Mary as a 'paradigmatic figure', like other saints, it is as a real human being who can be a companion for others on the journeys of faith. She plumbs, in particular, the scriptural richness that the references to Mary in the Gospels offer.

Paul names: compassion, kindness, forgiveness, patience, resilience, gratitude, hospitality, and joy. All these will be signs of the indwelling Spirit's irrupting. Again, it will be credibly personified in those who lead, how they relate, and how they build community.

Thus, to be Marian in leadership is to be someone whose authority is derived spiritually, and for whom the spiritual leadership of a community of mission precedes, underpins, and infuses all other aspects of leadership. It is to have a self-awareness, in all humility, of being *Theotokos*. It is not to be Marian in any idealised sense, let alone a devotional one. It is, rather, to be someone who can live and lead joyfully and prophetically in the spirit of Mary's *Magnificat,* singing it with her as a sister in faith, and doing so with such transparency that the faithfulness, mercy and justice of God are, in fact, magnified. It is this fidelity, mercy and justice of a distributed leadership through the school which gives life, and which incarnates *missio Dei*. The result is that Marian leaders will not only be people who lead authoritatively, but they will also lead inspirationally. Literally. They will be infused with God's Spirit, inspired. And the more they are, the more inspiring they will be for others.

LET THEM BE RECEIVED WITH THANKSGIVING: · AN ECCLESIAL RESPONSIBILITY

Whether these charisms be very remarkable or simple and widely diffused, they are to be received with thanksgiving and consolation since they are fitting and useful for the needs of the Church.[27]

In this simple sentence of *Lumen Gentium*, we read that the Church universally, and every local church, has been entrusted with a profound responsibility. Across the Church's ministry of Catholic education it is one that has been sometimes embraced wholeheartedly, sometimes accepted more reluctantly, and at other times misunderstood or just ignored. The 'reception' of charisms 'with thanksgiving and consolation', in order that the Church can be 'fit and ready' to be 'renewed and built up',[28] is not always seen as the responsibility of the whole community of the Church but, rather, something for individual spiritual families themselves to foster. When such whole-of-church welcome is weak or lacking, a causal factor is likely to be a failing of vision, understanding, or will in leadership, either or both within the spiritual family itself and/or in diocesan leadership. When spiritual families tend towards acting exclusively of the life of local churches,

---

27   *Lumen Gentium*, #12.
28   *Ibid*.

and frequently also of each other, it can be the result of failure of their leaders to be sufficiently broad and inclusive in their vision, understanding, and will. Such blinkeredness in leadership can, in turn, have its own roots, often found in local ecclesial history and culture. Whatever its causes, however, it is unlikely to be for the benefit of God's mission in the Church.

The pastors of the Church have three leadership responsibilities when it comes to spiritual families and movements. First is to discern the 'authenticity' of spiritual families as genuine promptings of the Spirit; second is to welcome and encourage their 'particularity' and 'novelty' without 'straitjacketing' them by any 'monolithic conformity'; and third, is to 'integrate' the spiritual families 'harmoniously' into communion with the pastoral program of the local Church.[29] Discernment, nurturance, integration. The opposite would be prejudice, imposition, and ostracism. The points along these spectra at which individual spiritual families find themselves in parishes, dioceses, or provinces of the Church are likely to be a mix of their own readiness to proceed in a spirit of mutuality, and also a function of how those in pastoral leadership understand their responsibilities. When it comes to Catholic education, such pastoral leadership is often exercised through Catholic education bureaucracies, sometimes quite large and labyrinthine. Bureaucrats do not always do multiformity and novelty easily or intuitively. This is not a comment on those people personally because experience suggests that they are typically quite committed and faith-filled women and men. It is, rather, a comment on bureaucracy *per se*. This can be problematic because, in the context of the discussion in Chapters 2 and 3, this is how the vivifying action of the Spirit mostly plays out. The Spirit is irruptive, and calls for agility and responsivity.

It is the way of bureaucracy that it tends naturally to inhabit the domain of management more easily than that of leadership. It can work well to ensure compliance, thoroughness, and diligence – all of which are important and necessary – but it can also make for uniformity, little taste for mould-breaking or, worse, torpor and sclerosis. In Western countries such as Australia, public funding has allowed for the growth of significant Catholic educational bureaucracies at diocesan and State/Territory levels. These have served and do serve Catholic schools professionally and comprehensively in the range of services, expertise, advocacy, cohesion, efficiencies, professional learning, specialist support, strategic planning, and the governance oversight they provide. The growing influence of these bureaucracies has strengthened, however, at the same time as the collapse in the numbers and moral authority of the religious institutes which had

---

29   Cf. *Iuvenescit Ecclesia*, #9, 17, 23.

previously administered most Catholic educational institutions, at least at the secondary and tertiary levels. It is increasingly common that the staff and even the leaders of Catholic education agencies and offices have had little or no direct personal knowledge of religious, either as teachers or as professional colleagues, or even in their wider participation in the Church. The growth of more inclusive and more broadly based spiritual families that have been a focus of this book, and the involvement of these groups in Catholic education, has been more of a latter-day phenomenon. There can also be a disconnection between such ecclesial communities and those who have the practical administration of Catholic education, at least on behalf of dioceses.

A litmus test for the collective influence of religious institutes and newer ecclesial communities in the Catholic education sector is to look at the proportion of Catholic schools they conduct. At the primary and tertiary levels, it is tiny, and at the secondary level it is a minority, albeit still sizable in some dioceses. But, taken overall, most Catholic schools in Australia are conducted by parishes (either individually or collectively) and dioceses, or through corporate entities established civilly by them.[30] Another test is to look at how the spiritual families of the Church participate structurally and collectively in the leadership of Catholic education at diocesan, provincial and national levels. Do they have a seat at the table in the ways that they might have done when such families were almost entirely religious institutes and their leaders were major superiors? More pointedly, do they want to have a seat at the wider Catholic education sector table? If the answer to the latter question tends towards the negative, then further enquiry into local ecclesial culture should be undertaken.

A challenge therefore presents itself. First it is a challenge for the episcopate, because most Catholic education councils, commissions, offices, and other entities derive their authority from individual bishops or a conference of bishops. They act on behalf of bishops. The bishops – both personally and through whatever agency it may be that they exercise their pastoral oversight of the Church – have the responsibility to welcome and encourage those spiritual families of proven spiritual and evangelical fecundity to share responsibility for the overall project of Catholic education, and to share this responsibility in all their diversity and distinctiveness, with due freedom to exercise this through governance and management.

The ecclesial vitality of dioceses will be advantaged if they can maximise the diversity of their spiritual gene pools. It is one of the great riches of the Catholic Church that such diversity exists, a catholicity that has often helped

---

30   Cf. D'Orsa and D'Orsa (2013) *op. cit.* p. 125.

it to avoid the insularity, stagnation, and narrowness that has marked some other Christian churches. For a local Catholic diocese or province, there will be not only structural ways for their enriching diversity to flourish, but there will also be an ecclesial culture that facilitates it, that seeks and fosters it, and that does not insist on the 'monolithic conformity' that *Evangelii Gaudium* warns can be debilitating for evangelising vitality.[31] This is not to suggest that a diocesan educational community cannot be vibrantly and effectively engaged in evangelisation without the involvement of the Church's spiritual families. Nor is it to infer any kind of simplistic dualism between the hierarchical and the charismatic because the institutional arms of the church need always to be led by men and women of personal charismic giftedness – by Marian leaders. Equally, the spiritual traditions of the Church will need their own canonical and civil structures and all that goes with that. It is, rather, only to acknowledge the added dimensions that tapping into the diversity and proven fruitfulness of the Church's spiritual traditions can potentially offer those in leadership of a local Church.

The bishop – again perhaps through his specialist agencies and offices – has the concomitant responsibility to ensure that such families are attending well to the spiritual formation and theological education of their members, and those who act on their behalf, so that they have readiness for mission engagement and mission leadership. It is always incumbent upon each bishop, and on conferences of bishops, to call the Church to unity. This means that there is an episcopal duty to try to proactively keep Catholic education authorities in the same educational tent. In practical terms, this will usually mean structural and cultural means to bring the schools of the various charismic traditions – both their governing bodies and their local principals – into an interdependence with diocesan and parochial schools. Such structures are likely to involve professional, financial and industrial connectedness and co-responsibility. So much will depend on the ecclesial culture, relationships, and mutual respect that can be built and maintained. Unity does not imply uniformity, but it does mean a living and defining sense of collaboration and cooperation, and of interdependence.

On the other hand, a dysfunctional ecclesial culture will be one where there develops a 'false juxtaposition' or a 'false contradistinction' between the hierarchical and the charismatic dimensions of the Church,[32] between the Petrine and the Marian. The discussion in Chapter 2 which explored not only their co-essentiality in the life and mission of the Church, but the primary place of the Marian, is pertinent here. The fundamental concern

---

31   *Evangelii Gaudium*, #131.
32   Cf. *Iuvenescit Ecclesia*, #7-8, 10.

for any local church should be its attentiveness to the movement of the Spirit in its existential realities. In the context of Catholic education, misconceived contradistinctions sometimes emerge at the local level when the responsibility for Catholic schools is in the hands both of diocesan/parochial authorities and authorities associated with other ecclesial communities. The former can see themselves aligned with the institutional arm of the Church, the latter with its spiritual families. It is antithetical to communion when any sense of dichotomy or competition develops between them, or any sense that the first group of schools constitutes the real local church while the others are content to have a looser Catholic connection.

One crucible where the two principles can interact is in the shaping of the identity of schools that may be governed by parishes or dioceses, but at the same time seek to draw on one of the spiritualities of the Church and to remain closely connected with one of its spiritual families. Indeed, the leadership and staff of these schools may be members of such families. This can be the case for an existing school that was founded or previously conducted by a religious institute, or perhaps where a diocese and a religious institute/PJP have partnered to establish a new school. Ideally, such situations create opportunity for the hierarchical and charismatic dimensions of the Church to manifest the mutuality and complementarity that should mark them, and which can grace the Church's realising of *missio Dei*. In many local Church situations that happens well, but sometimes historical and/or cultural factors work against complementarity and it flounders on the rocks of misunderstanding, mistrust, and power plays. Sometimes it is just muffled and stymied by bureaucracy. This is something for those in leadership both of spiritual families and dioceses to work on proactively and collaboratively, for the Church is richer when they do so.

Both culture and structures are important and, of course, they impact on each other. Leaders have a responsibility to shape and influence both. It will always be advantageous for those in leadership positions in the Church's ministry of Catholic education to have a piercing eye on the overall culture and structures of the Catholic education sector. This monitoring will enable assessment of the degree to which they work to be inclusive or exclusive, nurturing of the Church's spiritual traditions in education or dispiriting of them, and responsive to new paradigms of holiness and of ecclesial life rather than anchored by older ones. To heed recurring papal calls,[33] it falls to both bishops and leaders of spiritual families to ensure that the Church's charismic traditions in Catholic education do not retreat – either culturally

---

33   For example: *Novo Millennio Ineunte*, #22; *Evangelii Gaudium*, #131.

or structurally – to become the private domain of individual communities, but that they remain at the service of the whole Church, and healthily so. A measure of such health will be their involvement in the growth of the Catholic education sector, not just the governance and animation of existing schools. Another measure will be the participation of their leadership at the levels of dioceses and provinces of the Church. New models of overall leadership and animation of Catholic education need to remain conducive to this, as in the past they did when such leaders were almost entirely the major superiors of religious institutes. Within spiritual families themselves, especially those which have evolved from these education-oriented religious institutes, avenues for leadership and strategies for leadership succession need to continue to evolve to allow and encourage lay people to assume genuine roles as leaders, and for this leadership to have authority and authenticity.

AUTHORITY IN AND FOR MISSION

Leadership theories and complex conceptual frameworks can sometimes lose touch with the reality that leaders are people. Leadership within a charismic tradition, as leadership in any context, will certainly benefit from taking heed of the insights of scholarship and the evidence of research. It will be more effective if it is informed by the principles, orientations, and approaches that such learning reveals. Additionally, its practitioners will be better leaders if they expand their knowledge, taper their behaviours, and hone their skills by drawing on the wisdom of proven practice, for there is also a craft to leading well. It is a craft that can be learned and practised. Leaders need to be professional, contemporary and clever. But their authority will not be sourced in any of that, not primarily. It will be found, rather, in who they are. It was so for Jesus, and it will be for his disciples. It will be sourced spiritually, because the most fundamental aspect of their leadership is leadership of a community for mission that needs to be attuned and responsive to the Holy Spirit. The mission is God; God is the mission. God revealed in Jesus. At the core of their leadership, therefore, will be their personal Christian discipleship, something that can be nourished and lived by the very spirituality to which they are called to animate in others. Discipleship will immerse them in that spirituality so that they come to personify it. They will be able to take a lead in the realisation of *missio Dei* in their school situation because they will be alert to how *missio Dei* is unfolding in them personally.

Each spiritual family, and each ministry of that family such as a Catholic school, will benefit from a consideration of where, how, and in whom real authority is exercised. It can then pose critical questions about those who have to exercise leadership: Is it an essentially spiritual authority that defines the identity and mission of the community? Does such spiritual authority permeate all levels of the community or school, and those who share its leadership? For an individual school, there will be authority figures who need to be active at various levels. These will include, of course, the principal and leadership group who will be, it is to be hoped, adept at distributing their leadership throughout the school – in middle leaders, in classroom teachers, in sports coaches and co-curricular instructors, in counsellors and student mentors, in anyone who has influence over other members of the school community. There may also be others in governing and supporting roles – a school board, the members of an incorporated entity, and perhaps directors and team members that work at the level of the sponsoring spiritual family.

Wherever and however they find themselves in the leadership of a school, charismic leaders are people who are enthused. In God. Their leadership will help others to become similarly enthused, and will draw them into Christian community. This is more than simply exciting them, or galvanising their collective resolve, like Harry does in Shakespeare's *Henry V*. Excitement for a shared and noble purpose may ensue, and it would be well that it does, but enthusiasm is more than that. Enthusing leadership opens a way for the reign of God to capture the hearts, minds and hands of the school community.

7

KEEPING ENTHUSED

It shall come to pass in the latter days that I will pour out my spirit on all people, and your sons and daughters will prophesy, your elders will dream dreams, and your young ones will see visions

Joel 2:28

People. It all turns on people. Who they are, how they are, where they are, when they are, and why they are. It is not yesterday's people or tomorrow's. It is not in some nostalgic hankering for what was, or some idealised construct of what might be. It is not found in an educational philosophy or a theoretical framework. It is not in another time or place, but here and now: these people, this school, this culture, this state of church and society, this time. This is the who, the how, the where, the when and the why of Christlife seeking incarnation. To have vitality and integrity, a spiritual family will know that it comprises real people. It will want to help them attune to the movement of God's Spirit in the heart of that existential reality. These people will have their personal and professional stories, their families and relationships, their learning and ignorance and all their experiences of trust and betrayal, of joy and heartbreak, of fulfilment and failure, of life and loss. They will have their careers and their mortgages, their hopes for their children and their fears for them. They will live in a society and a culture, with all its trends, assumptions, influences, prejudices, and dominant ways of making meaning. And they will have their spiritual journeys threading through all of that.

The spiritual families of the Church, at their best, foster spiritualities that speak cogently to the real-life contexts of people. These spiritualities are paths of evangelical living that lead people to transform their understanding of those contexts, and to be transformed themselves in Christ. They provide language, symbols and rituals ways of associating and ways of serving the needs of others, all of which make sense in the real lives of the people. God abides in that time and place and in those people, each of them. God's Spirit seeks to irrupt there. It is from this premise that any thinking around how a spiritual family remains *enthused* needs to emerge.

As discussed in Chapter 2, the fate of many spiritual families is that they last in the life of the Church for between one and three centuries. They arise, often in response to a need in the Church for evangelical revitalisation or reform, and they remain active and fruitful for a time; but as contexts and needs change, they diminish and other groups with fresher insights and means emerge to take their places. People no longer find these older communities relevant and meaningful personally, communally, and/or ministerially. Some communities, however, do endure. They are those in which the spiritualities evolve and are recast to address new contexts and, through this recontextualising, continue to offer paths of Christian living – both to their own members and to the people with whom they minister. Their evolving spiritualities continue to bind them and mission these communities. Henri Nouwen has suggested that the basic principle of a person's fruitful following of a spiritual life is to be attentive to the movements of the Spirit, and to reflect on the experience of life in ways that lead the person to being reunited with God, with others and with one's truest self.[1] This is to live spiritually: in the Spirit and of the Spirit. Such an understanding could be extended to the collective spiritual life of an ecclesial community, one in which one of the Church's spiritual traditions abides. The challenge is the same: to remain attentive to the Spirit's movements – for the Spirit will be continually active and vivifying – and so to open perennially fresh ways for the Spirit to give evangelical life to each person, to each community and to their sharing in God's mission among those in need.

Many of the spiritual families that have been involved in Catholic education have their origins in apostolic religious institutes that were founded in the eighteenth and nineteenth centuries. Others have longer histories associated with monastic and mendicant orders, but ones which later adopted similar approaches to life and ministry as the apostolic foundations. Many of them, perhaps most of them, are now at critical phases in their stories. If history is predictive of what is likely to unfold, a high proportion of them will fade away.[2] They will go the way of the eighteenth-century monks of La Chaise-Dieu described in Chapter 2. Alternatively, those that rekindle their

---

1 See Nouwen (2010), *op. cit.* for an extensive consideration of this concept, and how Nouwen proposes that it is most effectively pursued. Some of this will inform the discussion below concerning formation.

2 For a sobering study concerning the life-cycles of organisations, with particular reference to religious institutes, see that by Liz Murphy. Dr Murphy looks at how a range of religious institutes in Ireland, which appear to be in terminal decline, are managing their transition to 'completion'. Most of these institutes were founded in the eighteenth and nineteenth centuries. Hers is not a study that finds much evidence for hoping there will be a continuity of a spirituality from which these institutes derived their ecclesial and spiritual identities. See: Murphy, E, *Organizational Demise: Survival, Terminal Decline, or Graceful Surrender of Apostolic Religious Congregations in Ireland Today*, PhD thesis submitted in the University of Ulster, September 2014.

vitality will be those that maintain the integrity of the evangelising impulses for which they were founded. They will do so by their recontextualising the *who* and *how* of their ways so that they will be relevant to the *where* and *when* of their changing contexts. But the *why* will always be the same. Indeed, it will be the degree to which this *why* – *missio Dei* – remains their heartbeat, that will be most critical for their vitality and integrity. For the *why* to be their heartbeat, they will need to give great care to the formation of their members. When done well, spiritual formation can be the major factor that helps them to continue to be vibrant schools of authentic Christian spirituality, of community, and of mission.

FORMATION, FORMATION, FORMATION

There is arguably no greater concern in contemporary Catholic education than the spiritual formation of those who are educators in Catholic schools.[3] If the fundamental purpose of Catholic schools is sourced in *missio Dei*, it is self-evident that those who most fruitfully lead those schools and educate in them will be people who not only understand this mission, but who are themselves consciously and intentionally caught up in it. The integrity of the school, and the passion with which it evangelises, will depend on this. This addresses the two primary issues in the shaping of any spiritual formation strategies: for whom is it intended and to what end? Ideally, all who have an educative role in Catholic schools – a wider group than only the professional teachers – share consciously in its missional purpose. Others who are less directly involved with students – such as members of a school's board, those in back-of-house administrative roles, or those in diocesan offices – also have a significant impact on a school's authenticity and vitality through the strategic decisions they make, the leaders they appoint, and the priorities they resource. Whatever their roles, people will be serving

---

3   For example, much of the Congregation for Catholic Education's 2007 document on the shared role of religious and lay people in Catholic schools is given over to the importance of spiritual formation, re-emphasising a theme that had marked every publication since *The Catholic School* in 1977. In Australia, in the same year, the Bishops of New South Wales and the Australian Capital Territory, in discussing the future for Catholic Schools, focused on the preparation of teachers. *A Renewing Passion* (the *instrumentum laboris* for the Church's 2015 International Catholic Education Congress) also emphasised this. The National Catholic Education Commission, at the prompting of the Australian Catholic Bishops Conference, has highlighted the critical importance of formation for mission in its 2017 document: *A Framework for Formation for Mission in Catholic Education*, NCEC, Sydney. Commentators such as Gerald Grace have long argued for the attention that needs to be given to what he has termed the building of 'spiritual capital' in schools, something that will happen through spiritual formation having at least the value and time of professional formation, as it did in previous generations for members of religious institutes. See: Grace (2010), *op. cit.* One of the three of Jill Gowdie's (2017), *op. cit.* 'fundamental criteria' for contemporary mission formation includes the need for it to be 'strategically effective', something echoed in two of her 'principles of implementation' – 'strategic alignment' and 'engagement of school leadership'.

the purpose of the school most effectively when they are motivated to do so from their own lived encounter with Christ,[4] and their own sense of belonging to Christ's disciples in an ecclesial community. Individual dioceses, other Catholic education authorities, professional associations and Catholic peak bodies have become quite committed to the spiritual formation of these people. Significant resourcing and expertise have been built.

'Formation' is an unusual term in everyday English, at least in the way it is used in Church parlance, and so it can be a misunderstood one. To those unfamiliar with the way the word is used, it may suggest a passive process, something that happens to an object or person as a consequence of circumstance, as in 'sedimentary rock formation' or 'character formation'. For some people, it evokes a sense of a type of mysteriously religious experience or process that takes place behind closed doors and which only initiates can either undertake or understand. Secret church business. Other programs in which teachers might engage to build their capacity as Catholic educators can be usually categorised without a second thought as 'professional learning', but when it comes to anything religious or spiritual then the descriptor 'formation' is employed. In the Latin languages – such as Italian, French and Spanish – from which the term has been sourced, it is a more normal word; it simply means training or skilling for a particular task or job. It does not attract the same mystique that Anglophones often give it, even when the adjective 'spiritual' is attached to it.

In the same way that the spiritualities of the Church gathered momentum from their facility to connect cogently with the immediacy of the lived experience of people, so formation within those traditions is best conceived when it is rooted in people's ordinary life experience. Little is achieved through language, concepts, story, ritual, accompaniment, symbol, art, music or other resources and programs if they are framed in a hermeneutic that is disconnected from how people make their meaning. Spiritual formation needs to work for people in the normal ways they go about their to day-to-day lives in families and homes, in the opportunities they can have for prayer and worship, in their work and their professional lives, in the ways they have to gather, in when and by what means they read and discuss, and so on.[5] It should also be approached holistically.[6] Part of the engagement of spiritual

---

4   Cf. *Deus Caritas Est*, #1. Benedict XVI begins his Encyclical with this oft-quoted sentence: 'Being Christian is not the result of an ethical choice or a lofty idea, but the encounter with an event, a person, which gives life a new horizon and a decisive direction.' He returns a number of times in the encyclical to the theme of this fundamental and personal encounter.

5   Sicari, *op. cit.*, emphasises this point in the context of Carmelite formation for people who are seeking to live a Carmelite spirituality as lay people (pp. 297ff).

6   In their guidelines for the formation of lay ecclesial ministers, the US Catholic Bishops draw on the same principles as those used in the Church for the formation for clergy, naming the four areas that

formation with the lived reality of adults is the integration with other dimensions of who they are as human beings and as professionals. Their attentiveness to God's Spirit in their lives, in the lives of others and in the world, is not something removed from who they are psycho-emotionally, intellectually, relationally or physically, nor is it apart from their professional involvements.[7] Integrated spiritual formation will be concerned with all a person is.

While there is nothing secret or abstruse about the concept of spiritual formation, nothing that should be understood as anything other than entirely human and healthy, there is still merit in approaching it as more than just another element of professional learning or professional development. This is because it is more than simple skill acquisition, even though there are skills to learn, and disciplines to develop. Spiritual formation is more than knowing more and understanding better, even in the area of theological literacy. But there is, nonetheless, knowledge and understanding to build, especially in theology. From this perspective, focused learning is indeed part of formation.[8] The very word *disciplus* in Latin means learner.[9] And when such learning involves adults, then principles of adult learning should be followed. Jesus, who only taught adults, knew about such principles: he engaged people where they were and in terms that were relevant to their life-situations; he was invitational, dialogical, respectful; but he was also intentional and ultimately transformational. Spiritual formation approaches that employ such principles have become common in Catholic education and in church contexts more generally.[10]

---

need to be included and integrated: human, spiritual, intellectual and pastoral. Their summary of the elements and methods that apply to each area offers a useful précis for an integral formation for anyone in ministry. See: USCCB (2015), *Co-workers in the Vineyard of the Lord. A Resource for Guiding Lay Ecclesial Ministry,* USCCB, Washington DC, pp. 33–53.

7   Masters of the spiritual life such as Henri Nouwen have built their approach to spiritual formation on multi-disciplinary scholarship. Gowdie (2017), *op. cit.,* from her survey of various approaches to understanding spiritual formation, also develops strategies sourced in a range of perspectives of human development. Other commentators on spiritual formation of teachers and also students critique theories of learning, identity and faith development such as those of Erikson, Piaget and Fowler. See, for example, Astley (2018), *op. cit.* and Wolfe, A (2018), 'Journeys of Faith, 'Multi-logue' Narratives, and Faith Formation in Schools', in Stuart-Buttle and Shortt, *op. cit.*

8   Many writers on spiritual formation like to emphasise its learning or educative dimension. Henri Nouwen, for example, while understanding the spiritual life and spiritual formation in terms of the 'heart' (in the Biblical sense of body, soul and spirit) and encounter with Christ, speaks of the 'discipline' that is required to deepen one's spiritual life. For Nouwen, the spiritual life is a 'journey inwards' and a reciprocal 'journey outwards'. The former requires the discipline of solitude, silence, prayer, meditation, contemplation, and attentiveness to the movements of one's own heart; the latter requires the discipline of care, compassion, witness, outreach, healing, accountability, and attentiveness to the movements of others' hearts. Cf. Nouwen (1975; 2010), *op. cit.* See also: Roebben, B (2016), *Theology Made in Dignity,* Peeters, Leuven.

9   For a discussion of this concept, see: Astley, J (2018), 'The Naming of Parts: Faith, Formation, Development and Education', in Stuart-Buttle and Shortt, *op. cit.*

10   See, for example: the 'Transforming Encounters' or Emmaus-inspired methodology used in the 'Catching Fire' program used by the Brisbane Catholic Education Office, described by

It is, nonetheless, more than just learning; spiritual formation is concerned with conversion. And conversion is about turning to the gospel. Spiritual formation in a Christian context ultimately leads to a deepening of personal discipleship of Jesus Christ, to a sense of belonging and critical engagement ecclesially, and to being impelled from both to share actively in God who is mission.[11] It is here that the spiritual traditions of the Church have much to offer, perhaps have most to offer. It is because they inspire and attract. They ground it. It is what they can do best, when they are at their best. Spiritual traditions can present a doable discipleship, an inspirational and accessible way of being Christian, a space where people feel at home and where there is a prevailing style of ministry that they feel can be their own. It is in spiritual formation that all of this happens most keenly: in programs and courses, in spiritual direction and accompaniment, in gatherings and companionship, in pilgrimages and rituals, in stories and heroes, in reading and approaches to praying, and in the whole range of other wisdom and opportunity that a spiritual family may have to offer. Spiritual traditions will profit, of course, from drawing on the scholarship and wisdom of other masters of the spiritual life; they will benefit if they adopt and adapt proven methodologies and contemporary approaches; and it is incumbent on them that they heed the discerned priorities of the Church universally and locally, and work in collaborative ways with the wider Church community. However, their x-factor will be, or should be, in the inspirational and attractional dimension they bring. People connect intuitively, humanly. It is what gave rise to these spiritualities in the first place.

This attraction is not spin or smart marketing. It is the Spirit at work, incarnating the reign of God in culture – in story, in place, in human wisdom, in ways of acting, in a community, in a work. For many teachers and other staff, especially younger ones, their encountering of this culture will be a door that leads them to a spiritual awakening or a spiritual deepening. It will be a doorway through which they find themselves walking, because it opens from where they are standing.

Jill Gowdie in (2017), *Stirring the Soul of Catholic Education: Formation for Mission,* Vaughan Publishing, Mulgrave, VIC. For examples of other-than-Catholic contexts, see: Sargent, W (2015), *Post-Modern Faith Formation: Christian Education and the Emerging Church,* Pickwick Publications, Eugene, OR; Roberto, J (2015), *Reimagining Faith Formation for the 21st Century,* Lifelong Faith Publications, Naugatuck, CT. Both emphasise the importance of working with the lived reality of people.

11   The fostering of Christian discipleship is the focus suggested by the NCEC's formation framework, something it proposes in a hexagonal way, rather than the tridimensional understanding that has been the recurring theme of this book and which frames the discussion of this chapter. The framework of NCEC is not inconsistent with the content presented here, but expands the third element of mission into preaching, witnessing and serving. Its five elements are: *koinonia* (living a spirituality of communion), *leiturgia* (engaging in worship), *kerygma* (preaching Christ), *martyria* (witnessing to Christ), and *diakonia* (serving Christ). The document supporting the framework also emphasises the importance of 'formation of the heart' and an individual's personal encounter with Christ. Cf. NCEC, *op. cit.,* 2017, p. 17.

There are three doors. People will be attracted initially to enter a spiritual family through one of them. As short-hand labelling, let us call them the ministry/professional door, the community/belonging door, and the personal faith/mystery door. Some people will intuitively connect first with the ministry style of a school for its educational priorities and approach, its distinctive pedagogy and accumulated expertise, its ways of relating and its pastoral care, its sense of innovation, its emphases on addressing particular needs, and other cultural attributes. They will intuitively feel that this is the kind of school in which they can flourish professionally and work productively. They may or may not be aware of the deeper rationale or sense of gospel-mission as they first enter, but what they do see and feel sits well with them. The second door will attract people who feel a strong sense of belonging and community among the faculty and students and perhaps more widely in the school. They intuitively feel at home and among people with whom they relate easily. They feel they can be themselves with these people. They identify readily with the school community, and are soon comfortable when speaking of it in the first-person plural. Experience suggests that these two doors, the ministry door and the community door, will be the most commonly used ones.

The third door, that which gives a glimpse into a personal spirituality and draws people interiorly into the mystery of God, will also be initially attractive to some, perhaps to those who have been more actively or consciously engaged at times in their lives in a quest to touch into the deeper meaning of their lives, whether or not this has been specifically through a religious faith framework. These people may be more alert to the distinctive spirituality that is alive in the school or, more pointedly, in members of the school community. They will feel drawn to it. Its language, its emphases, its style, its prayer and worship, its wisdom figures, its integrity – these will make sense to them. and may trigger a desire to learn more, to go more deeply.

A person's coming at least a little way through one of these doors tends to take place without much intentional effort from anyone. People just do it intuitively. Indeed, it is helpful when it happens this way. Purposeful spiritual formation needs, however, to follow on. People cannot be left at the door without any invitation to come further into the house, into a deeper engagement with the spiritual family that is at the heart of the way the school is sharing in God's mission. This invitation to go more deeply unfolds through reflection and dialogue, accompaniment and inspiration. It is not helpfully a one-way thing, some kind of inductive or pre-packaged approach on the part of the spiritual family, but one of genuine engagement that begins with where and who a person is. When it is invitational and inspirational rather than mandated and imposed, and dialogical rather than didactic, it aligns more closely to the approach of Jesus who always worked in the context of the people. He began where and how he met them. The inviting to go more deeply will also be a source of vitality and recontextualising for the spiritual family itself. Some writers on spiritual formation describe this movement as 'narthical', a reference to the narthex of a church.[12] People who find themselves drawn through the outer doors, are engaged right there, as adults with their own life stories, for that is where they are and who they are. There are reasons why they are not already in the nave with the worshipping community. Perhaps the encounter will lead them further in, and will draw them to the other open doors.

If a spiritual family, either collectively or in the specific context of one of its schools, is content to leave people at the edges, it is not only being negligent with the spiritual giftedness with which it has been entrusted by the Church, but it is also likely to be a community whose charismic vitality and viability could be at risk. Every family needs to renew and revitalise, and one of the principal ways to achieve this is through the comprehensive and relevant spiritual formation that it offers. It will have its narthical aspects, but it will also have rich and proven ways for others to be nurtured and sustained more deeply in their ongoing personal relationship with Christ, ways for community to be bonded and enlivened, and ever-fresh methodologies for engaging in the work of evangelisation. Discipleship is life-long. It will have its twists and turns, its ups and downs, its times of great joy and its times of disenchantment, for that is the way that life typically unfolds. Formation, therefore, is likely to be iterative and multi-faceted.[13] Like the nature of the spiritual family itself – the nature, indeed, of the Church itself as reflective of the triune God[14] – it will be tridimensional.

---

12 The phrase was coined by Bert Roebben in reference to religious education, and promotes the value of respectful adult dialogue, in a not dissimilar way to the emphases of the post-critical dialogue school advocated in the Enhancing Catholic Schools Identity Project. 'Narthical learning' parallels the 'Courtyard of the Gentiles' concept mentioned in Chapter 2, and favoured by Pope Benedict XVI. See: Roebben, B (2009) *Seeking Sense in the City: Perspectives on European Religious Education,* LIT Verlag, Berlin; (2018), *op. cit.* Richard Rymarz (2018), *op. cit.* has also supported the concept based on his research of younger teachers (under 30 years of age) in Catholic schools. Rymarz found that, while their personal connection to Church was minimal outside their professional responsibilities and their sense of personal faith was variously expressed, they were happy to be engaged in the religious activity of the school, and quite supportive of its purposes. This openness, argues Rymarz, is reason to 'leave the door open'.

13 Spiritual masters, from the medieval mystics to contemporary spiritual writers, frequently address this reality, situating a person's spiritual journey in everything else that is transpiring in a person's life, interiorly and exteriorly. See Rolheiser and Nouwen, *op. cit.* for accessible descriptions of this and for links to other writers. This has led to the development of formation strategies that are rooted contextually in people's actual lives. See Gowdie, *op. cit.* (Chapters 8-10) for how the Archdiocese of Brisbane has developed an approach that is 'personally meaningful', 'ecclesially faithful', and 'strategically effective', one that seeks to be both person-centred and theologically-based.

14 For a useful opening up of this see Leahy (*op. cit.* 2000, pp. 33-66) who explores the 'Trinitarian logic' of God – as mystery, communion and mission – at the heart of the ecclesiology of Balthasar. In his later study of ecclesial movements and communities within the Church (2011), *op. cit.* he points to the same essential ecclesial nature, as an icon of the Trinity.

It will be concerned with assisting people to encounter personally the indwelling and unfathomable mystery of God, accompanying them in the most challenging of all journeys – the personal inner journey – and helping them to live resonantly with God's Spirit. Second, it will be take place communally, in and through the graced giftedness of a living community of faith. Third, it will take them out to 'the least of these brothers and sisters of mine',[15] and to do so to bring joy, justice, peace and mercy.

Sensitive, engaging, respectful, integrated and inspiring spiritual formation will touch and move hearts, by bringing people into touch with their own hearts and the hearts of others.[16] Formation is about the heart.[17] It is about the full heart – mind, body, spirit. It can, in this concern with fullness of heart, bring people to see what each of the three doors can open for them.[18] God revealed in Christ. The spiritualities of the Church, and the families in which they abide, have an enormous responsibility when it comes to formation. An important factor in their assuring good formation will be their continuing to nurture people who can hold and pass on the accumulated wisdom of their particular spiritual family. In this way spiritual families are more likely to remain communities defined by their founding evangelising impulses. Let us revisit the three loci for discipleship in which they need to nurture Christian discipleship.

AS SCHOOLS OF HOLINESS, COMMUNITY, AND MISSION

Membership of a spiritual family should provide both inspiration and means by which people can deepen their personal encounter with the mystery of God, live more communally and ecclesially, and serve in love with purpose and connection. It is for this that the Spirit has called spiritual families into life in the Church. They show what Christian discipleship can look like; they teach it. So also, other people who serve in or are served by a ministry with which a spiritual family is involved, such as a Catholic school, should have the opportunity to find inspiration and accessible pathways to come into touch with God in their lives, to have a sense of Christian community, and to nurture reason and means for their bringing about the reign of God in their spheres of influence. The invitation to these people,

---

15 Matthew's theme of discipleship culminates in Chapter 25 – spiritual formation.
16 Again, this is the emphasis of Henri Nouwen.
17 This is the emphasis of the extensive treatment of formation in Congregation for Catholic Education (2007), *Educating Together in Catholic Schools*. It is something it links with the Encyclical of Benedict XVI, *Deus Caritas Est*, #31, which is also where our discussion began in Chapter 1.
18 Gowdie prefers the word 'levers', and uses them in a similar way. Her first three levers for formation for mission are calling/vocation, community and service. To these she adds two others, which also align with the above discussion: that there are individual entry points, and that it depends on reflective praxis.

mediated in ways they understand, is for each to be become a *disciplus*, a learner. Through that which they see, think on, touch, feel and breathe, they learn something of holiness, of community, and of mission. It is a sharp but essential line of self-reflection for any spiritual family, ecclesial community, or any individual ministry such as a school, to ask if people's experience of it in this place or this organisation is one that leads people to personal and communal encounter with Jesus Christ. Or, alternatively, are people left figuratively more in the narthex, with feel-good but fairly shallow experiences of the numinous? Do they have a sense of welcome, inclusion and belonging but little appreciation of being part of a community of faith or a community of mission?

Saint Augustine's concept that the restless human heart can only find peace by finding God is one way of expressing the fundamental principle of Christian anthropology, which is that it is in, for, from and towards God that human life is fulfilled.[19] Other masters of the spiritual life also tend to use verbs that capture something deeply seated at the core of the human psyche: to yearn, to long for, to thirst, to pine, to ache, to hunger, to burn.[20] For Augustine it was all about desire, and what people did with that desire. It is this driving desire that permeates his *Confessions* and his understanding of what it means to be human: 'Let me know myself; let me know you,' he prays.[21] The human desire for connection, communion, and ultimately for love is one that Augustine and other spiritual guides recognised as a manifestation of their Divine make-up. Knowing God and knowing oneself were not only inextricably bound for Augustine, but he felt a force that urged towards that knowing. The Latin original of his frequently quoted line is perhaps stronger than its usual English translation: *Fecisti nos ad te, Domine, et inquietum est cor nostrum donec requiescat in te.* The Latin preposition '*ad*' has a sense of direction, of momentum, of wanting to head towards, that the English 'for' may not have. It also neatly counterpoints the '*in*': '*ad te ... in te*'. The spiritualities of the Church offer wisdom and facility for this restlessness to be quieted, and this journey to be undertaken.

Those people who are attracted to a spiritual family or tradition through the 'mystery' or 'faith' doorway, can be those who may be more ready or open to a praxis around how a particular spirituality may help to satisfy their innate restlessness of heart, and assist them to interpret, integrate and transform their human desire. Such readiness or openness needs to be engaged, and the wisdom and accompaniment of the spiritual guides

---

19 This is also the anthropological underpinning of the National Catholic Education Commission's approach to formation for mission in Catholic schools. Cf. NCEC (2017), *op. cit.*, p.8.
20 See also the *Catechism of the Catholic Church*, #27.
21 Perhaps the succinct Latin original has more poetic power: *noverim me, noverim te.*

of the family offered to them. Some part of the journey is likely to play out through intuition and osmosis, and well that it does, but the efficacy of a spirituality is that it can intentionally and compellingly offer language, insight, wisdom and guidance. And so it should. It can teach people to pray, to contemplate, and to encounter Christ in scripture, sacrament, and daily life. And so it should. It can lead them to fall in love with Christ, time and again, as a child, as a young adult, as a person in middle years and in senior years. And so it should. It will articulate naturally into ongoing theological education and deeper spiritual formation. And so it should.

A spirituality that is being lived in ways that continue to connect with immediacy and relevance to the context of people's lives will attract through this 'mystery' door not only people who are more alert to their spiritual yearnings, but also those who may not yet name their longings in this way. But without strategies and resourcing to invite such people further in and to bring their lives and the gospel into conscious dialogue, it is likely that they may be left in the narthex – in their wonder but somewhat removed from the transformative possibility of encounter with Jesus Christ and his gospel. Signs and wonders, which can be the mark of rich liturgy or powerful prayer experiences, can also mislead people into shallowness and even superstition. It may take them little further than an emotional engagement. This can be a risk in the event culture, which can be attractive to young people, in particular. A school needs to be alert to this, asking itself if it is offering more than a 'bread and circuses' entertainment or diversion but rather a purposeful invitation to people – both students and staff – to understand their inner lives more deeply. A spiritual family's vitality and future will be at risk if it has weakened in its willingness, agility, or even capacity to be a genuine school of holiness and life-long conversion for people at all stages of life's journey.

Informed by a Catholic anthropology, Catholic schools are also intensely communal. They are called to be such. A recurring theme of the Church's hopes for Catholic schools is that they be places defined by community, by interdependence, and by a spirituality of communion. In contrast to the insidious individualism that has been promoted in Western culture from early modern times, and indeed by some strands of Western Christianity, a Catholic school has a mandate to practise and to foster community, at all levels. This will be done not only in its social and cultural ways of being and acting, but also through its approaches to learning and teaching, to prayer and worship, and to its range of co-curricular pursuits. A school which draws consciously on one of the Church's spiritualities is likely to have well-honed traditions for going about this. Indeed, such schools are often known and experienced as places of quite strong community.[22] Their climate, their hospitality, their sense of inclusion, and their capacity to engender bonding and belonging, are frequently among their strongest drawcards. Because of this, it is the 'community' doorway to which many students and faculty can be initially most attracted. They want to belong; they want to become members of this community. The question therefore emerges: what underpins the community in practice?. To what extent does it have a conscious sense of being a Christian community, a community of faith? The degree to which a positive answer can be given is likely to determine the extent to which someone attracted through the community door is likely to be schooled in what it means to live communally and ecclesially as a Christian.[23]

It is well for a spiritual family (and equally an individual school community associated with it) to reflect on the defining characteristics of the community that it is affirming. Strength of bonding or of owned identity are not of themselves measures of evangelical authenticity. While Saint Paul speaks of unity and complementarity,[24] they are in the context of other traits: forgiveness, tolerance, compassion, humility, kindness, gentleness, patience, gratitude, a permeating love, and, critically, where Jesus Christ abides deeply and explicitly, and is worshipped joyfully.[25] 'Let the word of Christ dwell in you richly.'[26] These Pauline attributes always emanate from personal encounter with Christ. Strength of community can, alternatively, lead to insularity, elitism, exclusion, even to prejudice and fear. Such developments are obviously not fruits of God's Spirit. A genuinely Christian community will not only be witnessing to the inverse of these, but it will be schooling its members that way – through both experience and teaching.

Insularity and exclusivity are lurking dangers for charismic communities as they are for any human communities. When a group has a compelling narrative and binding identity it can carry a risk of drifting towards some sense of being removed, privileged, and even self-serving. Cultism would be not very much further down that path. Purpose and identity are critically important for any culture, but they can also develop a degree of toxicity. In the context of *ekklesia*, a single Christian community is, however, a

---

22 The social capital of Christian school communities has been recurringly found to be a significant factor in their integrity and effectiveness. Ann Casson, for example, in the 'Ten Leading Schools Project', a study of how schools contributed to the spiritual development of students and staff, found that a 'sense of belonging' was a key factor, something she detailed as being part of an inclusive, worshipping, Christian community. See: Casson, A (2018), 'A Sense of Belonging: Spiritual Development in Christian-Ethos Schools', in Stuart-Buttle and Shortt, *op. cit.*

23 Cf. *ibid.* An important element in the 'sense of belonging' above was the explicitly spiritual and liturgical expression of it.

24 Cf. Rom 12:3-8; 1 Cor 12:12-27.

25 Cf. Col 3:12-17.

26 Col 3:16.

manifestation of the entire Church and takes both its identity and its purpose from it. It cannot conceive of itself apart from the Church, or the mission of God within the Church. It will seek to include, to reach out, both to other ecclesial communities and to vulnerable people in need and on the margins. It will be enriched and enlivened, not threatened or intruded upon, by 'the other'. It will even be emboldened by its encounter with the other, ready, like Jesus, to reach beyond social borders and to challenge stereotypes. Among the 'other ecclesial communities' are included, of course, those associated with other spiritual traditions of the Church. Saint Paul's counsel is that any hint of rivalry or elitism should be absent, but rather a sense of being part of the one building that is Christ.[27] Wherever spiritual families, and their schools, have developed a culture of what has been termed a 'communion of charisms', the healthier the local Church will be.[28]

Another challenge, and often a bigger one, is for a spiritual family to stay connected across its individual communities. People can identify strongly with the immediate community of their school or institution but have a more tenuous relationship with other communities of a particular spiritual tradition. This one challenge that every spiritual family needs to acknowledge and address. It may be the most critical challenge today facing spiritual families, both those that have emerged from religious institutes as well as those associated with newer ecclesial movements. Their future viability and integrity will be at risk if they are not able to achieve this. Narrow and closed gene pools are not only fatal biologically, but also spiritually and ecclesially. Without a lived sense of community, a spiritual tradition has no future. Even a Christian spirituality with a grand tradition, with libraries of written wisdom or centuries of history, risks becoming a spiritual house of cards if there is not a living, praying, worshipping community of Christian disciples. Spiritualities live in spiritual families of the Church, or they no longer live.

Such a living, breathing community first requires that the basics of a human community are functioning: people need to know one another, and well. They need to identify with something of the contexts of other places where the spiritual family lives and ministers, and so have some sense of co-

---

27 Cf. 1 Cor 3:3-23.
28 In her presidential address to the 2017 conference for the Leadership Conference of Religious Women in the United States, Sister Mary Pellegrino CSJ spoke of the growing sense of a 'communion of charisms' in the US Church, and the imperative for religious institutes to work co-operatively and supportively, especially with the 159 'emerging lay movements and communities of consecrated life' in that country. Pellegrino, M, 'The Future Enters Us Long Before it Happens: Opening Space for an Emerging Narrative of Communion', Presidential Address at the Annual Assembly of the Leadership Conference of Religious Women, Orlando FL, 10 August 2017. Available from the Conference's website: https://lcwr.org.

responsibility for the life and mission of the family more broadly than just their own school or ministry. In the past, when a community may have been mainly comprised of members of a religious institute or an administrative unit of such an institute, people came to know each other much more easily. They shared similar formation journeys through the same institutions, they were likely to have been assigned to a number of common schools and ministries during their lives. As they crossed paths with others, they regularly gathered, they told and retold stories, and they had their common heroes and folklore. As spiritual families have become broader and more inclusive, their predominantly lay membership can be inevitably more anchored, simply as a function of how people live.

Even in an era of increased mobility and global shrinkage, many people have family and financial ties to a geographical place. While spiritual families and ecclesial movements today have the advantage of being more representative in their ecclesiality – by including all states of life, and being mainly lay – they need to address the question of how to maintain a sense of community across their whole organisation. Strategies such as conferences, seminars, pilgrimages, formation programs, effective communication plans, retreats, itinerant support teams, options in social media, journals and news sharing, frequent dissemination of spiritual resources, online daily prayer and reading, and inclusive strategic planning, are all likely to be part of how a spiritual family addresses this imperative for building knowledge of one another, and a wider sense of belonging.

The fostering of a functioning community of faith can also be problematic at the local level, particularly when many people's identification with a spiritual family is principally through their professional lives or their employment. This is typically the case with schools. There are often real issues concerning how, when and where people can associate spiritually, can gather as spiritual companions of one another, can pray together, and can share faith experience and mission perspectives – and can do so not simply as part of their employment but as fellow disciples. How is such a group of disciples best led and supported? How does, for example, a school principal who is the employer, or the agent of the employing authority, exercise a Marian style of leadership, or develop a sense of being a fellow disciple, with members of staff whom he or she is professionally overseeing? How do people who work in different parts of a school, at different hours, and who socially may be in different cliques, come together with sufficient frequency, depth of encounter, or even willingness, to be a genuine community of faith? How do the resources, organisation and the culture of a school, or a network of schools, nurture and encourage the building of such a community?

The third doorway into a spiritual family – that of mission – also brings its opportunities and challenges. A teacher, for example, may be intuitively attracted to the pedagogical practices or pastoral style of a school in a particular tradition. It is likely there will be a language for that – the named characteristics, emphases, or touchstones of the tradition – and which: The teacher may learn this language as part of an induction; the same language may be embedded in school policy documents or appear on walls around the campus. All of these may be ritualised and reinforced by how members of the school community are formally honoured. School leaders who are smart cultural leaders will be adept at creating ways to do such things. Language, ritual, and educational approach are constitutive of the charismic culture that the spiritual family has developed. At its most authentic, this culture will not only be evangelical in its style, but will also be evangelising in its intentionality. It will bring the gospel alive for people. Again, there is 'narthical learning' that can take place. Or not. The challenge is for teachers and students to be inspired and have the means to go more deeply into the missional purpose of the school. This may well lead to a deeper engagement with the spiritual family itself.

The same twin question permeates all three dimensions: what is being taught and what is being learnt? It is a question by which the individual institution or the wider group is called to reflect continually: to what degree is it a genuine school of Christian holiness, community, and mission? One measure of this is likely to be found in the age profile of the membership of those who consciously identify with the spiritual family. Is the family being rejuvenated? Who is seeking to join and to belong to it, and how? Who are the people who most readily use the first-persons when they speak of the ecclesial community in which they find themselves? If the younger members of the group are not significant among those who do, then warning lights should be flashing. In the context of the school, for example, are younger teachers being attracted not only to one or other of the doorways, but are they seeking to enter right in and, in doing so, be invited through the other doors?

Since it is the younger teachers who are more likely to be creatures of the culture of the present time, they can offer a helpful barometer for taking a reading on how effectively a spirituality is or is not alert to its cultural contexts, and with what agility and relevance it is engaging with them. Not all spiritual traditions were begun by relatively young men and women but many were. Jesus himself is presented this way, particularly in the Synoptic Gospels. It is not surprising. While there is often a treasury of wisdom and perspective in age, there is connectivity and agility in youth.

They represent the *who*, the *where* and the *when* of God seeking incarnation today, and they are likely to be able to keep a spiritual tradition alert to the *how*. An investment in the community from across the generations is likely to be healthy.

Christian discipleship is the means and end of all of this, a discipleship that is expressed communally and lived out missionally.

8

CONCLUSION

Woe betide me if I do not proclaim the Gospel

1 Cor. 9:16

There is something of an *apologia pro vita sua* in the middle of Saint Paul's first letter to the Corinthians.[1] We can only conjecture as to all that could have been playing out in the Church of Corinth that prompted Paul to write what he did, but we do know from Acts that he knew the members of this nascent Christian community well, having helped them to establish it and having lived with them for the best part of two years.[2] From the standpoint of another culture and a time two thousand years removed, they present as a quite fractious, petty, inconstant and even licentious group of people. Paul certainly seems to have had some trouble getting traction for 'The Way' among all of them. Perhaps, in the context of their port-city Hellenic culture and the yet-to-be-paved path of Christianity, their attitudes can be more easily understood, but there is no doubting that Paul had his hands full with Corinth. As he also did also in Galatia, Ephesus, Colossae and elsewhere. Yet these people were 'saints' for Paul, and he treasured great hope for them. In this Letter, he calls the Corinthians to unity and to the big picture – the resurrection of Christ and all that that implied. He calls them to truth and to love, and powerfully so. But let us pause for moment on Chapter 9, because Paul's citing of his own approach to evangelisation here is something that can be heeded by a church of any time and place.

Paul was a recontextualiser. Although by birth and life-commitment a Jew,[3] Paul is ready to become 'all things to all people' – to the Jews a Jew,

---

1 1 Cor 9:1-23.
2 Acts 18:1-11
3 Cf. Phil 3:5-6; 2 Cor 11:22. Paul's Jewish self-identity is a subject of scholarly debate, fuelled by passages such as Philippians 3. A traditional perspective is that Paul rejected Judaism in order to embrace Christianity. Some people (not least Martin Luther) justify or explain later European anti-Semitism by reference to Paul. Later discourse, however, favours a view that Paul never renounced his Jewishness but simply reinterpreted it, leaving behind one strand of Judaism to help forge a new and more inclusive one. In this understanding, he could not conceive of himself except as a Jew. For an interesting and accessible exploration of this subject see: Eisenbaum, Pamela (2009), *Paul Was Not a Christian: The Original Message of a Misunderstood Apostle*, Harper-Collins, New York. For a summary of scholarship see John Gager's *Reinventing Paul*. Gager, JG (2002), *Reinventing Paul,* Oxford University Press, New York.

to the Gentiles a Gentile, to the weak someone in weakness, and to those 'inside' the Law as much as to those 'outside' that is where Paul will be.[4] There is a humility in this, an intentional vulnerability, that puts 'the other' at the centre of Paul's concern. He does so without any acquiescence or compromise to his own integrity as an Apostle: 'I have made myself a slave although I remain free.'[5] His integrity is rooted in singularity of purpose, because for Paul there is only one thing that matters: the gospel of Jesus Christ. He remains free, not free *from* but free *to*. It is a freedom born of his complete openness to be transformed by God's indwelling Spirit. In order to lead others to be captured by what has captured him, he is ready to interpret the message of Jesus into cultural terms that make sense to them. It is not that he turns himself into some kind of religious chameleon as if hiding in plain sight, for that would be surreptitious and dishonest. It is, rather, to incarnate the Good News in time and place, in people and events. In Paul's teaching, living 'in Christ' is strongly about doing so in the here and now: in interpersonal relationships, in moral behaviour, in marriage and family life, in social and civil order, in prayer and liturgy, in serving and teaching, in discerning the prevailing discourse and competing truth-claims of the time, in attitudes to wealth, in daily work, and above all in what it means to love one another. Even in an age that was somewhat absorbed by apocalyptic concerns, Paul writes about such existential realities as these. There was, for him, an immediacy and cogency about living in Christ. From this perspective, Paul is a model for all founders and for leaders of renewal in the Church. Radically open and responsive to the life that the Spirit brings, he is able to speak to the time and place, to the people and events, in which he finds himself. He gives the gospel a context, and facilitates its being incarnated.

In addition to this missional imperative that the time is now and that the place is here, and that the gospel has first priority, there are two other drivers for Paul's apostolic life that he reveals in this chapter. Both are found in its opening verse:

'Have I not seen Jesus our Lord? Are you not my work in the Lord?'[6]

Let us take them in reverse order.

Paul is covenanted to the community at Corinth: 'You are the seal of my apostolate in the Lord,' he tells them.[7] The 'you' is plural; he is speaking to them collectively. Although the chapter carries something of Paul's

---

4   1 Cor 9:22.
5   1 Cor 9:19. Paul's sense of spiritual freedom is a core theme of his writings, and is a study in itself.
6   1 Cor 9:1.
7   1 Cor 9:2.

individual struggle in the life of faith, an inner wrestle in which everyone must engage, and to which he returns a number of times in his letters,[8] Paul's instructions more usually have a communal cast to them. Unity, mutuality, and the gifts of the Spirit that make for strength in community: these are Paul's more frequent topics. 'Belonging to Christ', to use the Pauline terminology, means belonging to one another, and caring for, forgiving, trusting, and believing in one another. It is not just a message to a fraction of the community, but to the whole. Paul cannot conceive of the Christian life other than in communitarian terms. It is in and through relationships and community that the Body of Christ exists.

The other rhetorical question he poses in this verse goes to the heart of everything for him: his personal encounter with the risen Christ. Here is the key driver for Paul. His writings are not informed by reading about Christ, or from any theologising or philosophising about him; Paul has met the living Christ, and that is what has transformed his life. Paul brings us back to the same enduring truth with which Benedict XVI famously begins his Encyclical *Deus Caritas Est*, one which has been a recurring theme in the documents of the Congregation for Catholic Education, and to which we have returned recurringly in this book:

> *Being Christian is not the result of an ethical choice or a lofty idea, but the encounter with an event, a person, which gives life a new horizon and a decisive direction.*[9]

It is Paul's personal experience of the living God who is love, encountered through his vulnerably allowing God's indwelling Spirit to pray and to act within him, that is fundamental. From this comes everything for Paul; without it he would be 'an empty gong clanging'. And no less so would we – each of us individually, and the educating or ecclesial community of which we are part. Paul's response, as is ours, can only be to become an apostle of love.

Paul thus draws us once more into the three interconnected dimensions for all Christian living: the personal, the communal/relational, and the missional. The Pauline concept of 'charisms', and equally the Church's ongoing development of this term in the post-conciliar period, can only be understood in this perspective. To the degree that any of these three elements is missing, weak or disproportionate, then an individual's or a community's expression of Christianity will be distorted. This is true for the Church universally, and for each of its communities, including those which

---

8   For example: Rom 6:1-14; 7:14-25; Eph 6:10-20; Phil 1:13-24; 2 Tim 1:6-2:13.
9   *Deus Caritas Est*, #1

have formed around particular traditions of Christian spirituality.

At their most authentic and most compelling, the spiritualities of the Church have provided people with means to be Christian in this tri-dimensional way. They have been inspired and inspirational in how they have done this. They have enthused. *Missio Dei* has taken flesh, in time and place. The spiritualities of the Church have perennially reimagined Christian discipleship. They have helped the Church to be strengthened, enlarged, reformed, and revitalised, for there has been congruence of deep purpose between these particular spiritualities and those of the wider Church. Typically, new spiritualities have emerged at times and in places of evangelising need, where the gospel of Jesus has demanded to be planted or refreshed by the Church in new ways. With Pauline passion and spiritual freedom, they have been able to recontextualise the gospel. The intergenerational communities in which the spiritualities have been nurtured have, over time, accumulated wisdom, agility, and tested methodologies for giving effect to this. They have embedded these in their mythologies and cultures. In such stories are the power and grace of God. The degree to which these community cultures remain open and responsive to new contexts and new evangelical needs will determine their continued relevance and indeed justification as communities of the Church. Their mandate is predicated on their continuing to be conducive to keeping people in touch with the evangelical intuitions of their founding so that they can have both capacity and readiness to read and respond to the signs of the times, and attract people to Jesus.

Many of these spiritual families have become involved in education as one element or the major focus of their ministry in the Church. As they have brought their spiritualities to the work of Catholic schools, new traditions of Catholic education have developed which have proved efficacious for evangelisation. It is a misconstruing of their identity, however, to isolate this ministerial activity from the community itself, or the distinctive manner of faith-life that is shared by its members. The ecclesial identity of these spiritual families has the same tri-dimensional foundation as all spiritual families, and needs to retain this.[10] For an individual group, or indeed the wider Church, to focus solely or principally on what it *does,* is to risk the integrity of this activity because it risks weakening its sense of primarily being a community of faith. Since a school's culture is such an influential factor in how the

---

10 As discussed in Chapter 3, a distinction should be made between groups that are established by diocesan bishops or under their authority, and those whose principal purpose is best understood within the context of the pastoral program of a diocese or an ecclesiastical province. The primary identity of the latter – whether comprised of consecrated persons or not – may not reside in any distinctive spirituality or spiritual family as those terms have been used here, but may lie in a local Church community.

school realises its purposes, the retention of a Christocentric heartbeat in this culture is essential. The questions that the members of an educating community need to be able to ask themselves, individually and collectively, and with as much rhetorical assurance as Saint Paul did, are the same ones as those of 1 Corinthians 9:1 – 'Have I not seen Jesus our Lord? Are you not my work in the Lord?'

For the most part, until the second half of the last century, the spiritual families involved in Catholic education comprised consecrated women and men who were members of monastic, mendicant and apostolic religious communities. One of the most profound signs of the times to which these communities have since needed to be attentive and responsive is the post-conciliar imperative in the Church to live *communio*. The universal call to holiness and everyone's baptismal responsibility to participate in the essentially missionary purpose of the Church have reshaped how ecclesial life and ministry are understood and undertaken. Many older religious communities are coming to see how their spiritualities can be more inclusively embraced by a wider group and, in the process, how they can be reimagined conceptually beyond the consecrated life. People who were formerly excluded from membership, but nonetheless attracted to ways in which that group approached the spiritual life, related communally and went about educational ministries, have sought to belong and to share responsibility for the life and mission of the community in new ways. Indeed, they have taken leadership in new paradigms within the spiritual families. Many interpret this as the providential activity of the Spirit. A plethora of new ecclesial movements has also emerged, something similarly read as God's Spirit active in our times. For both the older and newer groups, these developments have offered opportunity to live ecclesially in new ways. This has been especially gracing for lay people as they have taken their rightful places at all levels of these Church communities, both in their institutional and their charismatic dimensions. Potentially, it has allowed for the enriching and even the refounding of older spiritual families, many of which had been more tightly defined by the consecrated life. It has also provided a challenge for how spiritual families – both the newer and older – can continue to shape and contribute to the Church's ministry of education, and work in communion with one another.

The make-or-break challenge is the building and sustaining of communities of faith. A Christian spirituality has no life, and lacks a living integrity, unless there is a vital Christian community which sustains and grows it. Such an *ekklesia* will be a school of Christian holiness, community, and mission for its members. This is the nexus that cannot be broken.

A Christian spiritual tradition is not a theory or a philosophy, not a set of values or principles, much less a set of educational characteristics. It may have a history, but it is not historical. It is, rather, the distilled and evolving way that a real group of like-hearted Christian disciples come to encounter the transforming gospel of Jesus Christ, and how they respond in the circumstances of their life and ministry to this ongoing *metanoia*. Being enculturated in an actual ecclesial community, in real people of this time and place, is the only way that a spiritual tradition of the Church can continue to be in touch with the times and speak the language of the day. If a spirituality is to continue with authenticity and relevance in the life of the Church, then it needs a community of faith. It needs people who are spiritually invested in it, intentionally and co-responsibly.

The critical issue, therefore, for spiritual families that are involved in Catholic education, and for every school that is associated with such spiritual families, is how to form and support communities where their graced paths of Christian discipleship can be lived and nurtured, where people can say, 'I have seen Jesus our Lord' and feel, like Paul, a compelling urge to be evangelisers. They will need to be clear on purpose and therefore on identity. The principal ways for pursuing this include comprehensive and continuing spiritual formation strategies, distributed leadership that is imbued with charismic authority, effective means for people to know one another and have a sense of belonging, continuing rejuvenation from new and younger members, ongoing development of written and other resources, and structures for exercising collegial co-responsibility at the level of the spiritual family or ecclesial community. These will need to be supported by a broader ecclesial culture in which the primary Marian principle of the Church prevails, fostering the charismic giftedness of the Church and drawing these communities into a whole-of-church communion. It makes for a rich ecclesial life.

A telling mark of evangelical vitality, as Pope Francis reminds the Church, is joy. It is a *Magnificat* joy, where the impulsion to head in haste into the hill country, with prophetic news for those in need of hope and love, is sourced in a mystical attentiveness and responsiveness to the indwelling God who calls forth life. It is a joy that magnifies this God in the here and now, a God of *rahamim*. Joy evokes colour and vividness and movement. It captures hearts. The charismic stories of the Church are replete with such evangelical joy, and their next chapters can be written by people who are enthused with it.

INDEX

193

OTHER BOOKS IN THE MISSION AND EDUCATION SERIES

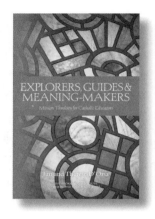

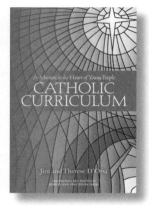

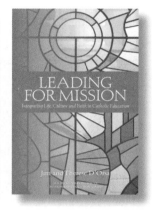

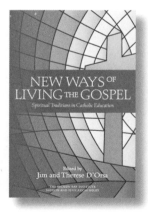

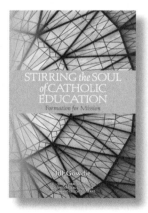

For more information see www.vaughanpublishing.com.au